Cognitive Coaching: A Foundation for Renaissance Schools

Arthur L. Costa, Ed.D.

and

Robert J. Garmston, Ed.D.

Professors Emeriti
California State University, Sacramento
and
Co-Directors
The Institute for Intelligent Behavior

CREDITS

Excerpt from "Fighting for Life in Third Period," in *Diversity in the Classroom: A Casebook for Teachers and Teacher Educators*, copyright © 1993 by Lawrence Erlbaum Associates, Inc. Reprinted by permission.

Quote from "Reflective Pedagogical Thinking: How Can We Promote it and Measure it?" in *Journal of Teacher Education*, Volume 41, Number 4, copyright © 1990 by Georgea M. Langer. Reprinted by permission.

Select material from "Linking Ways of Knowing With Ways of Being Practical," in *Curriculum Inquiry*, Volume 6, Number 3, copyright © 1978 by John Wiley & Sons, Inc. Reprinted by permission of John Wiley & Sons, Inc.

Every effort has been made to contact copyright holders for permission to reprint borrowed material where necessary. We apologize for any oversights and would be happy to rectify them in future printings.

Christopher-Gordon Publishers, Inc.
1502 Providence Highway, Suite 12
Norwood, MA 02062
1-800-934-8322

Printed in the United States of America

12 13 14 15 16   98 99 00 01 02

ISBN: 0-926842-37-4

Contents

Foreward

In the late 1970s, I spent much of my research time studying interactions between supervisors and teachers. I noted that most of the literature in supervision was void of the personal, cognitive, and developmental nature of human interactions. My own work in developmental supervision was an attempt to address this void by putting humans, with all their magnificent complexities, into the supervision equation. I believed supervision should enhance the thinking of professional educators rather than make them conform to particular practices. My initial attempts were limited, though, and I knew that additional information, techniques, and skills were needed to move clinical supervision beyond the ordinary recipes, steps, and external procedures being advocated.

In the early 1980s, I came across the work of Art Costa and Bob Garmston. Many school practitioners raved to me about attending their workshops and using the information presented there to make practical applications to their work. I immediately set about making the acquaintance of Professors Costa and Garmston, realizing that they were onto something important in redefining supervision as "cognitive coaching." Their command of counseling, clinical supervision, organizational development, teaching effectiveness, and cognitive psychology was impressive. Little did I know that their work was a harbinger of new educational demands, expectations, and reforms in the 1990s.

As my own research moved away from individual supervisor-supervisee interactions to a focus on schools working together for democratic renewal, I saw even more clearly the importance of Costa and Garmston's work in remaking teaching as a dignified and thoughtful profession. I am so pleased that they have put their years of studies and applications into a highly accessible book for all school leaders: teachers, supervisors, and administrators.

Readers will find *Cognitive Coaching* to be an intellectually stimulating resource for assisting individuals and groups in becoming more thoughtful and purposeful about the core of our profession: teaching and learning. If I were asked to refer school practitioners to the definitive guide for enriching thinking about teaching practice, this would be the source. The challenge of remaking public schools to educate all students must begin with each one of us. Costa and Garmston show us how to move from theory to practice. They give us direction for how we as individuals can think, speak, and behave toward one another to create the thoughtful educational environments that all our children deserve.

Carl Glickman
Professor, Department of Educational Leadership
Executive Director, Program for School Improvement
University of Georgia at Athens

An Introductory Note

This book takes the reader on an extensive intellectual (and emotional) tour, with many interesting side trips and many marvelous opportunities to do some broad-gauged idea-collecting and shopping along the way. There is, however, a well-defined destination and your tour guides have a surpassing command of the terrain plus a passionate commitment to it. No reader can travel this journey without being invigorated.

Writing an introduction for a book written by personal friends is a bit tricky, since one must balance objectivity (one's obligation to the profession at large) with the admiration that has built up over years of colleagueship. Fortunately in this case, my cognitive responses to the material were never in conflict with my cheerleading tendencies: this is, simply stated, a very fine book. I envy the readers, especially those in early stages of the professional awareness that these authors seek to define, who will be transported to the high terrain on which tomorow's schools—Renaissance schools—will hopefully be built.

The three goals of Cognitive Coaching as identified by Art and Bob are TRUST, LEARNING AND HOLONOMY. The latter term, borrowed from Arthur Koestler, is skillfully used to represent the twin goals of individual autonomy, on the one hand, and collaboration (working interdependently with others), on the other. The simultaneity of these behaviors is seen as crucial, and the coach's role in helping individuals to thrive, not only on their own terms but also as members of the professional community, is a recurring theme in the book.

The history and underpinnings of cognitive coaching are well developed in the opening chapter. The stage is set for a major message for coaches, namely that their work mediates individual growth toward the "five states of mind" on which the volume concentrates: efficacy, flexibility, craftsmanship, consciousness, and interdependence. These states of mind, sources of holonomy, are particularly developed in the seventh chapter and illustrated in the eighth.

The concept of renaissance refers to reinvention; new vision; a new paradigm. The term, which is built into the book title, is predominant in the text and serves as a symbol for the vitalization and redefinition of schools as well as the human beings who serve in them, or are served by them. The term is apt, since most persons use "renaissance" in a positive and salutatory manner. All the same, it may be useful for me to observe that the wonderful schools Art and Bob seek to describe and promote have never before existed. Rather than a "rebirth" of excellent schooling, they are in fact anticipating an educational genesis or origination. Granted, many elements of intelligent and enlightened practice can be found in educational history, but full-fledged and authentic models are yet to be developed. We should all be grateful to Art and Bob for providing such practical and persuasive advice as we pursue this developmental opportunity.

Having been continuously involved for more than thirty years in definitions and applications of growth-oriented supervision, or coaching (much the better term), I found myself stretched and re-educated by much that is in this volume. Art and Bob take us to a higher level, or in their terms they have made a quantum leap, in understanding the role and the power of coaching. The adjective "cognitive" is very appropriate, and in addition the dimensions of trust and caring within the coaching function seem increasingly relevant when elaborated by these obviously caring authors. This book reads well. It is a nice mixture of informal, conversational material and scholarly depth. The breadth and the currency of referenced works confirm that the authors are well in command of the expanding literature. The skill with which they have selected quotes and ideas from that literature confirms their excellent sense of what really matters as we think about improving the educational world we inhabit. That world will be a better place if we take their views seriously.

Robert H. Anderson
Anchin Center Professor
University of South Florida

Origins of Cognitive Coaching

Cognitive coaching has its source in the confluence of the professional experiences of Arthur L. Costa and Robert J. Garmston, who both began their educational careers in the late 1950s, a time of great ferment in American education.

In the early 1970s, Nabuo Watanabe, then Director of Curriculum Services of the Contra Costa County Superintendent of Schools Office, convened a group of California educators to develop a strategy for assisting school administrators in their understanding and application of humanistic principles of teacher evaluation. Art was a member of that group. Based on the clinical supervision model of Cogan and Goldhammer, the group outlined the basic structure of the pre- and post-conference. They also identified three goals of evaluation: trust, learning, and autonomy, goals and processes that foreshadowed key concepts in cognitive coaching.

At about the same time, Bob was a consultant and principal for the Arabian American Oil Company Schools in Saudi Arabia. He was implementing a system-wide innovation in computer assisted individualized instruction which cast the teacher in the roles of facilitator and mediator for student learning. Simultaneously, he and his colleagues were applying the pioneer work in clinical supervision developed by Cogan, Goldhammer, and Anderson at the Harvard Graduate School of Education. Additionally, Bob was teaching communication courses in Parent and Teacher Effectiveness Training, developed by psychologist Thomas Gordon and a forerunner to some of the nonjudgmental verbal skills found in cognitive coaching today.

In his early years as a teacher and curriculum consultant, Art was highly influenced by leaders in education and cognitive development. Art's doctoral work at the University of California, Berkeley, emphasized curriculum, instruction, and developmental psychology. He conducted courses based on the curriculum and instructional theories of J. Richard Suchman, Hilda Taba, Jerome Bruner, and Reuven Feuerstein. Bob's early pedagogical mentors included an exceptional group of professors at San Francisco State University, Santa Rosa Center, who operated as an interdisciplinary team and the national leaders in humanistic psychology. After 20 years in the roles of teacher, principal, director of instruction, and district superintendent, Bob completed a doctorate at the University of Southern California with an emphasis on educational administration, sociology, and staff development.

About the same time that the emphases of cognition, instruction, and supervision were beginning to coalesce for Art, Bob was piecing together principles of counseling practices and strategies of group dynamics for school improvement. He joined the faculty at California State University as Professor of Educational Administration, and taught courses in curriculum development, school improvement, supervision, and neuro-linguistics. Art was also teaching curriculum and supervision of instruction at California State University, and he and Bob were assigned to the same office. They developed the first formal expression of cognitive coaching one summer afternoon while sailing near Sacramento, and that December they tested their ideas with staff developers in a presentation at a statewide conference. The enthusiastic reception led to further conceptual work and publications as well as invitations to present seven-day "trainings" to educators.

By the summer of 1985, it became clear that the interest in cognitive coaching far exceeded Art and Bob's capacities to inform others about it. This stimulated the formation of the Institute for Intelligent Behavior, an association of persons dedicated to enabling educational and corporate agencies to support their members' growth toward the five states of mind. Currently, six Senior Associates and approximately 30 Associates provide seminar programs in cognitive coaching to interested school districts and private-sector organizations throughout North America, Europe, and the Far East.

For information concerning Cognitive Coaching seminars and other services provided by the Institute, contact:

Institute for Intelligent Behavior
720 Grizzly Peak Blvd.
Berkeley, CA 94708
(510) 528-8678

Acknowledgments

This book evolved from the work of many people, particularly Senior Associates of the Institute for Intelligent Behavior who have contributed to the continuing evolution of cognitive coaching concepts and practices.

Diane Zimmerman, principal at West Davis Intermediate School in Davis, California, contributed to our original thinking when she was a graduate student with us at California State University in Sacramento. She and other Senior Associates continue to test, refine, and develop these concepts as they conduct seminars in cognitive coaching, work directly in schools, and provide assistance to educators throughout North America.

Together, we and the Senior Associates have dedicated ourselves to living the principles of the Renaissance organization described in this book. We feel especially fortunate to be working with and learning from such exceptional people. They each enjoy demanding roles in a variety of educational pursuits in addition to their Institute responsibilities.

Bill Baker, Director of Group Dynamics Associates, provides management services to the Institute. Formerly of the Alameda County Superintendent of Schools office, he and Stan Shalit have provided the most concentrated and comprehensive cognitive coaching training services in any location to date.

Laura Lipton, Director of Educational Consulting Services in Yorktown, New York, has extensive expertise in instruction, thinking skills, and organizational development. She constantly focuses us on the critical questions we should be posing and links the group's explorations to current literature in a variety of fields.

Peg Luidens is an educational consultant from Holland, Michigan, who, in addition to cognitive coaching, specializes in helping teachers develop expertise in the writing process and is deeply involved in leading several school restructuring efforts. She adds keen intelligence, grace, and invaluable courage and social consciousness to the group.

John Prieskorn is President of Leadership in Human Behavior, a consulting firm specializing in self-esteem for adults and leadership development programs. John brings to the Institute his gifts in neurolinguistics and his rich experience as a superintendent. He skillfully redirects us to practical matters whenever we get lost in obtuse theoretical rhetoric.

Bruce Wellman is Director of Science Resources, a consulting firm in Lincoln, Massachusetts. He consults with school systems, professional organizations, and publishers on teaching methods and materials in science, thinking skills, skillful teaching, and facilitating learning organizations. He keeps us laughing, committed to quality, and focused on the big picture.

Taken together, this group of senior associates is as bright, talented, and diverse a group as either of us has ever had the pleasure of working with. We are extremely grateful for our association with them, what we learn together, and what we create together.

A host of other colleagues have added to our understandings: Linda Lambert and Marilyn Tabor have made special and enduring contributions; Bill Sommers has been generous with editing, quotations, and bibliographic material. We have learned from each of our esteemed colleagues in the "Leather Apron Club," too numerous to mention, but they know who they are. Rosemarie Liebmann has assisted via her doctoral dissertation and has offered validation through her conversations with Peter Senge and research of Arthur Koestler's concept of holonomy. We also wish to acknowledge and celebrate the growing numbers of dedicated people who are infusing the principles and practices of cognitive coaching in their classrooms, schools, districts, and communities.

We are indebted to scholars, practitioners, and researchers in many fields whose work has informed us, raised provocative questions, and guided our search. Most notably, we would like to thank Carl Glickman, at the University of Georgia, for his scholarship, inspiration, modeling, encouragement, and friendship.

Anne Meek graciously donated her time in editing an early version of the book, René Bahrenfuss saw us through several later versions, and Ardie Christian, Debbi Miller, and Mary Yaeger gave untold hours of professional assistance in formatting, typing, and correcting numerous drafts of the manuscript. We are grateful for their patience and skills. Undoubtedly, the two persons who have been the most patient with us, and have continuously extended their support and love, are our wives, Nancy and Sue.

—Art Costa and Bob Garmston
November 1993

1

What Is Cognitive Coaching?

The Butterfly Effect: A butterfly stirring the air today in Peking can transform storm systems next month in New York.[1]

Like the tiny air disturbances created by the butterfly's wings, very small and often invisible adjustments to a system can radically redirect its entire course. A physical therapist, for example, will sometimes spend an entire session massaging a foot, knowing that the spine, muscles, and tendons will make corresponding adjustments toward alignment in the week that follows.

Schools and educational organizations are also systems, influenced by a wide range of dynamics that shape the direction, capacities, and production of those who work within them. Enlightened educators who seek to influence far beyond the moment create, ever so gently, minuscule turbulences like those of the butterfly's wings. Cognitive coaching is one such consistent, positive disturbance that can bring profound changes to the classroom, school, district, and community.

Metaphors for Coaching

Think of the term *coaching*, and you may envision an athletic coach, but we have quite a different metaphor. To us, coaching is a conveyance, like a stagecoach. *"To coach means to convey a valued colleague from where he or she is to where he or she wants to be."* [2] Skillful cognitive coaches apply specific strategies to enhance another person's perceptions, decisions, and intellectual functions. Changing these inner thought processes is prerequisite to improving overt behaviors that, in turn, enhance student learning.

Cognitive coaching is a nonjudgmental process—built around a planning conference, observation, and a reflecting conference. Anyone in the educational setting can become a cognitive coach—teachers, administrators, department chairs, or support personnel. A coaching relationship may be established between teachers and teachers, administrators and teachers, and/or administrators and fellow administrators. When a cognitive coaching relationship is established between two professionals with similar roles, or *peers*, it can be referred to as *peer coaching*.

In an increasing number of educational communities, custodians, school secretaries, bus drivers, parents, students, and cafeteria workers are learning the skills of cognitive coaching. In one Michigan school district, the director of maintenance coaches an elementary principal, who in turn coaches a teacher. While it is important to recognize the value of cognitive coaching for everyone in the educational community, we have chosen to use the principal and teacher relationship to illustrate the coaching process.

Three Goals

 Cognitive coaching is organized around three major goals:
  - establishing and maintaining *trust*, an assured reliance on the character, ability, or strength of someone or something;
  - facilitating mutual *learning*, which is the engagement and transformation of mental processes and perceptions;
  - and enhancing growth toward *holonomy*,[3] which we define in two parts: individuals acting *autonomously* while simultaneously acting *interdependently* with the group.

Developing and maintaining trust is fundamental to achieving the other two goals because it creates a safe atmosphere where learning and change can occur. Trust is not an end in itself, but it is prerequisite for success in the coaching relationship. We discuss the issue of trust in greater depth in Chapter 3.

Learning—by the teacher *and* the coach—is perhaps the obvious goal of cognitive coaching. Cognitive coaches encourage and support individuals as they move beyond their present capacities into new behaviors and skills. To achieve the goal of learning, the coaching process incorporates the basic principles of knowledge construction by Jerome Bruner, Jean Piaget, and Hilda Taba; the adult learning theories of Malcolm Knowles; human development sequences based upon the work of Jean Piaget, Lawrence Kohlberg, Frances Fuller, and Eric Erickson; the neurolinguistic studies of Richard Bandler and John Grinder; and the mediational theories of Reuven Feuerstein. Chapter 5 details the coach's role in facilitating learning.

The heart provides a useful example of the third goal, holonomy, which is derived from two Greek words: *holos* meaning whole and *on* meaning part. The heart performs a unique function with its own intricate rhythm and pattern of functioning. Even when it is transferred to another body, the heart asserts its characteristic pattern of activity. Yet the heart's activities are regulated or modified by the autonomic nervous system, hormones, and other influences. The individuality of the heart operates within the wholeness of a larger system, and, in turn, affects the entire system.

Likewise, the most effective teachers are autonomous individuals—self-asserting, self-perpetuating, and self-modifying. However, teachers are also part of a larger whole—the school—and are influenced by its attitudes, values, and behaviors. (And in turn, the school is an autonomous unit interacting within the influence of the district and the community.)

The goal of developing holonomy consists of two outcomes: parts and whole. The first outcome is to support people in becoming autonomous and self-actualizing. The second outcome is for members of the school community to function interdependently, recognizing their capacity to both self-regulate and be regulated by the norms, values, and concerns of the larger system. And, of equal importance, recognizing their capacity to influence the values, norms and practices of the entire system. Five states of mind provide the energy sources for the actualization of holonomy, which we will discuss more in Chapter 6: efficacy, flexibility, craftsmanship, consciousness, and interdependence.

Toward a Renaissance Definition of Coaching

> *The current management culture, with its focus on controlling behavior, needs to be replaced by a management culture in which skillful coaching creates the climate, environment, and context that empowers employees and teams to generate results. . . . Coaching...that conversation which creates the new management culture, not as a technique within the*

> *old culture. Coaching, a people-based art which is defined as the heart of management, occurs within a relationship that is action oriented, result oriented, and person oriented.*[4]

For many years, supervisors were expected to install, redirect, and reinforce overt behaviors of teaching. This is compatible with the long-held metaphor of teaching as labor where management sets standards, directs how the work is to be done, monitors and reviews for compliance, and then evaluates and rewards the completed work.

But a quiet revolution has been taking place in corporate offices and industrial settings across America. Writings by Senge, Block, Toffler, Pascarella, Covey, Deming, Wheatley, Bracy, and numerous others have highlighted a need for greater caring for the personal growth of each individual. There is a growing desire to enhance individual creativity, to stimulate collaborative efforts, and to continue learning how to learn. The new paradigm of industrial management emphasizes a trusting environment in which growth and empowerment of the individual are the keys to corporate success.

We are seeing a corresponding revolution in schools as well. It is a revolution of relationships and a revolution of the intellect, placing a premium on our greatest resource—our human minds in relationship with one another. The relationship presumed by cognitive coaching is that teaching is a professional act and that coaches support teachers in becoming more resourceful, informed, and skillful professionals. Cognitive coaches attend to the internal thought processes of teaching as a way of improving instruction; coaches do not work to change overt behaviors. These behaviors change as a result of refined perceptions and cognitive processes.

 Teachers who wish to continually improve their craft never lose their need to be coached. And interestingly, the coach "need not be a more expert performer than the person being coached; . . . technical expertise frequently is less relevant than the ability to enable or empower" people to move beyond their current performance.[5]

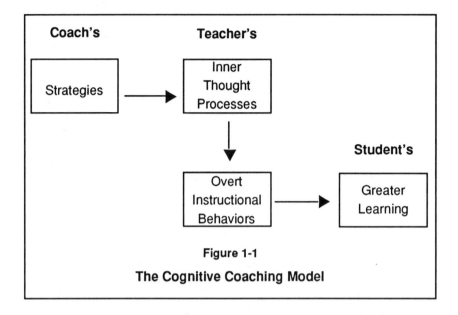

Figure 1-1
The Cognitive Coaching Model

Why Coaching?

In a decade when many schools are pressed for time and money, why is coaching so important? We have identified four compelling reasons:

 1. Cognitive coaching enhances the intellectual capacities of teachers, which in turn produces greater intellectual achievement in students. Research shows that teachers with higher conceptual levels are more adaptive and flexible in their teaching style, and they have a greater ability to empathize, to symbolize human experience, and to act in accordance with a disciplined commitment to human values.[6] These teachers choose new practices when classroom problems appear, vary their use of instructional strategies, elicit more conceptual responses from students,[7] give more corrective and positive feedback to students,[8] and produce higher achieving students who are more cooperative and involved in their work.[9]

Witherall and Erickson[10] found that teachers at the highest levels of ego development demonstrated greater complexity and commitment to the individual student; greater generation and use of data in teaching; and greater understanding of practices related to rules, authority, and moral development than their counterparts. Teachers at higher stages of intellectual functioning demonstrate more flexibility, toleration for stress, and adaptability. They take multiple perspectives, use a variety of coping behaviors, and draw from a broader repertoire of teaching models.[11] High-concept teachers are more effective with a wider range of students, including students from diverse cultural backgrounds.

We know that adults continue to move through stages of cognitive, conceptual, and ego development[12] and that their developmental levels have a direct relationship to student behavior and student performance. Supportive organizations with a norm for growth and change promote increased levels of intellectual, social, moral, and ego states for members. The complex challenge for coaches, of course, is to understand the diverse stages in which each staff member is currently operating; to assist people in understanding their own and others' differences and stages of development; to accept staff members at their present moral, social, cognitive, and ego state; and to act in a nonjudgmental manner.

 2. Few educational innovations achieve their full impact without a coaching component. Conventional approaches to staff development—workshops, lectures, and demonstrations—show little evidence of transfer to ongoing classroom practice. Several studies by Joyce and Showers[13] reveal that the level of classroom application hovers around only 5 percent even after high-quality training that integrates theory and demonstration. This figure increases a bit when staff development includes time for practice and feedback and when the curriculum is adapted for the innovation. But when staff development includes coaching in the training design, the level of application increases to 90 percent. With periodic review of both the teaching model and the coaching skills—and with continued coaching—classroom application of innovations remains at the 90 percent level.

 3. Working effectively as a team member requires coaching. A harmonious collegial effort needs coordination. Consider a symphony orchestra. Its members are diversely talented individuals: an outstanding pianist, a virtuoso violinist, an exquisite cellist. Together, they work diligently toward a common goal—producing beautiful music. Likewise, each member of a school staff is an extremely talented professional. Together, they work to produce a positive learning environment, challenging experiences, and self-actualized students.

In an orchestra, the musicians play, rehearse together, and come to a common vision of the entire score, each understanding the part they play that contributes to the whole. They do not all play at the same time, but they do support each other in a coordinated effort. In the same way, members of the school community support each other in helping to create and achieve the organization's vision. Teachers do not teach the same subjects at the same time, nor do they approach them in the same way. Cognitive coaching provides a safe format for professional dialogue and develops the skills for reflection on practice, both of which are necessary for productive collaboration.

4. Coaching develops positive interpersonal relationships which are the energy sources for adaptive school cultures and productive organizations. The pattern of adult interactions in a school strongly influences the climate of the learning environment and the instructional outcomes for students. Integral to the cognitive coaching model is the recognition that human beings operate with a rich variety of cultural, personal, and cognitive style differences, which can be resources for learning. Cognitive coaching builds a knowledge of and appreciation for diversity and provides frameworks, skills, and tools for coaches to work with other adults and students in open and resourceful ways. Cognitive coaching promotes cohesive school cultures where norms of experimentation and open, honest communication enable everyone to work together in healthy, respectful ways.

Jack Frymier (1987) states:
> In the main, the bureaucratic structure of the workplace is more influential in determining what professionals do than are personal abilities, professional training or previous experience. Therefore, change efforts should focus on the structure of the workplace, not the teachers.[14]

Benefits of Coaching

We believe organizations adopting cognitive coaching will see a variety of broad, positive changes:

• **Developing holonomy will become the school's new mission.** As coaches work to mediate the five states of mind as energy sources for individuals and the environment, teachers will work to enhance students' knowledge, skills, problem solving abilities, self confidence, and contributions to society in holonomous classrooms.

• **The overburdened curriculum will be selectively abandoned and new curriculums will be judiciously adopted for their contributions to one or more of the five states of mind.** Schools will no longer focus on the learning *of* content objectives; students will learn *from* the objectives. The fundamental values of efficacy, flexibility, craftsmanship, consciousness, integrity, and interdependence will become sources of information for the curriculum as well as resources for staff development, which will be refocused on producing teacher, student, and organizational growth in these areas.

• **Evaluation of teachers, students, and organizational effectiveness will change from performance review to the assessment of development toward greater holonomy.** If we believe that teaching is decision making, then the evaluation of teaching should become evaluation of teachers' growth in the decision-making processes and intellectual functions of teaching.[15] Research will focus on indicators of growth toward greater holonomy, not just test scores.

• **Staff developers will devote their efforts to enhancing teachers', administrators', parents', and support staff's leadership skills in a variety of areas.** All members of the school community will grow in areas such as communication and collaboration, action research, decision making, problem solving, and networking.

• **Systematic and sustained energies will be directed to making each school and each district a learning community where the culture of the workplace itself— the intellectual ecology—is continually evolving.** The twin goals of individual development and organizational development will live side by side.[16] Both the individual and the organization will continuously change, refine, and improve as a result of learning from experience.

The Renaissance School

The last major re-organization of American public schools occurred during the mid-1800s, but we believe a new philosophy is arising. We call it the Renaissance School.

The Renaissance School is not a restructured school. The buzzword "restructured" has very definite meanings for people. For some it calls to mind a new organization of the daily schedule. For others it means community involvement in decision making. Schools of choice and site-based management are also types of restructured schools.

The Renaissance School we envision is defined in broader terms, capturing some of the spirit we associate with the Italian Renaissance of the 1600s. For us, Renaissance represents a rebirth into wholeness, rejoining the mind and the soul, the emotions and the intellect, forging new practices and dreaming new potentials for all humans. The Renaissance School celebrates learning at all ages for all persons in all disciplines, including art, music, mathematics, language, the sciences, technology. Schools today are being influenced by a variety of new perspectives that challenge our notions of learning and relationships, and a modern Renaissance view would hold that:
- The human mind has no limits except those we choose to believe in.
- Humans are makers of meaning, and knowledge is constructed—both consciously and unconsciously—from experience.
- All people at all ages can continue to develop intellectually.
- All members of the school community are continual and active learners.
- Leadership is the mediation of both the individual's and the organization's capacity for self-renewal.

For us, such views have contributed to a new conception of schools. The Renaissance School acknowledges interdependent communities of autonomous human beings bound by core values, common goals, caring, respect for diversity, and the ability to struggle together. Its members are reflective, examining their products and processes in a continuing climate for self-renewal. The Renaissance School allows for the development and contribution of each person's unique personal and professional identity. Their personal history, culture, gender, race, interests, training, knowledge, and skills are all important to continued growth and change. Renaissance Schools are wellsprings of growth and self-renewal for all who dwell there.

Clearly, many of the attributes of the Renaissance School are reflected in the principles of cognitive coaching, and vice versa. Reflection, respect for diversity, and ongoing renewal are all-important principles of the coaching process and the Renaissance School. We discuss our vision of the Renaissance School further in Chapter 8, but we introduce it here because the vision has guided us through many of the chapters that follow. Just as the Peking butterfly influences those storm systems in New York, we believe cognitive coaching significantly contributes to the creation of Renaissance Schools.

Endnotes

1. Gleick, J. *Chaos: Making a New Science.* New York: Penguin Books, 1987, p. 8.

2. Evered, R. and Selman, J. "Coaching and the Art of Management." *Organizational Dynamics* (Autumn 1989): Vol. 18, pp. 16–32.

3. The origin of this word is drawn from the writings of Koestler, A. (1972). *The Roots of Coincidence.* New York, NY: Vintage Books, and Samples, R. (1981). *Mind of our Mother: Toward Holonomy and Planetary Consciousness.* Addison-Wesley Publishing Co., Inc. Samples, in 1981, described holonomy as the science or systematic study of wholes, of entire systems. Basic to holonomy is the assumption of unity and oneness as opposed to fragmentation, isolation, and separateness.

4. Evered, R. and Selman, J. "Coaching and the Art of Management." *Organizational Dynamics* (Autumn 1989): Vol. 18, pp. 16–32.

5. Evered, R. and Selman, J. "Coaching and the Art of Management." *Organizational Dynamics* (Autumn 1989): Vol. 18, pp. 16–32.

6. Sprinthall, N. and Theis-Sprinthall, L. "The Teacher as an Adult Learner—A Cognitive Developmental View." *Staff Development: 82nd Yearbook of the National Society for the Study of*

Education, Part II, Chicago, IL: University of Chicago Press, 1983.

7. Hunt, D. E. "Teacher's Adaptation: Reading and Flexing to Students," *Flexibility in Teaching*, New York: Longman Press, Chapter 4, 1980.

8. Calhoun, E. F. "Relationship of Teachers' Perceptions of Prescriptive and Descriptive Observations of Teaching by Instructional Supervisors," *Georgia Educational Leadership*, 1985.

9. Harvey, O. J. "Conceptual Systems and Attitude Change," *Attitude, Ego Involvement, and Change*, New York, NY: Wiley, 1967, p. 17.

10. Witherall, C. S. and Erickson, V.L. "Teacher Education as Adult Development," *Theory Into Practice* (June 1978): p. 17.

11. Hunt, D.C. "Conceptual Level Theory and Research as Guides to Educational Practice." *Interchange*, (1977–1978): Vol. 8, pp. 78–80.
    McNerney, R. F. and Carrier, C. A. *Teacher Development*. New York: MacMillan Publishing Company, 1981.
    Oja, S. N. "Developmental Theories and the Professional Development of Teachers," presentation at the annual meeting of the American Educational Research Association, Boston, MA, April 1980.
    Glickman, C. *Supervision of Instruction: A Developmental Approach*. Newton, MA: Allyn and Bacon, 1985, p. 18.

12. Sheehy, G. *Passages*. New York, NY: Bantam Publishing, 1979.
    Kegan, R. *The Evolving Self: Problem and Process in Human Development*. Cambridge, MA: Harvard University Press, 1982.
    Loevinger, J. *Ego Development Conceptions and Theories*, San Francisco, CA: Jossey-Bass, 1976.

13. Evered, R. and Selman, J. "Coaching and the Art of Management." *Organizational Dynamics* (Autumn 1989): Vol. 18, pp. 16–32.

14. Frymier, J. "Bureaucracy and the Neutering of Teachers," *Phi Delta Kappan*, (September 1987): p. 10.

15. For a discussion of this approach to evaluation, see A. Costa, R. Garmston, and L. Lambert, 1988, "Evaluation of Teaching: A Cognitive Development View," *Teacher Evaluation: Six Prescriptions for Success*, Alexandria, VA: Association for Supervision and Curriculum Development, pp. 145–171.

16. Garmston, R. and Wellman, B. "Developing Adaptive Organizations in a Holonomous Universe." In Progress.

2

Basics of the Coaching Process

In schools today, terms such as teacher evaluation, performance review, clinical supervision, reflective supervision, and reciprocal supervision connote vastly different systems. The verbs supervise, coach, observe, and evaluate tap different emotions in teachers. Role relationships such as colleague, supervisor, mentor, coach, catalyst, evaluator, consultant, and administrator all have a multitude of meanings in educators' minds. Administrators who are also coaches perform two distinct, but often conflicting, management functions: coaching and evaluation. Because coaching and evaluation may be confused, we contrast their characteristics in Figure 2-1.

We want to be clear with our definitions. At its most basic level, cognitive coaching is a set of nonjudgmental practices built around a Planning Conference, Lesson Observation, and a Reflecting Conference. At more complex levels, coaching is also the application of a set of assumptions, principles, and skills in both formal and informal interactions with faculty, students, and parents. An even more advanced level sees application of cognitive coaching principles to the larger community.

Attribute	Coaching	Evaluation
Who's Responsible?	It is possible to delegate this responsibility to department chairpersons, peers, mentors or colleagues.	By law, only personnel holding an administrative credential may be authorized to evaluate.
Timing	Coaching starts with the first day on the job and can be ongoing throughout the year.	Districts adopt policies and deadlines by which teachers must be evaluated.
Purposes	Improve instruction, curriculum, and student learning.	Quality control and meeting contractual requirements.
Sources of Criteria	The teacher determines what the coach shall look for as criteria for excellence in terms of student behavior and teacher behavior.	Quality teaching standards are usually developed, negotiated, adopted and made public on forms which are used in the evaluation process. While these statements vary from district to district, it is common practice for an evaluator to rate teachers' performance on these criteria.
Uses of the Data Collected	The data collected is given to the teacher.	Information written on the district-adopted forms are usually distributed to the teacher, to the district for placement in the employee's personnel file and another copy is retained by the building principal.
Topics Covered	Learning, classroom interaction, instruction, student performance, curriculum adherence, individual student behavior, teachers' behavior and skills, etc.	In addition, may include such performances as punctuality, willingness to participate in extra-curricular and professional activities, personal characteristics, professional attitudes and growth, etc.
Value Judgments	The teacher evaluates his or her own performance according to the criteria that were set out in the planning conference.	Within the word "evaluation" is "value." Teacher performance is rated by evaluations such as Outstanding, Adequate, or Needs to Improve.
The Role of the Observer	The teacher informs the coach of what to look for and what feedback information would be desired and helpful.	Equipped with the criteria from the district's evaluation system, the observer knows what to look for before entering the classroom. Evaluators are often trained in techniques of observing classroom instruction so that they can detect indicators of excellence or inadequacies in the specified performance criteria.
Empowerment	The power to coach is bestowed by the teacher. They "allow" themselves to be coached because of the respect, the helpfulness, and the leadership qualities of the coach.	The power to evaluate is bestowed by the Board of Trustees and the State or Province. It is a line staff authority position.

Figure 2-1
Coaching/Evaluation Distinctions

Can the administrator truly play both roles of evaluator and coach? Recent research by Carl Glickman of the University of Georgia provides some guidelines.[1] Operating under the assumption that these two roles were in conflict, Glickman conducted interviews with teachers that yielded some surprising results. He found that the administrator can perform both roles under three conditions:

- A trusting relationship has been established between the administrator and teacher.
- The teacher knows for certain which of the two functions is being performed—coaching or evaluation.
- The administrator's behaviors are scrupulously consistent with each of the functions. They should not be mixed.

Historical Background

In the late 1960s, Morris Cogan, Robert Goldhammer, Robert Anderson, and a group of supervisors working in Harvard's Master of Arts in Teaching program discovered a serious problem. At that time, traditional supervision placed the supervisor in an "expert" role superior to that of the teacher. Supervisors told the teacher what should be changed and how to do it. Supervisors offered solutions to problems that concerned them, which were not necessarily the problems encountered by teachers. All efforts to change the conference style in which the supervisor did the talking and the teacher did the listening had failed. The work of Cogan and his colleagues regarding this dilemma was the foundation for the clinical supervision model, and it is important to understand some of Cogan's work to appreciate the distinctive attributes of cognitive coaching.

Cogan[2] envisioned the purpose of clinical supervision as "the development of a professionally responsible teacher who is analytical of his own performance, open to help from others, and self-directing." Clinical supervision demanded a role change in which the teacher and the supervisor worked as colleagues, respecting each other's contributions. The intent of the process was to cultivate teacher self-appraisal, self-direction, and self-supervision.

Cogan's clinical supervision was conceived as a cyclic process, composed of eight phases organized around planning and conferencing with a teacher before instruction, the lesson observation, and a follow up conference after the lesson. Cogan and his colleagues believed:

- the act of teaching is a collection of behaviors,
- these behaviors can be observed singly and in interaction,
- teacher behavior can be understood and controlled, and
- instructional improvement can be achieved by changing or modifying certain instructional behaviors.

In American schools today, we find three applications, or adaptations, of the clinical supervision model. The first, nominal supervision, or supervision in name only, occurs in too many settings. Many teachers report that they are rarely, if ever, observed.

A second application of clinical supervision is practiced by proponents of Madeline Hunter, whose work deviates from Cogan and Goldhammer in several important aspects. The Hunter model eliminates the pre-conference. It preserves an expert-learner relationship because the supervisor's major contribution is sophisticated observation and analysis. While a stated goal is to enhance teacher decision-making skills, the weight of practice seems to lean toward installing some "certainties" based on a knowledge base of "a hundred years of research in human learning" and cause-effect relationships.[3]

The third type of clinical supervision, and most desirable, is linked to teacher reflection. Cognitive coaching is a modern expression of this orientation,[4] built on the foundation laid by Cogan[5] and Goldhammer.[6] There are, however, two significant departures. The first is in the conception of the teaching act. The second relates to the application of specific knowledge about teacher cognition and psycholinguistics. While the traditional model of clinical supervision[7,8,9] addresses overt teaching behaviors, we believe that these overt behaviors of teaching are the products and artifacts of *inner thought processes* and intellectual functions. To change the overt behaviors of instruction requires the alteration and rearrangement of the inner and invisible cognitive behaviors of instruction.

What do we mean by mediate? A mediator is one who:

- diagnoses and envisions desired stages for others;
- constructs and uses clear and precise language in the facilitation of others' cognitive development;
- devises an overall strategy through which individuals will move themselves toward desired states;
- maintains faith in the potential for continued movement toward more autonomous states of mind and behavior; and
- possesses a belief in his/her own capacity to serve as an empowering catalyst of others' growth.

Figure 2-2 is a basic map of the steps in a typical cognitive coaching experience: Planning Conference, Observation, and Reflecting Conference. Remember that this is a map, not a recipe. A recipe is prescriptive; it usually must be followed step-by-step. A map simply displays the territory, and travelers can chose different roads to get to their destinations. Skilled cognitive coaches know this map backwards and forwards so they can use it spontaneously and know exactly where they are in the process. Coaches may vary from or embellish the map, but it is always the basic structure of the coaching process. (The rationale for this structure will be elaborated in Chapter 5.)

When we've asked teachers what information they would like observers to have about their class prior to an observation, we get an extensive list of requests. These are situational, of course, and depend on many environmental and personal factors. But teachers often want coaches to know:

- Where this lesson fits into the teacher's overall, long-range plan for the students, and what's happened previously on this topic.
- Information about the social dynamics of the class.
- Behavioral information about specific students.
- Aspects of the lesson about which the teacher is unclear.
- Concerns about student behavior.
- Concerns related to trying a new teaching technique.
- Why this lesson concept is important to students.
- Events beyond the classroom experience affecting students.

While any of the above topics might be introduced into a planning conference by teacher or coach, the planning conference outline presented in Figure 2-2 represents the four cornerstones of any and all cognitive coaching planning conferences.

Planning Conference

I. **Planning:** Coaches mediate by having the teacher:
    - Clarify lesson goals and objectives
    - Anticipate teaching strategies and decisions
    - Determine evidence of student achievement
    - Identify the coach's data gathering focus and procedures

Lesson

II. **Teaching:** Coaches gather data by observing:
    - Evidence of student achievement
    - Teacher strategies and decisions

Reflecting Conference

III. **Reflecting:** Coaches mediate by having the teacher:
    - Summarize impressions and assessments of the lesson
    - Recall data supporting those impressions and assessments
    - Compare planned with performed teaching decisions, and student learning
    - Infer relationships between student achievement and teacher decisions/behavior

IV. **Applying:** Coaches mediate by having the teacher:
    - Synthesize teacher learnings and prescribe applications
    - Reflect on the coaching process; recommend refinements

Figure 2-2
Coaching Functions in Four Phases of Instructional Thought

The Planning Conference

The Planning Conference is both powerful and essential to the coaching process for five reasons:

1. It is a trust-building opportunity. Learning cannot occur without a foundation of trust, and establishing and maintaining this trust is one of the coach's primary goals. To this end, the Planning Conference agenda is controlled by the teacher. In the Planning Conference, the teacher suggests the time for a classroom visit, specifies which data should be collected during the observation, how data should be recorded, and even where the coach will sit, stand, or move about in the classroom. These specifics are especially important in the early stages of a coaching relationship.

2. The Planning Conference focuses the coach's attention on the teacher's goals. Art was once leaving a school when he noticed a classroom where the students were being especially loud. He saw children jumping on the desks, running about the room, yelling and screaming. Alarmed, he hurried to the principal's office: "You'd better get down to Room 14! Those kids are going wild and the teacher has lost control!" The principal calmly assured him, "Don't worry. They're practicing the school play. That's the riot scene." Without knowing a teacher's objectives or plan, an observer can make entirely incorrect inferences. Coaches cannot know what to look for in an observation unless they have met with the teacher before a classroom visit.

3. The Planning Conference provides for a detailed mental rehearsal of the lesson. As teachers talk with coaches about their lessons, they refine strategies, discover potential flaws in their original thinking, and anticipate decisions they may need to make in the heat of the moment. Specific questions in the Planning Conference can spark this mental rehearsal, promote metacognition, and prepare teachers with a repertoire of strategies for the lesson ahead. For example, "How will you know your strategy is working?" or "How will you know when it is time to move into the activity portion of the lesson?"

4. The Planning Conference establishes the parameters of the Reflecting Conference. Agreements in the Planning Conference establish the coach's role and the data to be collected during the lesson. This agenda is set by the teacher, and it provides the context for the Reflecting Conference. Without a Planning Conference, teachers can only evaluate their lesson in terms of what happened, rather than in terms of what their intentions were. You don't want to be in the situation of the rifleman whose targets Art and his wife saw as they traveled through Nevada. Every shot hit the bullseye! When Art and his wife stopped at a local general store, Art approached a couple of elderly gentlemen sitting on the porch. "Somebody around here's a really good marksman," Art observed. "I see all of these targets, and each one has a hole in the bullseye!" The men laughed and slapped their knees and one of them explained, "Let me tell you about that guy. He shoots first and draws the circles afterwards."

5. The Planning Conference promotes self-coaching. Our final reason for the Planning Conference may ultimately be the most important one, and it relates to the long-range goal of teacher automaticity. The coaching map represents a way of thinking about all instruction. After experiencing a number of Planning Conferences, teachers automate this way of thinking about most lessons. They internalize the conference questions, automatically asking themselves, "What's my objective?" "What's my plan?" and "How will I know students are learning?" They are activating the first step in self-coaching.

When the coach meets with the teacher before the lesson, she is seeking several kinds of information. First are the goals and objectives the teacher envisions, including the lesson plan and what the teacher wants to accomplish. We have discovered that as the coach probes and clarifies in an attempt to better understand the teacher's plan, the teacher also becomes clearer about the lesson. The coach is engaging the teacher in a process of mental rehearsal similar to what athletes do before their performances

The coach also invites the teacher to describe which strategies will be used to accomplish the goals. The coach leads the teacher to anticipate what students will be doing if they are, indeed, successfully performing the goals and objectives of the lesson. The coach helps the teacher specify what will be seen or heard within or by the end of the lesson to indicate student learning. Throughout the discussion, the coach clarifies her role in the process, the kind of data she is to collect, and the format of data collection.

We have found that in addition to the cornerstone information displayed in Figure 2-2, the two additional areas of Planning Conference talk *most frequently* useful to coach or teacher are: 1) information regarding the relationship of this lesson to the broader curriculum picture for the class, and 2) information about teacher concerns. The coach may ask the teacher, "Any concerns?" This artfully vague question allows teachers to say, "No," or to discuss anything that might be troubling them.

While the description of the planning conference described above appears to be focused on the lesson, the cognitive coach maintains her focus on the long-range outcomes: developing and automating these intellectual patterns of effective instruction.

Observing the Lesson

During the classroom Observation, the coach simply monitors for and collects data regarding the teaching behaviors and student learning as discussed in the planning conference and requested by the teacher. The coach may employ a variety of data-collection strategies including classroom maps of teacher movement, audio and video recordings, verbal interaction patterns, student participation, and on-task counts, or frequency counts of certain teacher behaviors. Of more importance, however, is the teacher's perceptions of the data and the format in which it is collected—both of which must be meaningful and relevant to the teacher's self-improvement efforts.

Coaches do not specify data-gathering instruments, nor do they offer their judgments of them. Instead, they assist the teacher in designing the instrument in the Planning Conference and in evaluating the instrument in the Reflecting Conference. The intent is to cast the teacher in the role of experimenter and researcher and the coach in the role of data collector. (A listing of those teacher and student verbal and non-verbal behaviors that teachers most often request be observed appears at the end of this chapter.)

Reflecting Conference

While the Planning Conference is best done just before instruction, when teachers are clearest about their objectives, we have found that the Reflecting Conference is most profitable when a period of time has elapsed between the lesson and the meeting. This intervening time allows the teacher to reflect on the lesson before participating in the conference, and it encourages deeper analysis and self-reflection.

Also the coach will use this time to organize the data and plan the reflective coaching strategy. The coach may wish to review the data collected and organize the rough notes in a more presentable form to give to the teacher. She may wish to reflect on the quality of trust with that teacher to decide which of the three goals (trust, learning, and holonomy) are paramount at this stage of their relationship. The coach may wish to plan and construct questions at an appropriate depth and level of complexity for the teacher at his present stage of professional development.

(1) As the Reflecting Conference begins, the coach encourages the teacher to share his impressions of the lesson and to recall specific events that support those impressions. We have found that it is important for teachers to summarize their own impressions at the outset of a conference. This way, the teacher is the only participant who is judging performance or effectiveness.

(2) The coach also invites the teacher to make comparisons between what he remembers from the lesson and what was desired (as determined in the planning phase) (3) The coach facilitates the teacher's analysis of the lesson goals by sharing data and using reflective questioning. The aim is to support the teacher's ability to draw causal relationships between his actions and student outcomes. Drawing forth specific data and employing a variety of linguistic tools are important coaching skills in supporting the teacher as he makes inferences regarding instructional decisions, teaching behaviors, and the success of the lesson. These coaching skills are elaborated in Chapter 6.

As the Reflecting Conference continues, (4) the coach will encourage the teacher to project how future lessons might be rearranged based on new learnings, discoveries, and insights. (5) The coach also invites the teacher to reflect on what has been learned from the coaching experience itself. The coach invites the teacher to give feedback about the coaching process and to suggest any refinements or changes that will make the relationship more productive.

Planning Conference, Observation, and Reflecting Conference: these are the basics of cognitive coaching. The map itself is simple, but the process becomes more complex as the coach tries to nurture a trusting relationship while understanding and facilitating teacher learning and movement toward the goal of holonomy. The following chapters describe the specific kinds of knowledge, techniques, and skills coaches need to achieve those goals. But before delving into the first of those, maintaining trust, we believe it is important to look at examples of actual coaching conferences. As you proceed in subsequent chapters, you may want to return to these interactions to see how the principles of cognitive coaching are applied.

Examples of Actual Sequences

The following transcripts are taken from the videotape series *Another Set of Eyes*.[10] As we begin, a high school chemistry teacher is meeting with his coach.

> **Marilyn:** *Hi, Lloyd.*
> **Lloyd:** *How are you, Marilyn?*
> **Marilyn:** *I'm looking forward to coming into your class-room today. What is it that you're going to be doing when I come in to visit?*
> **Lloyd:** *I'll be introducing the last unit that they'll be involved in this year. It's an acid/base unit. The main objective that I have is when we get done, hopefully they'll have developed two rules, one for being able to identify the formula of acids, and the other, to be able to identify the formula for bases.*
> **Marilyn:** *When you say develop these formulas, what do you mean by that?*

At this point, the coach is probing for specificity. Her responsibility will be to observe certain behaviors in the classroom during the lesson. Unless she knows what to look for in observable terms, she won't really understand her role as an observer. Probing for specificity also causes the teacher to be more precise about his objectives and to raise them to a conscious level in his mind. This helps him to identify operationally what his broad outcomes will be.

> **Lloyd:** *Well, I'm hoping to have them do this on their own. I'm going to use concept attainment with this group.*
> **Marilyn:** *Can I stop for just a second? When you say concept attainment, can you help me understand what you mean by concept attainment?*

Here again, Marilyn probes for specificity. Lloyd has used a term that may be open to interpretation, and Marilyn needs to understand what he means since she wants the picture in her mind to be clear and to accurately reflect his idea of the lesson. Later in the conference, Marilyn asks for additional information.

> **Marilyn:** *Okay. Now, you mentioned earlier that there was something you'd like me to look for. What is it that you'd*

like me to do today when I'm in your classroom?

The coach asks Lloyd what she should observe in his lesson that will help him later. The teacher knows best what information he needs, and he asks his coach to observe and collect this information for him. This critical question also signals to the teacher that the coach is there to assist him. The coach is coming into the classroom to observe what the teacher requests—not to make arbitrary evaluations.

> **Lloyd:** *One of the things I'd like you to do is watch what happens with the exemplars. As I mentioned, I don't use the concept attainment technique that much. It's not an easy one for me to develop . . .*

Lloyd plans to use a teaching strategy he admits he does not use very often. He displays vulnerability in seeking to increase his skill with the strategy. Some teachers may be reluctant to be observed while teaching lessons that are new to them, but Lloyd is willing to risk showing error or lack of knowledge in order to get feedback from Marilyn. This is one indicator of trust: in the relationship, in the process, and in the environment.

The coach is now prepared for the Observation. Because the coach and teacher have already determined exactly what data will serve as indicators of student learning, the coach knows where to focus data gathering. Following the lesson, the coach and teacher meet to compare what was desired and what actually happened. The Reflecting Conference frequently begins with an open-ended statement, which allows the teacher to decide how he will enter the conversation. This may be different from some supervision systems in which the coach reads back from a script of what was observed.

> **Marilyn:** *Well, how do you think it went, Lloyd?*
> **Lloyd:** *I'm not sure yet. I think I have to talk it through a little bit. I think it went well. During the first three minutes of interaction, I got back from the students what I expected to get back from this group—that they wouldn't have any specific gross misconceptions about the two concepts. When we started to do the exemplars, however, I felt as though, at least at one point, that I was losing them. I had the feeling I was talking with or working with only about five or six students.*

>**Marilyn:** *What did they do that made you feel that way?*

The second question in a Reflecting Conference is often something like this: "What are you recalling in the lesson that's leading you to those inferences?" Since the goal in cognitive coaching is to help the teacher self-modify, it's important to develop the ability to recall accurately and in detail what happened in a lesson.

Next, the teacher might be asked to do comparative thinking. For example, "How did what happened in the lesson compare with what you wanted?" Then the teacher might be asked to explain what he or she observed happening in the lesson in terms of cause-effect relationship.

The following excerpt from a Reflecting Conference shows how the teacher volunteers an evaluation and self-prescription in response to the coach's open-ended first question.

>**Diane:** *That was fun watching you in action today.*
>**Ellie:** *It was a lot more fun for me than I thought it would be. I thought I was going to be real aware of what I was doing, what the kids were doing. And actually, it was just like teaching a regular lesson. The kids acted like they always do.*
>**Diane:** *So you don't feel that having me there really got in the way?*
>**Ellie:** *I guess I'm getting used to you.*
>**Diane:** *That's good. How did you feel about the lesson in general?*
>**Ellie:** *Well, if I had it to do over, I would leave out the part about multiplying and having it be eight times bigger because that just seemed like one extra thing for kids to think about. And when I planned it, I thought that the ones that are really into art and math would choose that. But there were all kinds of people making, I thought, bad decisions about doing that.*

Later in the reflecting conference, the teacher is asked to apply what has been learned and to give the coach feedback about the process. This provides the coach with information about her skills and offers insight into what is happening in the teacher's mind as a result of cognitive coaching.

>**Diane:** *When you think back to this process, how did it feel to you? Is there anything that helped or got in the way of*

our working together?

Ellie: You didn't get in my way at all. I love this process because I like being able to ask you to look for things. I'm in that room by myself all the time with nobody noticing things that I do and always wondering, what's going on in other rooms or is there a better way to do this? I loved having the opportunity to say, "Diane, will you look at this, will you look at that."

Diane: So you liked to be able to direct what I'm going to focus on a little bit.

Ellie: Very definitely. I don't think I'd like it as much if you came in and told me what you were going to look at. Or if you came in and told me what you wanted me to teach. Now, I like having the chance to do different kinds of things when you're there, seeing what I'm most effective at, and what ways I can change it.

One goal in cognitive coaching is that the teacher, not the observer, judges what is good or bad, appropriate or inappropriate, effective or ineffective. Another goal is that the teacher becomes self-prescriptive, therefore, the coach invites the teacher to make suggestions for improvement. For coaching strategies with teachers with limited teaching repertoire see Chapter 7, Achieving Holonomy.

Getting Coaching Started

We are often asked, how do I get started, where do I begin, how do I find the time to coach, how much time should I allow, how long will it take to implement cognitive coaching, what should I do about reluctant teachers, how do I schedule the coaching conferences? While we have no prescriptions for each reader's unique situation, we have some general suggestions gleaned from working with numerous educators and school districts:

Deepening Skills. Skillfulness in cognitive coaching takes time and practice beyond the reading of this book. Other opportunities can help coaches acquire the skills and understanding of this complex process. Some staffs have used the ASCD videotape in-service program, *Another Set of Eyes: Conferencing Skills,* [11] as a centerpiece in skills training sessions for coaching. Others engage the Institute for Intelligent Behavior[12] to provide in-depth training in

Cognitive Coaching. The co-directors and the associates of the Institute for Intelligent Behavior conduct training sessions in Cognitive Coaching in many locations throughout the United States and Canada.

Getting Started. As a novice Cognitive Coach, begin with a colleague who is relatively secure and with whom you already have a trusting relationship. As your skills become more automated, you may wish to become more venturesome with new acquaintances and less experienced teachers.

For administrators whose staff have experienced a more traditional evaluative form of supervision, a demonstration in which staff members observe for differences between cognitive coaching and their previous experiences has been a highly successful strategy.

Communicate clearly at the outset that the purpose of cognitive coaching is to refine and automate the intellectual skills associated with effective instruction. Be equally clear that the coaching process is not evaluation. It is helpful to foreshadow your coaching behaviors—questioning, paraphrasing, probing—and explain why you remain nonjudgmental and do not give advice. The ASCD videotape in-service program, *Another Set of Eyes: Conferencing Techniques,* would also be helpful to acquaint the staff with cognitive coaching purposes and strategies

Some cognitive coaches have begun by switching roles—having the uninitiated teacher follow the coaching map presented in Figure 2-2 while the coach teaches a lesson to the teacher's class. Thus, the teacher becomes acquainted with the process by actually coaching the coach. Variations of this process have been used with student teachers and first-year teachers to model for them the basics of instructional thought.

Finding Time. That precious and rare commodity, time, must be allocated for coaching. For teachers engaged in peer coaching, many establish times for conferences before or after school, during planning periods, or even over lunch. Often, substitutes are hired or other resource teachers and administrators take the coach's class to free the teacher to conference and observe other teachers. Hiring a substitute teacher for a day, who spends one hour in each grade level or department to free that teacher, is a powerful and inexpensive way to free up time.

While the Planning Conference, Observation, and Reflecting Conference may consume extended time initially because both parties are learning the process, it has been found that the time condenses as the expectations of the teacher are better understood and the coach becomes more skillful. It has been found that highly proficient coaches working with teachers experienced in the process can conduct a planning conference in about 8 to 12 minutes. This does not mean speed is valued, however. It only points out that as experience is gained, there is a greater economy of time for coaching.

Administrators find time for coaching by incorporating it into their regular duties. They block out time on their calendars and inform their secretaries, staff, central office, and community that they will be in classrooms during these hours.

Scheduling. Arranging for peer coaching is most often done informally with teachers agreeing to meet at times convenient to them. Sometimes, however, substitutes need to be hired and teachers released. One school keeps a sign-up sheet in the faculty lounge to arrange for the substitute to take a class at a certain time. Often, the school administrator initially sets up a coaching session with the teacher both suggesting and agreeing on a suitable time. As trust develops, the teacher will request the conference with the administrator or other resourceful colleague.

What Are Teachers Interested in Having Observed?

When teachers are asked by the coach what concerns them and what they would like to have the coach observe, record, and provide feedback about, we have found, not surprisingly, that teachers request two rather distinct categories of behaviors: their own and their students'.

The following is a list of verbal and non-verbal behaviors, with examples of factors teachers most often want the coach to observe in their classrooms:

Non-Verbal Feedback Most Often Requested by
Teachers About Themselves

DESCRIPTION	EXAMPLE
A. Mannerisms	Pencil tapping, hair twisting, handling coins in pocket
B. Use of Time	Interruptions Transitions from one activity to another Time spent with each group Time spent getting class started, dealing with routines (such as attendance), etc. Punctuality of starting/ending times
C. Movement Throughout the Classroom	Favoring one side of the classroom over another Monitoring student progress and seatwork
D. Modality Preference	Using balanced visual, kinesthetic, auditory modes of instruction
E. Use of Handouts	Clarity, meaningfulness, adequacy and/or complexity of seatwork
F. Use of A.V. Equipment	Placement, appropriateness, operation
G. Pacing	Too fast, too slow, "beating a dead horse" (tempo/rhythm) Coverage of desired material in times allotted (synchronicity) Time spent in each section of lesson sequence (duration)
H. Meeting Diverse Student Needs	Considering/making allowances for gifted, slow, cognitive styles, emotional needs, modality strengths, languages, cultures, etc.
I. Non-verbal Feedback	Body language, gestures, proximity Moving toward or leaning into students when addressing them Eye contact
J. Classroom Arrangements	Furniture placement Bulletin board space Environment for learning Provision for multiple uses of space/activities

Verbal Feedback Most Often Requested by Teachers
About Themselves

DESCRIPTION	EXAMPLE
A. Mannerisms	Saying "O.K.," "ya know," or other phrases excessively
B. Sarcasm/Negative Feedback	Gender reference Criticism Put-downs Intonations
C. Positive/Negative Feedback	Use of praise, criticism, ignoring distractive student responses
D. Response Behaviors	Silence, accepting, paraphrasing, clarifying, empathizing Responding to students who give "wrong" answers
E. Questioning Strategies	Posing taxonomical levels of questions Asking questions in sequences
F. Clarity of Presentation	Giving clear directions Making assignments clear Checking for understanding Modeling
G. Interactive Patterns	Teacher—>Student—>Teacher—>Student Teacher—>Student—>Student—>Student
H. Equitable Distribution of Responses	Favoring gender, language proficiency, race, perception of abilities, placement in room, etc.
I. Specific Activities/Teaching Strategies	Lectures, group activities, lab exercises, discussion video, slide presentations

Non-Verbal Feedback Most Often Requested by Teachers
About Their Students

DESCRIPTION	EXAMPLE
A. Attentiveness	On task/off task Note taking Volunteering for tasks
B. Preparedness	Participation Sharing Homework Materials Volunteering knowledge
C. Movement	Negative: out of seat, squirming, fidgeting, discomfort, interfering with others Positive: following directions, transitioning, self-direction, taking initiative, consulting references/atlases/dictionaries, etc.
D. Managing Materials	A.V. equipment, textual materials, art supplies, musical instruments, lab equipment, care of library books, returning supplies, etc.

Verbal Feedback Most Often Requested by Teachers
About Their Students

DESCRIPTION	EXAMPLE
A. Participating	Positive: Volunteering verbal responses Speaking out—on task Student-to-student interaction—on task Requesting assistance Negative: Speaking out—off task Student-to-student interaction—off task
B. Social Interaction	Positive: Taking turns Listening, allowing for differences Sharing, establishing ground rules Assuming and carrying out roles Following rules of games, interactions, etc. Negative: Interrupting, interfering, hitting Name calling, put downs, racial slurs, foul language, etc. Hoarding, stealing
C. Performing Lesson Objectives	Using correct terminology Applying knowledge learned before or elsewhere Performing task correctly Conducting experiments Applying rules, algorithms, procedures, formulas, etc. Recalling information Supplying supportive details, rationale, elaborations
D. Language Patterns	Using correct grammar, spelling, punctuation, counting Using correct syntax Supplying examples
E. Insights into Student Behaviors/Difficulties	Learning styles: verbal, auditory, kinesthetic Cognitive styles: field sensitive, field independent Friendships/animosities Tolerance for ambiguity/chaos Distractibility

Summary

In this chapter the basics of the cognitive coaching processes of a planning conference, lesson observation, and reflecting conference are presented. Distinctions between the two traditional functions of evaluation and coaching were illuminated and an historical context regarding the development of clinical supervision and cognitive coaching was provided. Purposes, protocols, and examples for coaching functions in each of four stages of instructional thought—planning, teaching, reflecting and applying—were described.

This chapter also supplied start-up strategies for the novice coach and presented information about what teachers frequently ask coaches to observe.

Foundational research on teacher cognition, which supports the cognitive coaching processes will be found in Chapter 5, Cognition and Instruction. Chapter 3 addresses the first goal of cognitive coaching and the first building block toward a Renaissance School: developing and maintaining trust.

Endnotes

1. Glickman, C. Presentation at a National Curriculum Study Institute for the Association for Supervision and Curriculum Development, Scottsdale, AZ, April 1987.

2. Cogan, M. *Clinical Supervision.* Boston, MA: Houghton Mifflin Co., 1973.

3. Hunter, M. "Knowing, Teaching, and Supervising," in *Using What We Know About Teaching,* edited by P. Hosford, Alexandria, VA: Association for Supervision and Curriculum Development, 1984.

4. Pajak, E. *Approaches to Clinical Supervision: Alternatives for Improving Instruction* . Norwood, MA: Christopher-Gordon Publishers, 1993.

5. Cogan, M. *Clinical Supervision.* Boston, MA: Houghton Mifflin Co., 1973.

6. Goldhammer, R. *Clinical Supervision: Special Method for the Supervision of Teachers.* New York, NY: Holt, Rinehart, and Winston, 1969.

7. For a more detailed description of Clinical Supervision, refer to Anderson, R.H. "Clinical Supervision: Its History and Current Context." *Clinical Supervision: Coaching for Higher Performance*. Lancaster, PA: Technomic Publishing Co., 1993.

8. Pajak, E. *Approaches to Clinical Supervision: Alternatives for Improving Instruction* . Norwood, MA: Christopher-Gordon Publishers, 1993.

9. Bentz, M. and Bentz, R. "Development of Expertise in Teaching Prototypes: Non Advanced, Beginner, Expert." Presented at Annual Meeting of AERA (American Educational Research Association), April 1990.

10. For additional information about this videotape, contact the Association for Supervision and Curriculum Development at 1250 N. Pitt St., Alexandria, VA 22314 (703/549-9110).

11. For additional information about this videotape, contact the Association for Supervision and Curriculum Development at 1250 N. Pitt St., Alexandria, VA 22314 (703/549-9110).

12. For additional information about this videotape, contact the Association for Supervision and Curriculum Development at 1250 N. Pitt St., Alexandria, VA 22314 (703/549-9110).

13. Costa, A. and Garmston, R., Co-Directors, Institute for Intelligent Behavior, 720 Grizzly Peak Blvd., Berkeley, CA 94718, (510) 528-8678.

3

Developing and Maintaining Trust

Our colleague Marilyn Tabor once told us a story about her first assignment as a mentor teacher with responsibilities for staff development. She called a meeting at her school, and, because she was inexperienced in the process, she expected that everyone would attend. That wasn't necessarily so.

Gwen was one teacher who didn't come to the meeting, and she didn't attend a second one either. Marilyn decided to talk to Gwen privately, and, being apprehensive, she rehearsed exactly what she would say.

Marilyn went into Gwen's classroom one day when no students were there. Gwen looked up from her desk, crossed her arms, and said, "What do you want?" Her unexpectedly cool reaction destroyed Marilyn's prepared speech.

Marilyn searched for something else to talk about, and she saw a photograph of a young girl on Gwen's desk. When Marilyn asked who she was, Gwen answered, "That's my daughter."

"What's her name?" Marilyn asked, and they began to talk about the teacher's child. Marilyn discovered that Gwen was a single parent, and her daughter was the most important person on earth for her. They talked for quite a while, and though Marilyn remembered her speech, she was too embarrassed to say it. Instead she closed with, "Well, I'll see you later," and she left.

The next day, something remarkable happened. Gwen usually kept to herself in the faculty room, but that morning she called across the crowd, "Hi, Marilyn!" Over the next few weeks, Marilyn noticed that she and Gwen talked more, especially about Gwen's daughter. As their relationship changed, Gwen started to attend Marilyn's meetings without being asked. She even took a leadership role in certain activities.

In this situation, getting to know Gwen and being interested in what was important to her allowed the development of interpersonal trust. Trust is a vital element in all sorts of relationships, but especially so in cognitive coaching where teachers are encouraged to inquire, speculate, construct meanings, self-evaluate, and self-prescribe. These kinds of activities occur only when the coach helps create a low-stress environment where the teacher feels comfortable enough to create, experiment, reason, and problem solve. Building trust in four areas is one of the coach's most important tasks: trust in the self, trust between individuals, trust in the coaching process, and trust in the environment. Each of these four will be developed here and in later chapters.

Characteristics of Trust

We've asked hundreds of people to describe how they develop trusting relationships, and they report behaviors strongly consistent with the research: maintaining confidentiality, being visible and accessible, behaving consistently, keeping commitments, sharing personal information about out-of-school activities, revealing feelings, expressing personal interest in other people, acting nonjudgmentally, listening reflectively, admitting mistakes, and demonstrating professional knowledge and skills. Trust grows stronger as long as these behaviors continue, but a relationship can be seriously damaged when someone is discourteous or disrespectful, makes value judgments, overreacts, acts arbitrarily, threatens, or is personally insensitive to another person.

During the mid-1980s, researchers at Rutgers University studied teachers' perspectives on what makes principals trustworthy.[1] Three major characteristics emerged:

1. **Principals took responsibility for their own behaviors.** They admitted mistakes, and they did not blame anyone else.
2. **Principals were perceived as people first and roles second.** Trusted principals revealed personal information about themselves so others had a sense of who they were away from the job.
3. **Principals were perceived as non-manipulative.** Trusted leaders influenced directly, not covertly, and they had no hidden agendas.

This research also found links between interpersonal trust and trust in the environment. Teachers who had faith in the principal often trusted each other and the central office personnel.

Since cognitive coaching relies on trust, any manipulation by the coach is incompatible with this goal, and the related goal of learning. Should a principal have performance concerns about a teacher, those concerns are best communicated directly *outside* the coaching process. Coaching should never be about "fixing" the teacher. Inevitably, the motivation to "fix" is perceived, and defended against by the person being treated. For example, if you believe that your job is to fix Sara, despite all your pleasantries ("Hi Sara. I'm here to help you. How's it going today?"), Sara will accurately read your real intention. Sara gets the communication that you think something is deficient about her, or that she is not cared for.

To coach without manipulation, a principal changes the way in which she is regarding Sara. This may be difficult, but is even more necessary when you have been working over time with someone whose performance is problematic, who seems to be making limited growth, or not even making effort toward growth, or, it seems, is resistant to your assistance. It's more important because a natural outgrowth of these processes over time is frustration for the coach, and sometimes, even an unconscious blaming of the other person for remaining so resistant to change and rendering you so incompetent.

It is precisely at such times that coaches remind themselves that all behavior is motivated by positive intention from that person's point of view. Each person consistently and often unconsciously makes choices to maintain psychological benefits from existing actions and protect ego states. This reframes the interpretation of events into perspectives that free the coach from negative and debilitating emotions, enabling her to work empathically and rationally with the other person.

Now, setting aside this discussion of maintaining trust in the face of performance concerns, let's focus on what hundreds of educators and the literature[2] have to say about the practical realities of creating trust. Several themes have emerged.

Trust in Self

Self-trust is prerequiste to developing trusting relationships with others. The best coaches we've seen are conscious and clear about their own values and beliefs in areas such as pedagogy, philosophy, and spirituality. They manage their behaviors to be congruent with those core values. They experience a well-defined sense of personal identity, which comes, in part, from their ability to articulate their beliefs with precision and passion. They function at the highest stage of development on Krathwohl's Taxonomy of the Affective Domain,[3] characterization by a value or a value complex. They maintain the belief that, no matter what the situation, they will remain true to themselves. We would say that they have integrity.

Ultimately, these personal core values shape a coach's perceptions about leadership responsibilities, the meaning of learning, the potential for a school or community, and what motivates people.

Trustworthy coaches behave consistently in regard to these core values and beliefs. Because a principal's work is often fragmented, idiosyncratic, fast-paced, and unpredictable,[4] his long-term impact on a school occurs through the consistency with which he handles day-to-day interactions.

Trusting yourself also means being conscious of the ways in which you process and make meaning of experiences. For example, we relate easily to those with similar cognitive styles, but it requires great effort to withold value judgments about other people's attitudes and perceptions when their style differs from ours. Although we use all of our senses all the time, we often pay attention to one sense more than another. Knowing your modality strengths means being conscious of how you understand your experiences through visual, kinesthetic, and auditory channels.

Howard Gardner of Harvard University has proposed a schema of seven intelligences: verbal/linguistic, logical-mathematical, visual-spatial, bodily kinesthetic, music-rhythmic, interpersonal, and intrapersonal. Effective coaches become aware of their own intelligences and know how to work effectively with those who are stronger in different areas.

Effective coaches not only become aware of their own intelligences, they also know how to work effectively with others who possess other forms of intelligence as well. Wheatley[5] theorizes that the movement toward participation in organizations is rooted, perhaps subconsciously, in our changing perceptions of the universe. Knowing how to network; how to draw on the diverse resources of others; and how to value each person's expertise, diverse views, perceptions, and knowledge base is increasingly essential to survival. We might view this as a new form of interlocking intelligences: collaboratively melding the perceptions, modalities, skills, capacities, and expertise into a unified whole that is more efficient than any one of its parts.

Gender, culture, race, religion, geographical region, childhood experiences, and family history also predispose us to draw certain inferences and to attend to certain stimuli while blocking out others. And none of us leaves our emotions on the doorstep when we get to work. At times we function at less that 100 percent for a variety of spiritual or emotional reasons. Flexible coaches know when they're being influenced by their emotions, and they respect the fact that colleagues also experience emotional shifts that sap energy and distract attention.

Coaches who trust themselves are more capable of building trust with others.

Trust Between Individuals

A kindergarten teacher once told us the story of how she tried to develop trust with another teacher on the staff. "It seems the more I tried to express interest in her, reach out to her, let her know I cared for her, the more she put distance between us."

As Peg elaborated on the situation, it became clear that she had an image of how two people behave in a trusting relationship, and *she presumed the other teacher held the same vision.* As it turned out, Peg's image of trust included far more intimacy than the other teacher expected. Peg's colleague believed an emotional reserve and only a certain amount of self-disclosure characterized a comfortable, trusting relationship.

To see things from another person's point of view requires cognitive flexibility and is essential to any healthy relationship. Seeking to understand is one of the more important ways a coach can communicate that another person is valued. To support our efforts to understand, we should listen in three areas:

- What is important to the person in the long term: values, goals, ideals, interests, passions, and hobbies?
- What are the information-processing patterns the person displays, such as cognitive style, perceptual filters, and modality preferences? (We examine these in Chapter 4.)
- What are the person's current reactions, concerns, thoughts, and theories?

The expression of personal regard is also important to interpersonal trust building, especially in a cognitive coaching relationshop where praise is withheld because it interferes with thinking. (See the sidebar on "Criticism and Praise" on the following page.)

It's reported that Ken Blanchard, who wrote *The One Minute Manager*, was in San Diego, California, visiting Sea World, where they train whales and porpoises. Talking to some of the trainers, Ken said, "I understand that you are using some of my techniques; that you catch the animals doing something right and then you reward them."

The trainers said, "Yes." Blanchard was very pleased because this is what he recommended in his book when working with employees.

"However," they said, "we do something first." "What is that?" Ken asked. "When we first get the animals here to Sea World, we get into the water and play with them to convince them." Puzzled, Ken pursued, "I'm not sure I understand what you mean. What do you do in the water and what do you convince them about?" The trainers said, "We get in the water and we play with them to convince them we intend them no harm," and, the trainers added, "If we don't do that, the animals don't learn anything!"

The effect of personal regard on improved student achievement was dramatically demonstrated in one of the longest-running and most consistently successful staff development programs in education. The Teacher Expectations and Student Achievement (TESA) Program[6] found that teachers treated students perceived to be low-achieving differently from students perceived to be high-achieving. Differences in teacher expressions of regard and teacher feedback led "low-achieving" students to feel less involved and less valued. Simply correcting the imbalances in teacher communication improved learning for *all* students.[7]

Coaches signal personal regard by:
- spending time with the other person in activities not related to the coaching task,
- making inquiries or statements related to the other person's personal interests or experiences, and, of course,
- practicing all the fundamental behaviors of courtesy and respect—proximity, touch, courteous language, personal compliments—revealed in the TESA research.

Sometimes schools get so busy and task oriented, these little personal connections are abandoned and the teacher's day-to-day workplace becomes an emotional wasteland.

Trust in the Coaching Process

Nearly all relationship difficulties are rooted in conflicting or ambiguous expectations surrounding roles and goals. Whether we are assigning tasks at work or choosing a decision-making process for a meeting, we can be certain that unclear expectations will lead to misunderstanding, disappointment, and decreased trust.

 Skillful coaches maintain trust by signaling the purpose of their communications:

"*I'm not going to give you advice.* Let's explore some alternatives together."

"*My job is not to evaluate you,* but to help you reflect on your teaching."

Clear expectations are most important in dealing with the purposes and forms of classroom observations. Where principals perform the two supervisory functions of coaching and evaluation, it's important to be clear about the goals of a classroom visit. Confusion, suspicion, and even hostility arise when a teacher isn't certain which activity is occurring: coaching or evaluation. In Chapter 6, we elaborate on the information the teacher and coach need to develop trust in the coaching process.

Rapport and Its Relationship to Trust

There is one common flow, one common breathing, all things are in sympathy.

Hippocrates

Trust is about the whole of a relationship; rapport is about the moment. Trust is belief in and reliance on another person developed over time. Rapport is comfort with and confidence in someone during a specific interaction. Rapport may be naturally present or you may consciously seek it, even when you are meeting a parent, student, or colleague for the first time. You cannot manipulate someone into a relationship of trust and rapport, but you can draw on specific nonverbal and verbal behaviors to nurture the relationship.

Nonverbal Behaviors

On average, adults find more meaning in nonverbal cues than in verbal ones. A recent summary of communication literature supports the theory that nearly two-thirds of meaning in any social situation is derived from nonverbal cues.[8]

During the early 1970s a graduate student and a professor of linguistics at the University of California at Santa Cruz, Richard Bandler and John Grinder, conducted a series of investigations to learn why some therapists were almost magically effective in contrast to others who simply did a good job. They initially studied Fritz Perls, the father of Gestalt therapy; Virginia Satir, noted for her results in family therapy; and Milton Erickson, generally acknowledged to be the world's leading practitioner of medical hypnosis.[9]

The researchers discovered that Perls, Satir, and Erickson constantly mirrored their clients. For example, if the client had his legs crossed, the therapist crossed his legs. If the client leaned forward on his elbows, so did the therapist. When the client spoke rapidly, the therapist did too.

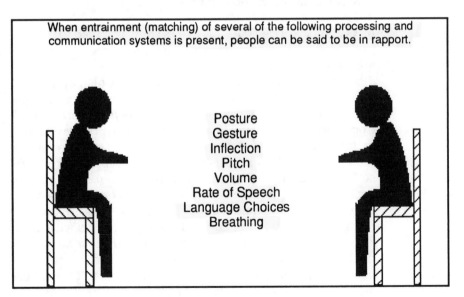

When entrainment (matching) of several of the following processing and communication systems is present, people can be said to be in rapport.

Posture
Gesture
Inflection
Pitch
Volume
Rate of Speech
Language Choices
Breathing

Figure 3-1
Manifestations of Rapport

Whether they were conscious of it or not, Perls, Satir, and Erickson were modeling the theory of entrainment, which was formulated in 1665 after a Dutch scientist noted that two pendulum clocks mounted side-by-side on a wall would swing together in a precise rhythm. It was discovered that the clocks were synchronized by a slight impulse through the wall.

Human beings also seek this kind of synchronization. George Leonard reports that human beings pulse at frequencies of oscillation as do the simplest single-celled organisms at the atomic, molecular, sub-cellular, and cellular levels.[10]

When two people "oscillate" at nearly the same rates, we observe entrainment, a manifestation of rapport. At the Boston University School of Medicine, William Condon studied films of many sets of two people talking.[11] Not only were the bodies of the speakers matched, but a "very startling phenomenon" was observed: entrainment existed between the speaker's words and the listener's movements. As one person would talk, the second person would make tiny corresponding movements.

As Condon expressed it, "Listeners were observed to move in precise shared synchrony with the speaker's speech. This appears to be a form of entrainment since there is no discernible lag even at 1/48 second. . . . It also appears to be a universal characteristic of human communication, and perhaps characterizes much of animal behavior in general. Communication is thus like a dance, with everyone engaged in intricate and shared movements across many subtle dimensions, yet all strangely oblivious that they are doing so."[12] An example of entrainment in a school setting might be: Lee says, "Fran, I've got some teachers on my staff doing things I am really excited about. I'm trying to figure out how I can get them to share some of their good ideas with other faculty." *While Lee is speaking, she gestures broadly with her hands and arms. Then she shrugs her shoulders as she notes her predicament.* Now Fran says, "Lee, tell me a little bit about what's so special about these teachers." *As Fran speaks, she mirrors Lee's gestures and body movements.*

Because Lee's nonverbal behaviors are congruent with her feelings and thoughts, each particular movement and gesture conveys specific meanings. When Fran borrows these same nonverbal cues, Lee subconsciously senses that Fran knows exactly what she's talking about.

Photo by Bruce Wellman, Science Resources, Lincoln, Mass.

Figure 3-2
Body and Gesture Matching as Manifestations of Rapport

Don't imagine you can trick someone into a trusting relationship. Babad, Bernieri, and Rosenthal conducted a study where five groups of judges viewed 10-second film clips of teachers talking to or about students. The judges, who ranged from fourth graders to experienced teachers, were asked to rate the students' scholastic excellence and the teacher's love for each student. In some cases the judges heard teachers talking about students; in other cases they simply watched—with no sound—as the teacher talked to a student (who was not seen). In each case, one was a good student of high potential and one a weak student of poor potential. The judges were asked to rate the student's scholastic excellence and the teacher's love for that student.

None of the judges had difficulty in detecting students' excellence and teachers' love. The negative affect teachers tried to conceal were detected by observers through "leaks" in communication channels not under as much conscious control as what the teachers said to the student.[13]

The teachers' words gave them away when they talked about students; their actions alone gave them away when they were talking to the students. We can consciously take actions to nurture trust and rapport, but we can't mask our true feelings.

Verbal Behaviors

Nonverbal communications may convey much of the meaning in an exchange, but the words we choose—and how we state them—also have a strong effect (see the sidebar "The Language of Coaching"). Through the cognitive coaching process, coaches must seek a nonjudgmental environment where teachers feel safe to experiment and risk. We have identified five nonjudgmental verbal approaches that contribute to interpersonal trust: structuring, silence, accepting, clarifying, and providing data.

The Language of Coaching

During the Reflecting Conference, coaches send clear messages that the relationship is one of coaching when they provide data without interpretation. For example:

"Seventeen students responded."
"You paused, walked to the other side of the room, and then responded."

Coaches also ask open-ended questions, which signals that there are no preconceived right answers:

"How did you feel about the lesson?"
"How did you decide what to do next?"
"What do you think might have caused that?"

Effective Reflecting Conference questions invite the teacher to state impressions, recall data, make inferences, develop cause-effect relationships, metacogitate, evaluate, predict, and self-prescribe.

Well-intentioned but poorly formed questions can cross the line from coaching to evaluation, upsetting rapport and weakening trust. For example, the question, "What two things went well?" implies that the observer has judged that only two things went well. This sets up the possibility that some things didn't go well.

Observers signal evaluation when they make value judgments. For example:
"That was a good job."
"You did a nice job using wait time."
"Your directions could have been clearer."

An observer also signals evaluation by interpreting data and lesson events:
"The lesson allowed students to apply the concept."
"Your questioning strategy produced complex thinking in your students."
"They understood because you modeled."

Structuring. A safe, trusting relationship exists when you know what the other person expects of you. When expectations are unclear, you spend your energy and mental resources interpreting cues about what the other person wants and detecting any hidden agendas. With structuring, the coach clearly and deliberately communicates expectations about the purposes for and use of resources such as time, space, and materials. Structuring generates a common understanding of the purposes for an Observation, the roles the coach should play, time allotments, the most desirable location for the conference, and the placement of the coach during the Observation. For example, a coach might ask, "Since you want me to observe the students' on-task behavior, I'll need to sit in a place in the room where I can see them all. Where would that be?" Or, "It will take us about 15 minutes for a Planning Conference. Let's set a time that would be convenient for both of us."

Silence. Some coaches make the mistake of waiting only one or two seconds after they ask a question before they ask another one or give the answer themselves. It may seem nothing is happening unless someone is talking, but silence is actually an indicator of a productive conference. A coach who waits communicates respect for the teacher's reflection and processing time and faith in the teacher's ability to perform a complex cognitive task. A coach who doesn't allow adequate time to answer subconsciously communicates that the teacher is inadequate and really can't reason through to an appropriate answer.[14] Waiting for an answer also models the same thoughtfulness, reflection, and restraint of impulsivity that are desirable behaviors for teachers to use with students.

Sometimes periods of silence seem interminably long. But if trust is the goal, teachers must have the opportunity to do their own thinking and problem solving. Coaches who wait only a short time elicit short, one-word responses. Coaches who wait for longer periods receive answers with complete sentences and thoughts. Coaches who allow time for thought see a perceptible increase in the creativity of the teacher's response.[15]

Criticism and Praise

We'd expect a statement like "Can you give me a *better* answer?" to weaken someone's trust. But what about saying "Your lesson was *excellent!*" Surprisingly, praise can be as damaging to trust as criticism and other put downs.

Criticism. We define criticism as negative value judgements. A coach who responds to a teacher's ideas or actions with such negative words as poor, incorrect, or wrong is signaling inadequacy and disapproval. This terminates the teacher's thinking about the task. Negative responses can be subtle statements, such as "You're *almost* right," or "You're getting *close*." Sometimes the intonation of the voice conveys sarcasm or a negative impression: "Why would you want to do it that way?" or "Where on earth did you get that idea?" However it happens, criticism leaves the teacher with a feeling of failure, cognitive inadequacy, and poor self-concept.

Praise. When we praise, we use positive value judgments such as good, excellent, and great. Some peer coaching and supervisory strategies advocate the use of praise to reinforce behaviors and build trust, but the research on praise indicates that the opposite is more often the case. While most of us enjoy rewarding and praising others, Brophy[1] found that the one person for whom praise has the most beneficial effects is the praise giver. When praise and rewards are given, experimentation is inhibited.[2] Teachers tend to acquire or exercise skills that the coach values rather than their own.[3] A skillful coach will avoid phrases such as:

"That was an *outstanding* strategy you used today, Linda."
"You're doing a *great* job, Leo."
"Yours was the *best* lesson plan that anybody shared."
"Your students are progressing *well* and certainly did a *good* job today."

Nonjudgmental Accepting Responses. A coach who *acknowledges* is simply indicating that she heard what the teacher said. For example, "I understand," or "Uh huh."

A coach *paraphrases* by rephrasing, recasting, translating, summarizing, or giving an example of what the teacher said. The coach strives to maintain the intent and accurate meaning of the teacher's idea, even while using different words and phrases. The paraphrase is possibly the most powerful of all the nonjudgmental verbal responses because it communicates that "I'm attempting to understand you, " and that says, "I value you."

Finally, a coach who *empathizes* acknowledges feelings and emotional states in addition to cognition. This does not mean that the coach agrees with the emotions or behaviors; she simply acknowledges that they are there. For example, "You're confused because those directions are so unclear." Or, "You're frustrated because the students are not doing their homework when you assign it."

Probing and Clarifying. Clarifying signals that the coach does not understand what the teacher is saying and needs more information. Clarifying is not meant to be a devious way of redirecting what the teacher is thinking or feeling. Nor is it a subtle way of expressing criticism of something the teacher has done. The intent of probing and clarifying is to help the coach better understand the teacher's ideas, feelings, and thought processes.

Clarifying is often stated in the form of a question, but it might also be a statement inviting further information. For example, "Could you explain what you mean by 'appreciate the music'? I'm not sure I understand." Or, "So you're saying that you'd rather have the students work by themselves rather than in a group. Is that correct?"

Clarifying contributes to trust because it communicates to the teacher that her ideas are worthy of exploration and consideration; their full meaning, however, is not yet understood.

Providing Data. One of the main objectives of cognitive coaching is to nurture the teacher's capacities for processing information by comparing, inferring, or drawing causal relationships. Data, therefore, must be rich and readily available for the teacher to process.

During the Observation, the coach will use whatever technique or instrument was agreed upon to gather information: for example, a television or an audio recording, a classroom map, or verbatim transcripts. In the Reflecting Conference, this information may be presented to the teacher in a nonjudgmental, nonconfrontational fashion: "You asked three questions within the first five minutes of your lesson," or, "Of the six students you wanted me to observe, Eric spoke four times, Bernadine spoke two times, Shaun spoke once, and the remaining three not at all." Suggestions for providing data will be presented in Chapter 6.

Trust in the Coaching Process

We've heard horror stories of supervisors observing classrooms without a Planning Conference, leaving teachers totally in the dark about why the supervisor is in the room. Teacher anxiety mounts, and the Reflecting Conference is nearly a disaster because there are no common expectations about the purposes, focus, and procedures of the Observation. The Planning Conference, Observation, and Reflecting Conference each play a vital role in cognitive coaching, and each offers an opportunity to further trust in the coaching process and relationship between teacher and coach.

Increasingly, as the coach and the teacher work together in a non-threatening relationship they place greater value in the coaching process. They realize the intent of this process is to grow intellectually, to learn more about learning, and mutually to increase their capacity for self-improvement. They realize that the process is not one which the "superior" does to the "inferior"; rather, they are two dedicated professionals striving to solve problems, improve learning, and make curriculum more vibrant. Furthermore, the teacher soon realizes that the coach is working at the coaching processes as hard as the teacher is in the teaching process.

In time, we find that teachers begin requesting the process because they find it helpful:
"That felt good."
"You really made me think."
"Could you come back?"

"Would you teach me how to coach like that?"

Soon, the process begins to spread. Word gets around through the school "grapevine." Principals call each other on the phone requesting to be cognitively coached through an upcoming parent conference; the director of staff development calls a principal to be coached through a forthcoming in-service. Teachers in grade-level or department meetings soon find that they are doing "it" spontaneously with each other, beyond the classroom situation.

Planning Conference

The Planning Conference is the time to clarify expectations for the coaching experience. Trust is enhanced when the coach and the teacher have agreed beforehand when the Observation will occur and what teacher and/or student behavior will be observed. During the Planning Conference, the teacher specifies what should be recorded and helps determine how the information will be recorded, including what type of instrument to use. The teacher also defines why the data are important and how she will use the information after it is collected. Throughout the Planning Conference, the coach is deliberately nonjudgmental in her questions and responses. Just as she will in the Reflecting Conference, she withholds both positive and negative value judgments about the content of the lesson and the decisions the teacher describes. Such a conversation might sound something like this:

    Coach: *I'll be happy to gather wait-time data for you. At what particular points in the lesson do you want me to do this?*

    Teacher: *During the open discussion I conduct with the class right after they've seen the film.*

    Coach: *What, specifically, would you like me to observe and record?*

    Teacher: *The time I wait after asking a question before calling on a student.*

    Coach: *So you'd like me to record how long you wait after your questions before you call on someone.*

    Teacher: *Yes, oh, and why don't you also measure my wait time after they respond.*

    Coach: *Do you want me to try to record your questions and/or the student responses too?*

    Teacher: *Yes, get my questions, because that will help me remember the parts of the lesson we were working on. But* *don't write any student responses.*

*   **Coach:** Wait time seems to be pretty important to you.*
Why is it significant for you in this particular lesson?

*   **Teacher:** I'm trying to get students to do more complex*
thinking and . . .

The Observation

During the lesson, the coach's role is to gather data related
to teacher behavior and student achievement that was
agreed upon during the Planning Conference. Trusted
coaches know that while they are providing a service to the
teacher, they are also guests in the classroom. They make
themselves as unobtrusive as possible. Where the coach sits
or wanders (depending on the Observation focus) has already been agreed to during the Planning Conference, and
the coach does not deviate from this.

How does the coach avoid making judgments during an
Observation? Actually, she doesn't. All humans are "judgment machines," constantly generating thoughts, opinions,
and attitudes about ongoing experiences. But making such
judgments public is counterproductive to any trusting
relationship. When skilled coaches notice they're mentally
making judgments, they set them aside. If related information is important to their data-gathering, they record that
information in terms free from judgment or inference.

Reflecting Conference

A coach can signal a trusting atmosphere in the Reflecting
Conference by starting out with a statement that shows
positive personal regard for the teacher or the experience of
being with the teacher. The coach might say, "I really
enjoyed being in your class," or "I had fun with the lesson,"
or "I learn something every time I watch you teach."
As in the Planning Conference, the teacher is the guide to the
conversation that follows. The coach may begin the Conference by inviting the teacher to summarize his impressions of
the lesson, but questions are deliberately open so the teacher
is free to communicate whatever is important to him and his
impressions of the lesson. If a teacher says, "I think the lesson
went great," the next logical question is something like, "What
are you recalling that leads to your impression that the class
went great?" This clearly signals that the coach intends to have
a nonjudgmental data-based discussion, which promotes

trust during the exchange that follows.

At any time during the Reflecting Conference, trust is diminished if the teacher draws the inference that the coach is making judgments about the teacher's performance. The coach's job is to provide data and ask questions in such a way that the teacher feels free to safely perform critical self-reflection. Criticism should only come from the teacher.

In the end, trust is further cemented when the coach asks the teacher to evaluate the coaching process and recommend refinements. This specifically signals that the exchange was a coaching situation, not an evaluation, and it shows the teacher that the coach is working to refine her behaviors, too. It also communicates that the teacher is the authority about which coaching behaviors are most appropriate and useful.

Endnotes

1. Kupersmith, W. and Hoy,W. "The Concept of Trust: An Empirical Assessment," presentation at the American Educational Research Association Annual Meeting, New Orleans, LA, 1989.

2. Such diverse authors as the following have described the essential nature of trust and the operation of trust in productive working relationships:

    Drucker, P.F. *The Effective Executive*. New York, NY: Harper & Row Publishers, 1967.

    Deal, T.E. and Kennedy, A.A. *Corporate Culture: The Rites and Rituals of Corporate Life*. Menlo Park, CA: Addison-Wesley Publishing Company, 1982.

    Likert, R. *The Human Organization: Its Management and Value*. New York, NY: McGraw-Hill Book Company, 1967.

    Gibb, J. *Trust: A New View of Personal and Organizational Development*. Los Angeles, CA: The Guild of Tutors Press, 1978.

    Ouchi, W. *Theory Z: How American Business Can Meet the Japanese Challenge*. Menlo Park, CA: Addison-Wesley Publishing Company, 1981.

    Bennis, W. and Nanus, B. *Leaders: The Strategies for Taking Charge*. New York, NY: Harper & Row Publishers, 1985.

Rosenholtz, S.J. *Teachers' Workplace: The Social Organization of Schools*. White Plains, NY: Longman, Inc., 1989.

Schmuck, R. and Runkel, P. *The Handbook of Organization Development in Schools, 3rd Edition*. Prospect Heights, IL: Waveland Press, Inc., 1985.

Senge, P. *The Fifth Discipline: The Art and Practice of the Learning Organization*. New York, NY: Doubleday, 1990.

Scearce, C. *100 Ways to Build Teams*. IRI/Skylight Publishing, IL, 1992.

Covey, S. *The 7 Habits of Highly Effective People: Powerful Lessons in Personal Change*. New York, NY: Simon & Schuster, Inc., 1989.

Bracey, H. et al. *Managing From the Heart*. New York, NY: Delacorte Press, 1990.

3. Krathwohl, D.R. *Taxonomy of Educational Objectives: The Classification of Educational Goals, Book 2: Affective Domain*. New York, NY: Longmans, 1956–1964.

4. Peterson, K. "The Principal as Instructional Leader," *The Peabody Journal of Education* (1985): Vol. 63, p. 1. This is expressed by Krathwohl and others in the Taxonomy of Education Objectives in the Affective Domain (1956) as the highest form of affective attainment. Krathwohl labeled it "characterization by a value or a value complex." This means the principal's consistency in action is an expression of a set of core values in a variety of settings over time.

5. Wheatley, M. J. *Leadership and the New Science*, San Francisco, CA: Berrett-Koehler Publishers, 1992.

6. Kerman, S. ESEA Title III Project, "Equal Opportunity in the Classroom Project Coordinator Training Handbook," Downey, CA: Office of the Los Angeles County Superintendent of Schools, 1977.

7. Joyce, B. and Showers, B. *Student Achievement Through Staff Development*, New York, NY: Longman, Inc., 1988.

8. Burgoon, J.K., Buller, D.B. and Woodall, W.G. *Nonverbal Communication: The Unspoken Dialogue*, New York, NY: Harper and Row, 1989.

9. Bandler R. and Grinder, J. *The Structure of Magic*. Palo Alto, CA: Science and Behavior Books, Inc., 1975.

    Lankton, S. *Practical Magic: A Translation of Basic Neuro Linguistic Programming Into Clinical Psychotherapy*. Cupertino, CA: Meta Publications, 1980, p. 38.

10. Leonard, G. *The Silent Pulse: A Search for the Perfect Rhythm That Exists in Each of Us.* New York, NY: Bantam Books, Inc. by arrangement with E. P. Dutton Publishing Co., Inc., 1978.

11. Condon, W.S. "Multiple Response to Sound in Dysfunctional Children," *Journal of Autism and Childhood Schizophrenia,* (1975): Vol. 5, Issue 1, p. 43.

12. Condon, W.S. "Multiple Response to Sound in Dysfunctional Children," *Journal of Autism and Childhood Schizophrenia,* (1975): Vol. 5, Issue 1, p. 43.

13. Babad, E., Bernieri, F. and Rosenthal, R. "Students as Judges of Teachers' Verbal and Non-Verbal Behavior," *American Educational Research Journal* (1991): Vol. 28, Issue 1, pp. 211–234.

14. Brophy, J. "Teacher Behavior and Its Effects." *Journal of Educational Psychology* (1979): 71, pp. 733–750.

15. Rowe, M. B."Wait Time and Rewards as Instructional Variables: Their Influence on Language, Logic, and Fate Control," *Journal of Research in Science and Teaching* (1974): Vol. 11, pp. 81-94.

Sidebar Endnotes

1. Rowe, M.B. (1974). "Wait Time and Rewards as Instructional Variables: Their Influence on Language, Logic, and Fate Control," *Journal of Research in Science Teaching,"* Vol. 11, pp. 81–94.

2. Rowe, M.B. (1974). "Wait Time and Rewards as Instructional Variables: Their Influence on Language, Logic, and Fate Control," *Journal of Research in Science Teaching,"* Vol. 11, pp. 81–94.

3. Lepper, M. and Greene, D. (1978). *The Hidden Cost of Rewards: New Perspectives on the Psychology of Human Motivation.* New York, NY: Erlbaum.

4

Flexibility in Coaching

It is estimated that at one mating, a pair of human parents can potentially produce 64 trillion genetically different offspring.[1] Is it any wonder that individuals are so varied?

We differ in temperament, tempo, signature, and thumbprint. We like different books, people, music, and work. Some of us are sloppy, some fastidious. Many are serene, many others stressed. We are light-skinned, dark-skinned, slim, and stout. Genetic and environmental histories combine to make each of us truly unique, specifically like no other.

Skilled coaches are sensitive to these differences, and they adapt the coaching process for each person with whom they work. Hand-in-hand with developing trust is knowing how to be flexible with people. To do this, coaches constantly sense, search for, and detect cues about another person's thinking processes, beliefs, modality preferences, and styles. Coaches constantly expand their repertoire so they can match their style to a variety of situations and individuals. Though we do not define it as a separate coaching goal, developing flexibility is also a prerequisite for understanding teachers' learning processes and seeking holonomy. In Chapter 7 we examine the state of mind of flexiblity. Here we present information about five areas in which coaches practice flexibility: perception, cognitive styles, belief systems, gender, and ethnicity.

Understanding Perception

None of us experiences the world in exactly the same way. In fact, all the information we receive through our eyes, ears, nose, mouth, and skin has been selected and distorted before it even reaches our brain. For example, the rods and cones of the retina respond not to light itself but to differences in that light. Reading this book, your eyes flicker so that the rods at the boundary of black and white are stimulated, which projects an upside-down image on the retina. This image is coded electrically and reassembled by the brain's visual cortex. Thus, we literally construct the images we "see."

Furthermore, the images we "see" are prescribed by the unique physical properties of the human eye. A honeybee's eyes cannot perceive the same waves of light we can, and they don't see the usual colors we do. If we are looking at flowers together, they sense the honey while we recognize the white petals and yellow center of a daisy. A dog would see the same flowerbed as if through a wide-angle lens and in black and white. A bat would experience the garden as an echo of ultrasound.[2]

Differences between human perceptions and the perceptions of other species are genetically determined, but they're also affected by environment. In an experiment at Harvard Medical School,[3] kittens were placed in a white box with only vertical black stripes. A second group lived in a world of only horizontal stripes, and a third group in a box that was simply left white. After being exposed to these conditions during the critical few days when sight develops, the kitten's brains conformed to them for life. For example, the cats raised in a horizontal world were unable to perceive vertical objects like furniture legs. Chopra remarks, "This was not because they didn't believe in the existence of vertical stripes, but because their brains did not have the connections to register those perceptions."[4] This phenomenon is termed a "premature cognitive commitment." Thinking that things are the way they appear to be is simply not true.

Similar selections, distortions, and constructions occur within each of our five senses: seeing, hearing, feeling, tasting, and smelling. It is for this reason that we describe the human processing of sensory information in terms of "representational systems." That is, what we hear is a representation in our mind of the original sound, and what we see is a representation of a picture. The reality is created deep inside our brain.[5] Furthermore, when we think, we re-experience the information in the sensory form in which we first experienced it: as pictures, sounds, feelings, tastes, or smells.

How do honeybees, "representational systems," and the five senses affect the cognitive coach? Understanding how we each create different perceptions allows us to accept others' points of view as simply different, not wrong. We come to understand that we should be curious about other peoples' impressions and understandings—not judgmental. The more we understand about how someone else processes information, the better we can communicate with them.

Representational Systems

Flexible coaches are sensitive to the unique ways each person processes information. We think in pictures, sounds, feelings, tastes, and smells, and we use the same neurological pathways to represent our experience internally as we do to experience it directly.

In Western culture, the primary systems in which we think are the visual, auditory, and kinesthetic. All persons think using these three primary representational systems, and we each favor one or two, even though we are often unaware of our thoughts in more than one of the systems. In addition to having a "highly preferred" representational system, each person has a lead system. Think back to your last birthday. Did you first see pictures, hear sounds, or experience feelings? This is your lead system, the jump start to your thinking process. Perhaps you saw a picture of a friend's face, followed by feelings of relaxation. In that case, your lead system would be visual and your preferred system kinesthetic.

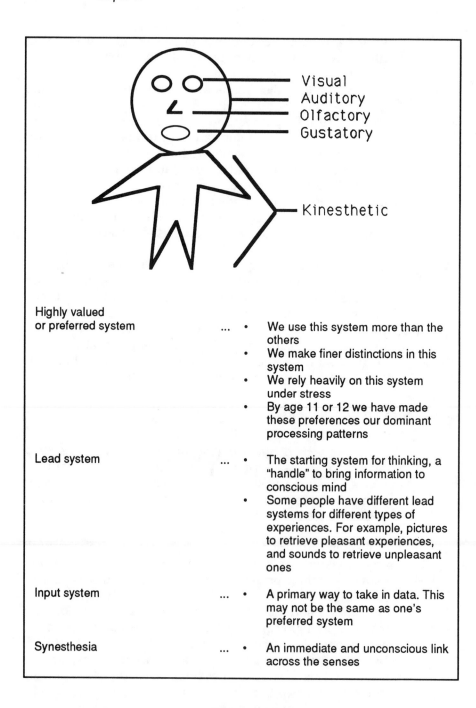

Figure 4-1
Representational Systems

The person with the greatest flexibility has the greatest influence in any system. The most effective coaches are conscious of their own and others' personal styles, patterns, and predispositions. They flexibly work in different ways with each individual according to the ways in which each is unique. This is important for the development of trust because across all stylistic differences we tend to be more comfortable with, and therefore trust more easily, people with similar styles.

Flexible coaches personalize and tailor each moment of communication to the individual, responding to the representational systems the other person is using. This has two benefits: deeper rapport and communication that requires no translation. Two types of cues indicate which representational system a person is using in the moment: language and eye movement.

Language Cues

Our words are often clues to our thinking processes, and we've heard several stories about how this was first discovered. In one version, Bandler and Grinder noticed certain speech patterns as they watched therapist Virginia Satir at work. One client said to Satir, "Virginia, I just can't *see* things *clearly*. I've lost my sense of *perspective*. My prospects are *dim*." Satir responded, "Let me *see* if I get the *picture*. Your horizons are *dark*. Your prospects are *cloudy*. You'd like to develop a *brighter focus*." Both the client and Stair spoke in rich, visual terms.

Another client told Satir, "I am feeling *low*. I'm just *down* a lot of the time. I've lost my *grip*. I can't seem to get *moving*." These words are primarily kinesthetic, referencing emotions, tactile sensations, and sensorimotor or positional aspects of experience. Satir responded, "What I *get* is enormous *depression*. It's like you're living *under* a rock and you have this great *weight* on your shoulders. You're feeling *pressure*. You'd like to *push* these *feelings* away and be *relaxed, at ease*."

As you listen to a person talk, you may discover there are times when a majority of his/her predicates (descriptive words and phrases—primarily verbs, adverbs and adjectives) are from one of the modality or representational systems listed below. This person is choosing, usually at an unconscious level, to isolate one system from his/her ongoing stream of representational system experiences. This is an indicator for you of how this person is best understanding his/her experiences and how you can best communicate.

Visual	Auditory	Kinesthetic
see	hear	feel
look	listen	grasp
observe	speak	handle
watch	tell myself	energetic
clear	verbalize	in touch
viewpoint	told	gut feeling
perspective	talk	firm
point of view	say	foundation
visualize	clear as a bell	on the level
eyeball	tune in	relaxed
hazy	resonate	tense
fuzzy	tone	weighty
murky	harmonious	heavy
vivid	volume	come to grips
light	loud	lightweight
transparent	dissonant	raise an issue
lighten up	pitch	grasp the situation
look something up	high pitched	let go
picture	low key	sleep on it
reflect	squeaky	hurt
acuity	singsong	touchy
see the light	ring my chimes	irrational
focus	unheard of	pushy
image	well said	pain in the neck
mirror	answer	itchy
insight	so to speak	foot the bill
foreshadow	drum it in	shoulder the blame
red	mellifluous	soft touch
purple		

Olfactory	Gustatory	Nonspecific
smell	taste	think
odor	tasteless	experience
scent	tasteful	know
aroma	salivate	intellectualize
fragrant	mouthwatering	understand
rotten	tip of my tongue	perceive
fresh	delicious	respond
	lip smacker	accurate
	sweet	solution
	spicy	resolve
	bitter pill to swallow	strategy
	bit off more than she/he	logical
	could chew	

Figure 4-2
Representational Systems:
Language Indicators of Modality Preferences

As coaches listen to a person talk, they may discover the majority of words are from one of the sensory-based representational systems listed in Figure 4-2. This is an indicator of how the person is representing this experience at this time. It is also a cue that you can best communicate by using metaphoric language from the same representational system.[6] We refer to this as language congruence. For example, when someone says, "They play hardball around here," you can respond by saying, "Yeah, it's really tough. Bases are loaded, you go up to bat, and the team is counting on you."

Following is an example of a discussion between two teachers in which the coach is intuitively matching the language of a colleague in her department. As you read, notice how Maria congruently matches Tom's visual style.

> **Tom:** *Thanks for agreeing to* **observe** *my third period Economics class.*
>
> **Maria:** *I'm* **looking** *forward to* **watching**. *What will I* **see** *students doing?*
>
> **Tom:** *What you will* **see** *is students taking notes from a video tape and lecture about the influence of political philosophy on economic policies preceding, during and after President Reagan's two terms of office.*
>
> **Maria:** *So I'll* **see** *students taking notes. What specifically do you want them to learn?*
>
> **Tom:** *The* **focus** *of today's lesson is on two world leaders: Ronald Reagan and Margaret Thatcher, Prime Minister of Great Britain, and how their political philosophy influenced their nations' economies. Today the students will* **watch** *a video program about the Reagan Era. I want them to understand the concept of conservatism and to* **see** *its relationship to world trade, domestic policy and inflation.*
>
> **Maria:** *Can you* **illustrate** *for me what you mean by "***seeing** *the relationship"? What will you* **observe** *students doing as evidence that they are* **getting that picture***?*

Regrettably, the research and literature on language congruence has been rife with misunderstanding and methodological errors. But several solid studies—and our own experience—have affirmed the relationship between language and representational systems.[7]

Eye Movement

With the advent of research in brain specialization, scientists have investigated the relationship between particular types of eye-movement patterns and variations in brain functioning. Several researchers agree that eye movements indicate differences in cognitive involvement and hemispheric dominance.[8] In an approach largely validated in our own informal and nonscientific observations, eye-movement patterns provide a kind of external graph of internal sensory activity[9] for a typical right-handed person. This information is reversed for many left handers.

- Eye movement to the upper left of the person's face indicates that past visual memories are being stimulated.
- Eye movement to the person's upper right indicates a visual construction of new or future images.
- Unfocused eyes reflect imagery.
- Eye movements in a lower-left direction indicate accessing of an internal auditory process.
- Eyes moving horizontally to the left or right indicate auditory processes.
- Eye movements to the person's lower right indicate accessing of kinesthetic experiences (see Figure 4-3).

The literature is rich with examples of therapists understanding and communicating with clients based on their attentive reading of eye patterns. Some eye movements indicate the duration of cognitive processing, which gives the coach information on the use of silence and how long to wait. Coaches can use eye-movement information to select language congruent with the representational system the teacher is currently using. More importantly, eye movements indicate when to use wait time and how long to wait. Eye movements signal that someone is focusing attention internally, and therefore additional comments or questions can't be processed.

Persons who process auditorily typically do so quickly. (Eye movements to either ear are much quicker than eye movements up or down.) Persons who process information visually take slightly longer, and processing kinesthetically takes longest (from two to five seconds, as described in research by Mary Budd Rowe). Readers interested in observing eye movements are encouraged to watch the planning and reflecting conference on the ASCD Video Tape, *Another Set of Eyes: Conferencing Skills. Practice Tape 1.*[10]

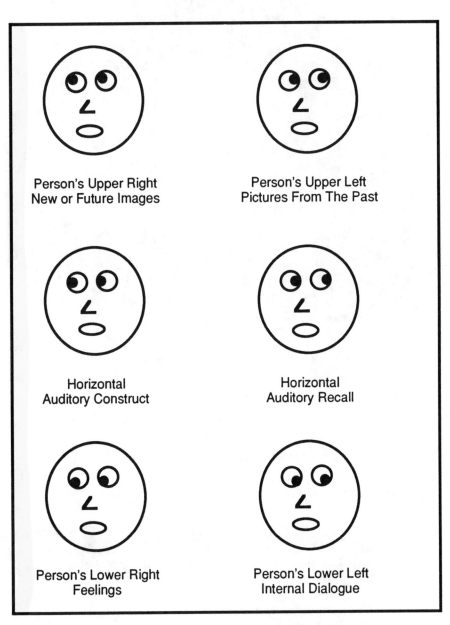

Person's Upper Right
New or Future Images

Person's Upper Left
Pictures From The Past

Horizontal
Auditory Construct

Horizontal
Auditory Recall

Person's Lower Right
Feelings

Person's Lower Left
Internal Dialogue

(Depicted as you are looking at a normally organized right handed person)

Figure 4-3
Eye Movements and Representational Systems

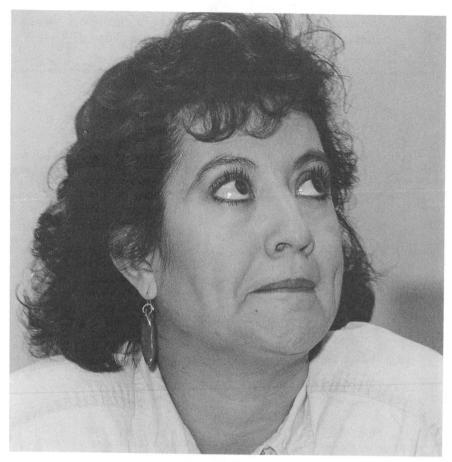

Photo by Bruce Wellman, Science Resources, Lincoln, Mass.

Figure 4-4
Accessing Her Visual Memory

Cognitive Styles

Perhaps the greatest accomplishment for the coach is maintaining flexibility with cognitive styles. If there is an area in which we are likely to be judgmental about others, this is it.

Two persons looking at the same invitation to a dinner party may literally see something different. Amy will notice the time, date, and location of the affair as well as the recommended dress. Jane will register with pleasure that she has been invited to a party by a friend. She notices that the event is planned for Thursday, an evening she is usually free. It wouldn't be unheard of for Jane to arrive at the party on the wrong Thursday or get lost on the way because she didn't pay attention to details. Amy's and Jane's readings of the party invitation illustrate differences in cognitive styles.

Numerous models and theories explain stylistic differences, but we have found that Herman Witkin's Field Dependence-Independence Theory of cognitive styles is a simple yet effective construct for learning how teachers' perceptions, intellectual processing, and instructional behaviors differ.[11] Witkin's work is also solidly founded. The results of more than 35 years of research on field dependence-independence are compiled in bibliographies listing over 2,000 studies.[12]

We define styles as behaviors, characteristics, and mannerisms that indicate underlying psychological frames of reference. Most of us lean toward one of two poles:
- exacting attention to detail where perception is not influenced by the background, *field independent*, or
- strong influence by the context of information—*field dependent.*

Over time, Witkin and his associates became convinced that field dependence-independence influences not only perceptual and intellectual functioning but personality traits such as social behavior, career choice, body concept, and defense.[13]

Field Independence

The field-independent person is task oriented and competitive. She likes to work alone and emphasizes getting the job done. This person works part to whole—perceiving analytically. The field independent teacher is logical, rational, and likes to figure things out for herself. She learns through books, is good at sequence and details, and likes theoretical and abstract ideas.

The field-independent person who is placed on a committee might say, "Just give me a job, and I'll go off and do it. Why are we talking so much? We don't need to get to know each other. We need to complete the task."

Strong field-independent people often hate workshops. If they could learn from a book, it would be more efficient.

We've heard of a man who taught himself to sail by reading a book. Why not? He was an engineering major, good at sequence and details.

 The field-independent person wants the coach to focus on tasks. She wants independence and flexibility to make decisions based on data and analysis. She looks to the coach to be knowledgeable about curriculum and instruction, to maintain a professional distance, and to give messages directly and articulately.

Field Dependence

The field-dependent person enjoys working with others and likes collaborative and mentor relationships. He takes in the overall scheme of something and can have difficulty with individual parts. He works from intuition and gut reactions but likes and needs concrete experience. Metaphors, analogies, patterns, and relationships appeal to this person, who likes to see things holistically.

Field-dependent persons are often oriented toward relationships, even seeking mentors in their lives. They have a sense of the large picture, and they know where they are going for the semester or the year. They often understand what is occurring in their class through intuition, reading subtleties of body language and voice.

The field-dependent teacher in a faculty meeting appreciates the discussion and interaction about ideas. It's important and valuable to share feelings on a topic. He is more tolerant of ambiguity than his independent peers and more skillful in process.

Field-dependent teachers want a coach to be warm and show personal interest and support. They want guidance and modeling, but they also want the coach to seek their opinion when decisions are to be made. They want the coach to have an open door, practice what she preaches, and use voice tones and body language that support her words. Though it is always possible to err by stereotyping using certain characteristics, these traits of field-independence/dependence are useful cues for communication in the coaching relationship.

Two Teachers' Responses to Cognitive Coaching

In a recent project, Bob coached two middle school teachers. One was field dependent, the other field independent. Each kept a journal of their reflections on the coaching processes over a four-month period. At the end of the project the three shared their journals. Here are some excerpts:[14]

Christina, a Field Dependent

A problem with trust was never really an issue for me. I was not overly concerned with the mechanics of cognitive coaching, and had even chosen to remain somewhat ignorant of the specifics of the coach's role in the process.

The most exciting result of my cognitive coaching experience was the improved quality in teacher-student interactions.

Jan, a Field Independent

Because of my personality type, I had a more difficult time establishing "trust" in the coaching process. I felt uncomfortable opening my teaching up for such intimate analysis and not knowing where this process would lead me.

I was interested in information that gave specific, quantitative answers like how many interactions were made during a class period, or how many responses were questions, probes, or paraphrases.

Both teachers found that they needed a combination of precision and art to develop their teaching and that they were each moving closer to balancing both. Jan had been extremely curriculum based in her approach to teaching, focusing her time and attention on the details of each activity. She was administering knowledge and successfully keeping the students busy, but at the expense, she said, of some aspects of the students' cognitive development and personal growth. At the opposite end of the spectrum, Christina's style of teaching focused almost exclusively on the affective domain. Because she encouraged a focus that was often subjective, her students learned through exploration, and often specific learnings were sacrificed in attainment of the broader goal. As the teachers reflected on subtle changes that had taken place during the course of their cognitive coaching experience, they saw a greater balance in the focus of their curriculum.

These teachers believed that cognitive coaching helped them access the "lesser used" sides of their brains. Through self-analysis, and "self-remediation" (their words), they searched every corner of their minds, bringing to the surface feelings and ideas that might have otherwise gone untapped. In becoming more bicognitive they became better thinkers and better teachers.[15]

Educational Belief Systems

Whether they verbalize them or not, educators hold deep beliefs about their work, their students, the role of schools in society, the curriculum, and teaching. Furthermore, these beliefs are grounded in and congruent with deep personal philosophies. These philosophies are powerful predictors of behaviors, and they drive the perceptions, decisions, and actions of all players on the education scene.

Pajares reports that beliefs are formed early and tend to self-perpetuate.[16] Changing beliefs during adulthood is a relatively rare phenomenon, and beliefs about teaching are well-established by the time a student gets to college. Because beliefs strongly influence perception they can be an unreliable guide to the nature of reality. The filtering effect of belief structures ultimately screens, distorts, or reshapes thinking and information processing.

Skilled cognitive coaches learn to recognize the prevailing educational beliefs of others through their vocabulary, metaphors, educational goals, evaluations of achievement, and teaching choices in the classroom. The following sections on the five primary education belief systems will be more meaningful to you if you first complete the short exercise in Figure 4-5.

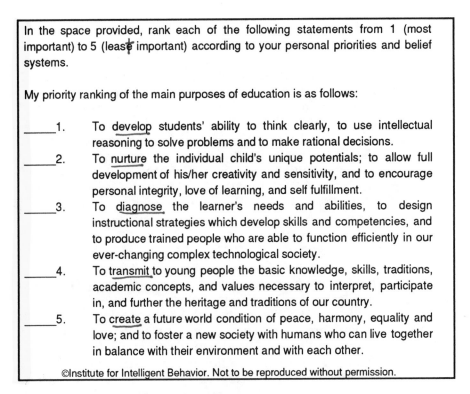

In the space provided, rank each of the following statements from 1 (most important) to 5 (least important) according to your personal priorities and belief systems.

My priority ranking of the main purposes of education is as follows:

_____1. To develop students' ability to think clearly, to use intellectual reasoning to solve problems and to make rational decisions.

_____2. To nurture the individual child's unique potentials; to allow full development of his/her creativity and sensitivity, and to encourage personal integrity, love of learning, and self fulfillment.

_____3. To diagnose the learner's needs and abilities, to design instructional strategies which develop skills and competencies, and to produce trained people who are able to function efficiently in our ever-changing complex technological society.

_____4. To transmit to young people the basic knowledge, skills, traditions, academic concepts, and values necessary to interpret, participate in, and further the heritage and traditions of our country.

_____5. To create a future world condition of peace, harmony, equality and love; and to foster a new society with humans who can live together in balance with their environment and with each other.

Figure 4-5
Goals of Education Inventory

Five Belief Systems

In their seminal work on educational beliefs, Eisner and Vallance[17] describe five belief orientations that guide teachers' instructional decision making and fuel the ongoing debate among policymakers and the public.

If you ranked statement one in Figure 4-5 as your first choice, you could probably be classified as a **cognitive processor**, drawn to educational theorists and authors such as Jerome Bruner, Hilda Taba, Robert Sternberg, Jean Piaget, Reuven Feurstein, Maria Montessori, and Edward deBono. With your orientation to cognitive psychology, you may believe that the central role of schools is to develop rational thought processes, problem solving, and decision making. You believe that the information explosion is occurring at such a rapid rate that it is no longer possible for experts in any field to keep up with new knowledge. Thus, we no longer know what to teach but instead must help students learn how to learn (see Figure 4-6).

You most likely select instructional strategies that involve problem solving and the inquiry method. When you talk about instruction, you use terms from Bloom's taxonomy: intellectual development, cognitive processes, metacognition, and thinking skills. You organize teaching around the resolution of problems, the Socratic Method, and bring in discrepant events for students to explore and analyze. You evaluate student performance by how well they perform in problem-solving situations. Your metaphorical model of education is that of information processing: Human beings are meaning makers and schools and teachers mediate those capacities.

If you marked the second item in Figure 4-5 as most important, you could be termed a **self-actualizer**. With an orientation to Gestalt psychology, you regard schools as child-centered. You probably view the teacher as a facilitator for learning, and you believe the purpose of teaching is to bring out the unique qualities, potentials, and capacities in each child. You like multi-sensory instruction with many opportunities for auditory, visual, and kinesthetic learning. You value student choice, whether it be for classroom topics, the nature of assignments, or classroom activities. You also value self-directed learning and individualized instruction.

To provide for students' multiple needs, interests, and developmental tasks, you use learning centers focused around themes. You value student autonomy and look for increases in autonomy as a central measure of your effectiveness as a teacher. You are drawn to such humanists as Abraham Maslow, Sylvia Ashton Warner, Arthur Combs, Carl Rogers, Sidney Simon, and George Leonard. Your vocabulary incudes words referring to the affective domain and terms such as the whole child, nurturing, peak experiences, choice, democracy, holistic, self-esteem, continuous progress, dignity, creativity, climate for learning, individualize, and caring. Because every child is different, you are concerned with developmentally appropriate curriculum, whole language, and creativity. Your metaphoric model of education is one of nurturing each child's potential.

If you ranked the third item on the survey as number one, it's likely that you have strong leanings toward the **tech-**

nologist position. You may be influenced by the behavioral psychology of Skinner, Pavlov, and Thorndike, and may be attracted to such education authors as Robert Mager, James Popham, and Madeline Hunter. You place strong emphasis on accountability and measurable learning. Your metaphor for education is as an input—throughput—output system in which data and opportunities to learn skills are provided. You are skilled at task analysis and the instructional materials that might interest you are computers and learning systems with opportunities to diagnose entry levels and prescribe according to what is known and what is yet to be learned. You are probably more field independent and skilled in detail, with great ability to analyze, project, and plan. You talk about accountability, evaluation, task analysis, time on task, mastery, templates, diagnosis, prescriptions, disaggregrated analysis, and percentiles.

If you ranked the fourth item as number one, you may regard yourself as an **academic rationalist.** Some of the philosophic company you keep includes Diane Ravitch, E.D. Hirsch, Arthur Bestor, William Bennett, and Chester Finn. You are drawn to teacher-centered instruction, believing that knowledgeable adults have the wisdom and the experience to know what is best for students. Your metaphor for education is the transmission of the major concepts, values, and truths of society, and you consider students as clay to be molded or vessels to be filled. You value and are highly oriented toward increasing the amount and rigor of student learning. You are probably drawn to essential truths, classics, the great books, and traditional values. You appreciate basic texts and the teaching strategies of lecture, memorization, demonstration, and drill. You evaluate students through summative examinations, achievement testing, and content mastery. You speak about discipline, authority, humanities, basics, scholarship, standardized tests, basic skills, and other aspects that value higher academic standards.

Finally, if you rated number five as your first choice, you probably are a **social reconstructionist.** You may be concerned with the problems of society, the shrinking world, the future of the planet, and major crises such as destruction of the food chain, the hole in the ozone layer, and the deforestation of timberland, protection of wildlife, and the threat of overpopulation. You view the learner as a social being: a member of a group, a responsible citizen, one who identifies with and is proactive regarding the environmental ills and social injustices of the day. You probably agree with Nesbitt, who reports that we have gone beyond the age of representative democracies. Because we no longer trust our elective officials to make important decisions, we have moved to a stage of participative democracies.

You believe this is a world where we must care for our neighbors and take action at the grass-roots level. As a teacher, you engage your students in recycling centers, contributing to social issues, cooperative learning, outdoor education, and global education. Your metaphor of education is as an instrument of change, and you believe that schools are the only institution in our society charged with the responsibility of bringing about a better future and a better world. You are drawn to Marilyn Ferguson, Willis Harmon, Alvin Toffler, Robert Samples, John Naisbitt, and Jean Houston. Your vocabulary includes terms such as environment, consumer education, peace, student rights, 21st century, multicultural, futurist, global intellect, pluralistic, change, save-the-Earth, ecology, and love.

All of these belief systems are necessary and valued aims of education. We want students to become good problem solvers; we want them to be self-actualized and to be knowledgeable, efficient, and concerned. So the task for coaches is to become at ease with a variety of educational beliefs and refine their ability to work with people whose styles may be different from their own.

Since belief systems don't change easily, the older we become, the less likely we are to change. However, change does occur in two instances. If the prevailing culture begins to shift its values persistently and pervasively, we may begin to move our thinking in like directions. For example, the 1960s saw the pervasive influence of individualized instruction, and many educators began to behave more like self-actualizers.

Teachers also adapt their belief systems to accommodate new realities. For example, a 12th grade history teacher may take a position as a kindergarten teacher, or an instructor may move from an affluent school to one of pervasive

ATTRIBUTES	COGNITIVE PROCESSORS	SELF-ACTUALIZERS	TECHNOLOGISTS	ACADEMIC RATIONALISTS	SOCIAL RECONSTRUC-TIONISTS
SOURCES OF GOALS	Scientific method, problem-solving thinking as basic	Individual needs, interests, abilities	Measurable learning, task analysis	Truths, classics structure of the disciplines, traditional values	Problems of society, now and in the future.
VIEW OF THE LEARNER	Problem solver, mind over matter, all learning in the brain	Within each individual are potentials to be nourished	Information processor, input—throughput—output	Container/vessel/to be filled/sponge to absorb	Social being—member of the group
EDUCATIONAL PSYCHOLOGY	Cognitivist	Humanistic/Holistic/ Gestalt	Stimulus/Response Skinnerian/behavioral conditioning	Imitative	Molding
MATERIALS ORGANIZA-TION OF	Problem focuses, data sources, discrepant events	Multiple, varied, student created, individualized	Learning activity packages, modules, systems computers	Basic tests, classical literature	Newspapers, current events, school problems
TEACHING STRATEGIES	Inquiry, critical thinking, problem solving	Self-directed learning centers, individualized	Diagnosis/prescription, management systems, task analysis, 5 steps	Lecture, notetaking, memorization, demonstration, drill	Simulations, role playing, values awarenesses
METHODS OF EVALUATION	Observation of performance in problem situations	Self-evaluation, demonstration of increased autonomy	Entry level/mastery level. Pre and post testing/gain scores	Content master, achievement testing summative	Social concern and cooperation, empathy
LEADERS IN THE FIELD	Suchman, Montessori, Bruner, Piaget, Bloom, Feuerstein, deBono Sternberg, Taba	Maslow, Combs, Rogers, Buzan, Leonard, Simon, Edwards	Skinner, Pavlov, Thorndike, Hull, Mager, Popham, Hunter	Bestor, Honig Hirsch, Bennett, Finn, Ravitch	Ferguson, Cremin, Tofler, Hutchins, Shane, Friere, Whitehead, Houston, Illich
VOCABULARY	Cognitive processes, cognition, thinking skills, intellectual development	Peak experience, nurturance, whole child, affective, individual, right brain	Task analysis, management by objectives, computer-assisted learning, teacher proof, competencies, accountability	Conceptual themes, traditional values, classics, rigor, humanities, basics, 3 R's, scholarly	21st century, student rights, survival, consumer education, peace environment

Figure 4-6
Belief Systems

poverty. In these cases the teacher's paradigm changes, and so do the beliefs they use to explain their role in their new environment.

The Influence of Gender

Sociolinguist Deborah Tannen[18] has reported many differences in the ways men and women talk, and we have found her work useful for understanding nuances in coaching relationships.

Tannen finds that men and women converse for different purposes. Men talk, she says, to establish independence and status and to report information. Women, on the other hand, tend to use talk to establish intimacy and relationship. In a sense, women's talk is about establishing the fact that we are "close and the same" and men's talk is to establish the fact that we are "separate and different."

Men tend to operate in conversations as individuals in a social world in which they are either one up or one down. Women tend to operate as individuals in a network of connections. That is not to say that women are not interested in status and avoiding failure, but those are not consistent goals. Tannen summarizes these differences as "men talk to report, women talk to rapport."

For example, a man and a woman are standing outside enjoying the sunset. The woman says, "What a beautiful sunset." The man answers, "Yes. Do you know what it is caused by? There have been several volcanic eruptions to the west of us, and what we are looking at is the volcanic ash in the air." If the second speaker were a woman, her response might be, "Yes, that's a lovely sunset. It makes you feel good, doesn't it?"

It's possible to overestimate these kinds of differences, which are actually overlapping tendencies on continuums of expression. In fact, the most successful coaches tend to be androgynous in their communications, drawing on both the male and female characteristics reported by Tannen and others. Still, gender-flavored language patterns show up in public conversation as well as in private talk. At work, men are inclined to jockey for status and challenge the authority of others. Many females lack experience in defending themselves against such challenges. Women may misinterpret challenges as personal attacks on their credibility. It is as if men ask, "Have I won?" while women ask, "Have I been helpful?"

In faculty meetings, men tend to talk more often and for longer periods of time. In one study of seven university faculty meetings, the longest women's turns were shorter than the men's shortest turn. And since women seek to establish rapport, they are inclined to play down their expertise in meetings rather than display it. Because men place more value on being center stage and feeling knowledgeable, they seek opportunities to gather and disseminate factual information.

Women tend to ask more questions and give more listening responses than men. In one startling study, Sadker and Sadker[19] reported that teachers who were shown a film of classroom discussion overwhelmingly thought the girls were talking more. In actuality, the boys were talking three times more than the girls.

Probably one of the most important coaching findings from Tannen's work relates to the misunderstandings that sometimes develop out of the different purposes of conversation. For example, many women feel it is natural to consult with a partner before making a decision. Men, however, may view consulting with a partner as tantamount to asking for permission. Since men strive for independence, they may find it more difficult to consult. This drive for independence may also explain their difficulty in asking a stranger for directions.[20] Women, on the other hand, are more comfortable in asking a stranger for directions when they are lost since it literally affords another person an opportunity to be helpful to them.

How many of these differences are culturally induced patterns or the result of evolutionary patterning? How much might be attributed to psychological differences between men and women? During the 1970s, it became almost unfashionable to suggest that physiological differences between the genders can lead to different abilities or predispositions. But three conclusions are now apparent.

One is that the whole of human history has been developed from a male perspective. This subconscious and pervasive filter has both hidden truths and perpetualized ways of thinking and being related to masculinity and femininity. Riane Eisler's remarkable work that reexamines history from a gender holistic perspective has given birth to a new theory of cultural evolution.[21] In her view, two basic models of society exist: a dominator model, in which one gender is ranked over the other, or a partnership model, in which diversity is not invested with interpretations of inferiority or superiority. Since the Paleolithic period (but not before), humans have primarily lived in dominator societies. Our earlier views of physiological gender differences spring from this source. For example, biologists in the 19th century believed that a woman's brain was too small for intellect but large enough for household chores.[22]

A second conclusion is that we have been guilty of overgeneralizing differences between males and females. For awhile, we believed certain brain differences led to girls' supposed inability to do mathematics. Today, we are sensitive to the fact that classroom and teacher behaviors may play a larger role than nature in differentiating the sexes.

The third conclusion is that recent studies are finding some real biological differences between men and women. At birth, more men than women are left-handed. By contrast, more women listen equally with both ears, while men favor the right one. A number of gender differences are found in the hypothalamus, the portion of the brain associated with sexual behavior.

Psychology tests consistently support the notion that men and women perceive the world in subtly different ways. Females are better at reading the emotions of people in photographs; males excel at rotating three-dimensional objects in their heads. Though some researchers caution that most gender differences are, statistically speaking, quite small,[23] recent brain scans from live, apparently healthy people have confirmed that parts of the corpus callosum are 23 percent wider in women than in men. Some researchers speculate that the greater communication between the two sides of the brain caused by a thicker corpus callosum could actually impair a woman's performance in certain specialized visual-spatial tasks. For example, the spatial ability to tell directions on a map without physically rotating it appears strong in those individuals whose brains restrict processing to the right hemisphere. Though research conclusions may sometimes seem to conflict, the bottom line for the coach is to be aware of gender differences that may—or may not—exist.

Race, Ethnicity, and Culture

We once taught a woman who was a vice-principal of a math-science magnet high school. On her staff was an Iranian male math teacher. This vice-principal couldn't understand why it was so difficult to coach this man until she realized that many Moslem men do not view the role of women in the same manner as other cultures.

Describing patterns related to any racial or ethnic group is highly suspect. Race and ethnicity intersect with geography, religion, economics, class, art forms, gender, language, folklore, world events, family patterns, personal history, and so on. But studies of race and culture do offer generalizations regarding cognitive styles and patterns of verbal and nonverbal communications. Skillful coaches educate themselves about different groups of people and their ways of communicating. Though this topic is far beyond the scope of this book, we offer several general assumptions that are useful guidelines for achieving communications free of gender, racial, or ethnic bias.[24] (See also "Black and White Styles in Conflict" by Thomas Kochman, University of Chicago Press and "Managing Cultural Differences: High Performance Strategies For Today's Global Manager" by P. Harris and R. Moran, Gulf Publishing Company.)

1. If your race or gender is different from mine, you carry experiences, perceptions, and meanings I cannot know directly.
2. The origins of your perceptions, processing, and communication styles emerge from personal experience. Because they are ecologically sound, they become persevering patterns.
3. To the degree that our personal histories are different, my communications may be misinterpreted by you and yours by me.
4. When we have misunderstandings about communication style differences, it doesn't make them go

away, but understanding the source of the differences can diminish mutual mystification and blame. This makes the world a more familiar and comfortable territory.

5. Our communication and the mutual interests that bring us together provide valuable opportunities to grow and learn from each other. Our differences enrich us both.

6. We all have unexamined prejudices and biases. We can work respectfully together and accomplish tasks important to us both to the degree that we can become conscious of and set aside these thoughts and feelings.

7. My most useful personal attributes in communicating with you are integrity, consciousness, flexibility, and interdependence manifested through respect, openness, curiosity, and inquiry. From these sources, you and I can continue to learn more about each other.

8. As a result of these assumptions, I strive to be free of ethnic, racial, and gender bias in my communications. Therefore, I use the following guidelines in my private and public communications:

    • I guard against making generalizations that suggest all members of a racial, ethnic, or gender group are the same. Universals, generalizations, and stereotypes may lead to insupportable or offensive assumptions while ignoring the fact that all attributes may be found in all groups.

    • I avoid qualifiers that categorize others and call attention to racial, ethnic, and gender stereotypes. A qualifier is added information that suggests an exception to a rule (for example, a "sensitive" man, a "mathematically gifted" girl).

    • I identify others by race or ethnic origin only when relevant. Few situations require such identification.

    • I consciously avoid language that to some people has questionable racial or ethnic connotations. While a word or phrase may not be personally offensive to you, it may be to others.

    • I am aware of the possible negative implications of color-symbolic words. I choose language and usage that does not offend people or reinforce bias.

Summary

Human diversity is valued in the Renaissance School. Coaches, therefore, not only promote diversity but also are effective in working with others who possess a wide range of human variables. This is critically important to developing trust, to accelerating the learning of the coach and the person being coached, and to enhancing interdependence and a sense of organizational community.

In this chapter we have identified a range of differences: beliefs, representational systems, cognitive styles, gender, race, ethnic and cultural differences. Effective coaches are knowledgeable about these differences and draw on their capacities of consciousness and flexibility. They are aware of their own and other's representational systems, cognitive preferences, belief systems, and/or communication styles; *and* they are able to flex—to draw upon a wide repertoire of strategies to communicate effectively in each divergent situation. Thus consciousness and flexibility are prerequisites to promoting the interdependence of the Renaissance classroom, school, and community. In the next chapter we will examine how consciousness, flexibility, interdependence, and two other states of mind contribute to holonomy and how coaches can enhance growth toward these desired states of mind.

I ka noho pu ana—a'ike i ke aloha
"It is living together that teaches the meaning of love"

In Hawaii, the sugar planters mixed ethnic groups on purpose, their idea being that different folks would not naturally mix, and dissension among the workers would make them easier to manage and less likely to band together against their bosses, the Lunas. But what actually happened is a tribute to the adaptability and resiliency of the human spirit—they not only got along, but of necessity shared the very elements that made them different, even as they maintained their ethnic integrity. First they had to adapt to their new situation. There were things they were used to in their home cultures that they simply couldn't get in Hawaii. Second, they adopted the good things from other cultures they were exposed to, but they retained some of the important cultural elements of their ethnic groups. Finally, they made special contributions to their new multi-cultural society on the plantation, a working class culture made up of many minorities.

Endnotes

1. Ornstein, R. *The Evolution of Consciousness: Of Darwin, Freud, and Cranial Fire—The Origins of the Way We Think.* New York, NY: Prentice-Hall Press, 1991, p. 188.

2. Chopra, D. "Escaping the Prison of the Intellect." Audio Tape. Quantum Publications. P.O. Box 598, South Lancaster, MA 01561, 1991.

3. Chopra, D. *Quantum Healing: Exploring the Frontiers of Mind/Body Medicine.* New York, NY: Bantam Books, 1989.

4. Chopra, D. *Quantum Healing: Exploring the Frontiers of Mind/Body Medicine.* New York, NY: Bantam Books, 1989.

5. O'Connor, J. and Seymour, J. *Introducing Neuro-Linguistic Programming: The New Psychology of Personal Excellence,* Hammersmith, London: Harper Collins Publishers, 1990.

6. Garmston, R. "A Guide to Neuro-Linguistic Programming and Counseling in Education," course syllabus, School of Education, California State University, Sacramento, 1988.

7. Einspruch, E. and Forman, B. at the Department of Psychiatry and the Department of Psychological Studies at the University of Miami, 1985.

   Einspruch, E. and Forman, B. "Observations Concerning Research Literature on Neuro-Linguistic Programming, *Journal of Counseling Psychology* (1985): 32, 4, pp. 589–569.

8. Galin D. and Ornstein, R. "Individual Differences in Cognitive Style—Reflective Eye Movements." *Neuropsychologia,* (1973): Vol. 12, pp. 367–376.

   Kinsbourne, M. "Eye and Head Turning Indicates Cerebral Lateralization," *Science* (1972): Vol. 58, pp. 539–541.

   Kocel, K., Galin, D., Ornstein, R. and Merrin, E. "Lateral Eye Movement and Cognitive Mode." *Psychonomic Science* (1972): Vol. 27, Issue 4, pp. 223–224.

9. Bandler, R. and Grinder, J. *The Patterns of the Hypnotic Techniques of Milton H. Erickson, M.D.,I.* Palo Alto, CA: Behavior and Science Books, 1975.

   Beck, C. and Beck, E. "Test of the Eye-Movement Hypothesis of Neuro-Linguistic Programming: A Rebuttal of Conclusions," *Perceptual and Motor Skills* (1984): Vol. 58, pp. 175–176.

   Dilts, R. *Roots of Neuro-Linguistic Programming,* Cupertino, CA: Meta Publications, 1983.

10. For information on this videotape, please contact the Association for Supervision and Curriculum Development, 1250 N. Pitt St., Alexandria, VA 22314 (703/549-9110).

11. Guild, P. and Garger, S. *Marching to Different Drummers.* Alexandria, VA: Association for Supervision and Curriculum Development, 1985.

12. Witkin, H.A., Oldman, P. K., Cox, W., Erlichman, E., Hamm, R.M., and Ringler, R. *Field-Dependence-Independence and Psychological Differentiation: A Bibliography.* Princeton, NJ: Educational Testing Service, 1973.

13. Witkin, H.M., Goodenough, D., and Cox, P. *Field Dependent and Field Independent Cognitive Styles and their Implications.* Princeton, NJ: Educational Testing Service, 1975.

14. Garmston, R., Linder, C. and Whitaker, J. "Reflections on Cognitive Coaching." *Educational Leadership* (1993, October) Vol. 51, No. 2, pp. 57–61.

15. Garmston, R., Linder, C. and Whitaker, J. "Reflections on Cognitive Coaching." *Educational Leadership* (1993, October) Vol. 51, No. 2, pp. 57–61.

16. Pajares, M.F. "Teachers' Beliefs and Educational Research: Cleaning Up a Messy Construct." *Review of Educational Research* (1992): Vol. 62, Issue 3.

17. Eisner, E. and Vallance, E. *Conflicting Conceptions of the Curriculum.* Berkley, CA: McCutchan Publishing, 1974.

18. Tannen, D. *You Just Don't Understand: Men and Women in Conversation.* New York, NY: Ballantine Books, 1990, p. 17.

19. Sadker, M. and Sadker, D. "Sexism in the Schoolroom of the '80s." *Psychology Today* (March 1985): pp. 54–57.

20. Goldberg, H. *What Men Really Want.* New York, NY: Penguin Books, 1991.

21. Eisler, R. *The Chalice and the Blade: Our History, Our Future.* New York, NY: Harper Collins Publishers, 1987.

22. Ehrenreich, B. "Making Sense of la Diffe'rence." *Time* (January 20, 1992): p. 51.

23. Gorman, C. "Sizing Up the Sexes." *Time* (January 20, 1992): pp. 42–48.

24. Adapted from material developed by the Anti-Defamation League of Southern California. This information is based upon excerpts of *Without Bias: A Guidebook for Nondiscriminatory Communication* (2nd ed.) prepared by Ellen Bettmann, ADL, Boston, Mass., and edited by Peggy O'Keefe, ADL, New York City.

5

Cognition and Instruction

Through the efforts of a number of researchers, we are coming to understand that the act of teaching is a highly intellectual process involving continuous decision making—before, during, and after classroom instruction.[1] Jackson and Coladarci[2] were among the early theorists who moved us beyond teacher behaviors toward a cognitive notion of teaching, and we now accept that the overt behaviors we observe in classroom performance are the results and artifacts of invisible decisions and complex intellectual processes in the teacher's mind.

Based on this cognitive perception of teaching, we regard coaching as a process of engaging, enhancing, and mediating the intellectual functions of teaching. A coach cannot achieve these goals without some understanding of what—and how—teachers are thinking as they plan for, execute, and evaluate instruction.

Five Findings

Through increasing research on teacher cognition, we gain valuable insights into what teachers think about as they teach. We also gain insights from research on human information processing, effective problem solving, human intelligence, and brain capacities and functions. Five major findings stand out:

•   **All behavior is rationally based on rather simple cognitive maps of reality.** For example, Swedish researchers Dahllof and Lundeen[3] discovered that teachers used a subset of the class ranging from the 10th to the 25th percentile as an informal reference group for decisions about pacing a lesson or unit. These mental constructs guided the behaviors of teachers toward the entire class, and it illustrates how teachers make simple cognitive maps to deal with complex situations.

•   **When teachers talk about their reasons for doing things and respond to questions about their perceptions and teaching decisions, they often experience a sense of professional excitement and renewed joy and energy related to their work.**

•   **Talking aloud about their thinking and decisions about teaching energizes teachers and causes them to refine their cognitive maps, and hence their instructional choices and behaviors.** Teachers have implicit theories about teaching and learning that are "robust, idiosyncratic, sensitive to [their] particular experiences, incomplete, familiar, and sufficiently pragmatic to have gotten [them] to where they are today."[4] Talking aloud about these causes examination, refinement, and the development of new theories and practices.

•   **Certain invisible, cognitive skills drive teaching performance.** These teacher thought processes influence their classroom behaviors, students' classroom behaviors, student achievement, and, reciprocally, the teacher's thought processes, theories, and beliefs.[5]

•   **The invisible cognitive skills can be categorized in four domains.** *Pre-active* thought occurs as the teacher plans before teaching. *Interactive* thought occurs during teaching. *Reflective* thought occurs when teachers recall and analyze a lesson. *Projective* thought is used to synthesize learnings and plan next steps.

These thought processes are influenced by deeply buried theories of learning, beliefs about education and student conduct, personal representational styles, and the teacher's cognitive style. Coaching can raise these deep-structure forms of knowing to a more conscious level so the teacher can elaborate, clarify, evaluate, and alter them.

A Basic Model

A basic model of human intellectual functioning is vital for the cognitive coach who wants to develop strategies, learning activities, and assessment indicators that focus on the intellect rather than superficial behaviors.[6] Figure 5-1 synthesizes many psychologists' and psychobiologists' concepts of human intellectual functioning. A variety of authors distinguish three to four basic thought clusters:[7]

- **input** of data through the senses and from memory,
- **processing** those data into meaningful relationships,
- **output,** or application, of those relationships in new or novel situations, and
- **metacognition,** or self-monitoring of one's own thoughts, actions, beliefs and emotions.

Every event a person experiences causes the brain to call up meaningful, related information from storage, whether the event is commonplace or a complex learning experience. The more meaningful, relevant, and complex the experience is, the more actively the brain attempts to integrate and assimilate it into its existing storehouse of programs and structures. The most complex thinking occurs when an external stimulus or problem challenges the brain to:

- draw on the greatest amount of data or structures already in storage,
- expand an already existing structure, and
- develop new structures.

A problem may be defined as any stimulus or challenge that has no readily apparent resolution. If there is a ready match between what is perceived by the senses and what is already in storage, no problem exists. For example, there's not much need to process information when you are asked your name because the response to the challenge is readily available. Jean Piaget called this *assimilation.*

If, however, the challenge or problem cannot be explained or resolved with existing knowledge in short- or long-term memory, the information must be processed. Some action must be taken to gather more information to resolve the discrepancy, and the resolution must be evaluated for its "fit" with reality. Piaget called this *accommodation*, and he believed it is the process by which new knowledge is constructed.

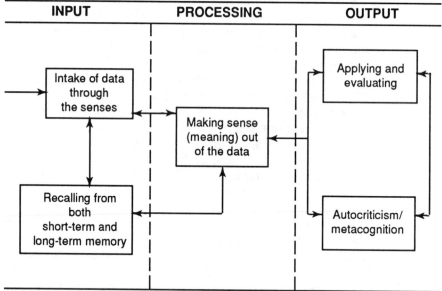

Source: A. Costa, "Towards a Model of Human Intellectual Functioning," in *Developing Minds: A Resource Book on Teaching Thinking* (Alexandria, Va.: Association for Supervision and Curriculum Development, 1984).

Figure 5-1
A Model of Intellectual Functioning

Our brains constantly strive to satisfy and resolve discrepancies perceived in the environment. Information that the brain has not processed remains in memory for very short periods of time. Merely experiencing something or memorizing without acting on that information commits it to short-term memory. This fact may explain the unusual power of cognitive coaching. Most data perceived by the brain are either not attended to (and therefore never enter short-term memory) or are not processed and are forgotten within 18 seconds.[8] Much of the daily experience of teaching, therefore, is forgotten and not explained, its potential influence for teacher learning lost.

For these reasons, it is the processing of the instructional experience that facilitates construction of new meanings and insights in the teacher. With this model of human intellectual functioning in mind the coach engages and mediates the teacher's cognition. When cognitive coaching is used, teachers process the same teaching event as least *six* times. Before the Planning Conference, teachers formulate their objectives and plans. During the Planning Conference, they engage in deep, pre-active mental rehearsal during which the coach questions, paraphrases, and clarifies in ways that help teachers be more precise in their lesson strategies. Instruction then occurs, with the teacher's conscious awareness about key elements greatly heightened. The teacher recalls the instructional event before and during the Reflecting Conference. Finally, the teacher continues to reflect and refine after the coaching conference, especially when closure was not reached on a subject or issue.

The long-range goal of Cognitive Coaching is the automation of the intellectual functions of effective teaching. In other words, the goal is self-coaching. It is for the teacher to continue growing intellectually by internalizing these intellectual processes and to experience them when the coach is not present—to be self-modifying, self-referencing, and self-renewing. Thus these intellectual functions of effective teaching become automated.

Four Stages of Instructional Thought

When we compare the research described above on human information processing from a variety of domains with research on teacher cognition, we are struck by the natural similarities. *Planning* (pre-active) consists of all the intellectual functions performed before instruction. *Teaching* (interactive) includes the multiple decisions made during teaching. *Analyzing and evaluating* (reflective) consists of all those mental processes used to think back on, analyze, and judge instruction. Finally, *applying* (projective) abstracts from the experience, synthesizes new generalizations, and carries them to future situations.

Pueblo Indians plan their house construction by means of quite a different set of priorities than other cultures. Before the ground is broken, all the right thoughts must be present. The Pueblos believe that thoughts are alive and that they become an integral part of any man-made structure.

Planning: Preactive Stage

Planning may well include the most important decisions teachers make because it is the phase upon which all other decisions rest. Planning basically involves four components:[9]

1. Anticipating, predicting, and developing precise descriptions of students' learnings that are to result from instruction. Ironically, this can be a low priority for many teachers.[10]

2. Identifying students' present capabilities or entry knowledge. This information is drawn from previous teaching/learning experience, data from school records, test scores, and clues from previous teachers, parents, counselors.[11]

3. Envisioning precisely the characteristics of an instructional sequence or strategy that will most likely move students from their present capabilities toward immediate and long-range instructional outcomes. This sequence is derived from whatever theories, beliefs, or models of teaching logic, learning, or motivation that the teacher has adopted. The sequential structure of a lesson is deeply embedded in teachers' plans for allocating that precious and limited resource: time.

4. Anticipating a method of assessing outcomes. The outcomes of this assessment will provide a basis for evaluating and making decisions about the design of the next cycle of instruction.

There is reasonable agreement among researchers that teachers do not adapt a linear form of planning (for example, specifying objectives first, then selecting learning activities, and so on). Instead, teachers seem to enter the planning process from multiple and varied entry points. In fact, several studies find that many teachers think about content first and objectives later.[12]

But even below this structure, what is going on in teachers' minds as they plan? Psychologists know that the human intellect has a limited capacity for handling variables. Miller[13] describes this as "M-space" or Memory Space. He found that humans have a capacity for handling and coordinating seven different variables, decisions, or disparate pieces of information at any one time (plus or minus two). This assumes the person has attained the Piagetian stage of formal operations, which not all adults achieve. It has been found that most adults can operate on four or so disparate variables simultaneously.

When humans approach the outer limits of their capacity, a state of stress begins to set in, and there's a feeling of loss of control. Most intellectual energy appears to be invested in techniques and systems to simplify, reduce, and select the number of variables. For teachers, certain planning strategies help reduce this stress.

During planning, a teacher envisions cues—definitions of acceptable forms of student performance for learning. This simplifies judgments about appropriate and inappropriate student behaviors. The teacher also selects potential solutions, back-up procedures, and alternative strategies for times when the activity needs to be redirected, changed, or terminated.

This kind of planning causes thought experiments during which a teacher can mentally rehearse activities to help anticipate possible events and consequences. This improves the coordination and efficiency of subsequent performance because systematic mental rehearsal prepares the mind and body for the activity and is the main mechanism for focusing attention on critical factors relevant to the task.

When a person thinks about an action, the brain sends electrical impulses to the nerves and muscles in the corresponding locations of the mind and body associated with the action. This is called the Carpenter Effect, and it is the scientific basis for the practice of mental rehearsal (see the sidebar "More About Mental Rehearsal"). Mental rehearsal is also beneficial for overcoming the psychological and emotional problems associated with performance. One common problem is failing to maintain effective concentration. Through mental rehearsal, we learn to direct attention to cues that are most important for performance, and at the same time to close down the perceptions of distracting external stimuli.[14] Much research concerns performance during short physical activities, but we also know that mental rehearsal of complex and interactive activities of longer duration also improves performance. This means that it is helpful to rehearse whole races, entire games, and, of course, entire lesson sequences.[15]

More About Mental Rehearsal

Much of the literature and research on mental rehearsal is drawn from the field of athletics. The famous French Alpine skier Jean-Claude Killy mentally rehearsed ski slopes with a stopwatch. He concentrated on every turn and part of the slope, timing himself as he envisioned his performance from start to finish. Killy claimed that the recorded time for his mental performance closely paralleled the time he actually achieved in the competition that followed.

Olympic gold medalist Greg Louganis mentally rehearses each dive. The activity prepares his mind for the coming dive and his body for the series of movements. Rehearsal also enabled him to forget everything else in the surroundings. Olympic pentathlete Marilyn King[1] reports using a combination of three kinds of visualization: visual imagery, being able to project a visual image of herself; kinetic imagery, feeling or physically sensing; and auditory imagery. These three forms of visualization are used by many high performers in three different areas: long-term goal orientation, envisioning a goal step-by-step, and centering, or concentrating, to eliminate outside distractions and focus inward.

Planning also demands that the teacher exercise perceptual flexibility—viewing learning from multiple perspectives. This requires a certain degree of disassociation or detatchment from the instruction in order to stand off and assume alternative perspectives. Highly flexible teachers have the capacity to view their lesson in both the immediate and long range. They are not only analytical about the details of this lesson (the micro mode), they can also see connections between this lesson and other related learnings. They know where this lesson is leading and how it is connected to broader curricular goals (the macro mode). Less flexible, episodic teachers, may view today's activity as a separate and discrete episode, unrelated to other learning events.

Flexible teachers see a lesson from a variety of points of view. The teacher may view the lesson:

- *egocentrically*—from his own point of view, including his goals, teaching strategies, and content background;
- *allocentrically*—from a student's point of view;
- *macrocentrically*— imagining how the entire interaction will appear from a "third" position, such as from a mental "balcony," overlooking the interactions between teacher and students; and
- *retrocentrically*—envisioning the end or completed product and backing up from that vision to form strategies and steps of how to achieve the vision.

Teacher Thought During Teaching

One of the great cognitive capacities of teachers is the ability to manage a multitude of activities in the classroom simultaneously. Take an imaginary tour of a classroom to observe this cognitive capacity at work during teaching:

As you walk in, you are immediately struck by all the activity. Some students are working on a salt and flour map; more are at the computer; some are helping each other with their homework; some are at the science table. The teacher sits at a round table working with a small reading group. She listens to Rebecca read; next she listens to and corrects Diane; she diagnoses Don, then Leroy. At that moment, an office monitor enters and delivers a note to the teacher. The teacher, still listening to Rebecca, reads the note, commends the monitor for coming in so quietly, composes a response, sends him out, and never misses a beat with Rebecca.

In a high school classroom, George arrives late, noisily, and apparently dejected. Glancing at George, the teacher instantaneously makes an assessment of his emotional state, assesses what's happening to the class discussion and George's potential for disruption. She tosses a humorous greeting, "Hi George. Good to see you. Make friends with that chair and turn to the chart on page 70." She locates in her mind some appropriate open-ended questions for students to work on. She instructs the students to think-pair-share on those questions for two minutes. Simultaneously she is providing George a chance to settle in and she provides students an opportunity to check their understanding of the concept just taught.

Planning a teaching strategy also requires the cognitive function of analysis: both structural and operational. Structural analysis is the process of breaking down the learning of the content into its component parts; operational analysis involves a seriation of events into a logical order of sequence.[16] To handle this information overload, teachers probably synthesize much of this information into "hypotheses" or best guesses about student readiness for learning. They estimate the probability of successful student behavior as a result of instruction.

While these studies are representative of the practices reported by researchers regarding teacher planning, Clark and Peterson[17] point out that the research is silent on which planning processes are most effective. From our experience, we agree with Shavelson that of the four stages of teachers' thought, planning is the most crucial because it sets the standard for the remaining three phases. We also place particular emphasis on the value of specifying clear learning objectives, and find that the more clearly the teacher envisions and mentally rehearses the plan, the greater are the chances that the lesson will achieve its purposes, the greater are the chances that the teacher will be self-monitoring during the lesson, and the more critically will the teacher analyze his own lesson during the reflective phase, assuming a greater internal locus of control.

Teaching: The Interactive Phase

Teaching has been described as the second most stressful profession (after air traffic controllers), and no doubt this stems from the fact that teachers are constantly interacting with students in an environment of uncertainty.[18] Teachers are constantly making decisions, and they may be subconscious, spontaneous, planned, or a mixture of any of the three types. They are probably modifications of decisions made during the planning phase, but now they are carried out on the spur of the moment in the fast-paced interaction of the classroom. Changes are probably not well-defined or as thoroughly considered as those made during the calmer stage of planning. Teachers have little time to consider alternative teaching strategies and the consequences of each.

Six time dimensions interact constantly with teachers' other thoughts and values and influence their daily decisions.

Two of these are sequence and simultaneity. (Time dimensions are further elaborated in the Appendix.)

1. Sequence refers to the seriation or ordering of instructional events within a lesson.

2. Simultaneity. More highly holonomous, flexible teachers have the capacity to operate under multiple classification systems at the same time. This means they can teach toward multiple objectives, coordinate numerous and varied classroom activities at the same time, plan a lesson incorporating several learning modalities, and think about multiple time frames. Research indicates that there are as many as six time frames that affect how teachers plan: weekly, daily, long range, short range, yearly, and term. Effective teachers relate information from all those time frames as they prepare daily lessons.[19]

Keeping a planned strategy in mind while teaching provides the teacher a backdrop against which to make new decisions. During the beginning of a lesson, for example, the teacher may emphasize structuring the task and motivating students to become curious, involved, and focused. Later in the sequence, the teacher may use recall types of thinking to review previously learned information and to gather data to be considered later. Farther into the lesson, the teacher may invite higher-level thinking and, finally, tasks for transference and application.

Clark and Peterson[20] describe the content of teachers' interactive thought related to: a) changing their plans, b) the influences on those decisions, c) the cues that teachers read in order to make decisions, and d) the relationships between teachers' interactive decisions, teacher behaviors and, ultimately, student outcomes. A relatively small portion of teachers' interactive thoughts deal with instructional objectives (14 percent or less across the four studies that used objectives as a category). A greater percentage of teachers' interactive thoughts deal with the content or subject matter. A still greater percentage of interactive thoughts deal with the instructional process. And the largest percentage of teachers' interactive thought concerns learning and the learner.

One of the great mental skills of teaching is simply the teacher's ability to remember the lesson plan during the press of interaction. Teachers suffer cognitive overload—too many things going on all at the same time—yet skillful teachers respond immediately, intuitively, and spontaneously. Highly conscious teachers are alert to what is going on in the classroom; less conscious teachers continue their lessons regardless of what occurs among the students. For example, alert teachers search for clues that students are prepared. Has the student acted on the information, digested it, and made meaning out of it or used it? Are students staring vacantly, or do body language and facial cues indicate attention? The alert teacher constantly observes, questions, probes, and interprets students' behaviors to gain information before making decisions about moving ahead in the sequence or remaining at the present step longer.

Metacognition refers to teachers' critically important capacities to consciously "stand outside themselves" and reflect on themselves as they manage instruction. During a lesson, teachers may ask themselves, "Are my directions clear? Can students see the overhead projector? Am I using precise words to make sure that the students are understanding? Should I speed up?" Such internal dialogue means that the teacher is constantly monitoring his own and students' behavior during instruction.

Metacognition also refers to the ability to know what we know and what we don't know. It is our ability to plan a strategy for producing the information that is needed, to be conscious of our own steps and strategies, and to reflect on and evaluate the productivity of our thinking. Perkins[21] has elaborated four increasingly complex levels of metacognition:
- the *tacit* level, being unaware of our metacognitive knowledge;
- the *awareness* level, knowing about some of the kinds of thinking we do (generating ideas, finding evidence, but not being strategic);
- the *strategic* level, organizing our thinking by using problem solving, decision making, evidence seeking, and other kinds of strategies; and
- the *reflective* level, not only being strategic but reflecting on our thinking in-progress, pondering strategies, and revising them accordingly.

The metacognitive skills necessary to successful teaching—

and that a coach may want to be alert for—include:
- keeping place in a long sequence of operations,
- knowing that a subgoal has been attained, and
- detecting errors and recovering from them by making a quick fix or retreating to the last known correct operation.

This kind of monitoring involves both looking ahead and looking back. Looking ahead includes:
- Learning the structure of a sequence of operations and identifying areas where errors are likely.
- Choosing a strategy that will reduce the possibility of error and will provide easy recovery.
- Identifying the kinds of feedback that will be available at various points, and evaluating the usefulness of that feedback.

Looking back includes:
- Detecting errors previously made.
- Keeping a history of what has been done up to the present and therefore what should come next.
- Assessing the reasonableness of the present and the immediate outcome of task performance.

Teachers monitor the classroom for conscious and subconscious cues, and sometimes they build up so much that they disrupt conscious information processing. Flexible teachers restrain their impulsivity by avoiding strong emotional reactions to classroom events. This is an efficient strategy to reserve the limited capacity for conscious processing of immediate classroom decisions.

Drawing on Repertoire

Flexible teachers have a vast repertoire of instructional strategies and techniques and call forth alternative strategies as needed. They are aware that in a math lesson, for example, Richard obviously isn't getting the concept of sequence. Sensing that Richard is a kinesthetic learner, they give Richard a set of blocks. "Here, put these in order."

In many classes there is a heterogeneous array of languages, cultures, and learning styles. Teachers may have within one group of students Vietnamese, East Indians, and the predominantly Spanish-speaking. Each must be dealt with employing different strategies, vocabulary, examples, and techniques. Efficacious and flexible teachers continually cast about in their vast repertoire for strategies that may prove effective.

Routines are also helpful in dealing with the information-processing demands of the classroom. Routines reduce the need to attend to the abundance of simultaneous cues from the environment. Efficacious teachers develop a repertoire of routine systems for dealing with many classroom management functions (taking roll, distributing papers and books). They also have systematic lesson designs (for example, spelling and math drills) and teaching strategies (for example, questioning sequences, structuring).

Analyzing and Evaluating: The Reflective Stage

After teaching the lesson, the teacher now has two sources of information: the lesson that was envisioned during planning and the actual lesson as performed. Analyzing involves collecting and using understandings derived from the comparison between actual and intended outcomes. If there is a great similarity between the two, there is a match. But a discrepancy exists when there is a mismatch between what was performed and what was planned. Teachers generate reasons to explain the discrepancy: cause-and-effect relationships between instructional situations and behavioral outcomes.

Teachers can either assume responsibility for their own actions or they can place the blame on external forces. Teachers with an *external locus of control* tend to misplace responsibility on situations or persons beyond their control. For example:

"How can I teach these kids anything? Look at the home background they come from. Their parents just don't prepare them to learn."

Efficacious teachers have an *internal locus of control.* They assume responsibility for their own successes or failures. "Of course the students were confused. Did you hear my directions? They were all garbled. I've got to give more precise instructions."

Seligman[22] suggests that persons develop "explanatory styles" with which they subconsciously form internal hypotheses or rationalizations to explain to themselves good and bad events in their environment. Hartoonian and Yarger[23] found that some teachers may dismiss or distort information indicating that students did not learn as a result of their teaching strategy. Less autonomous teachers may give themselves credit for student improvement but misplace blame when performance is inadequate.

Even with this analysis, the cycle of instructional decision making is not yet complete. The learnings must be constructed, synthesized, and applied, or transferred to other learning contexts, content areas, or life situations.

Explanatory Styles

Seligman[1] suggests that persons develop "explanatory styles" with which they unconsciously form internal hypotheses or rationalizations with which to explain to themselves good and bad events in their environment. His "ABC's" of explanatory style for coping with difficulties are:

A–adversity: For example, students are noisy and inattentive.

B–beliefs: For example, the teacher believes this has to do with the windy day.

C–consequences: For example, the teacher gets frustrated, angry and feels helpless, and may even yell at the students.

Explanatory style is the way you "explain to yourself" why an event is happening. Seligman finds that optimistic and pessimistic people explain events to themselves by assigning attributes differently to three critical dimensions: permanence, pervasiveness, and personalization.

	GOOD EVENTS		BAD EVENTS	
	Optimists	**Pessimists**	**Optimists**	**Pessimists**
Permanence:	Permanent "I'm always lucky."	Temporary "It's my lucky day."	Temporary "I'm exhausted."	Permanent "I'm all washed up."
Pervasiveness:	Universal "I'm smart."	Specific "I'm smart at math."	Specific "Mr. Scofield is unfair."	Universal "Administrators are unfair."
Personalization	Internal "I can take advantage of luck."	External "A stroke of luck."	External "I grew up in poverty."	Internal "I'm insecure."

Less efficacious teachers who are insecure, pessimistic, or who have low self-esteem, may allow such explanatory biases to enter their interpretations. For "bad" events, they may assign attributes of:

Permanence ("This always happens")

Universalness ("All students are like this") and/or

Internal personalized reasons ("There's something wrong with me")

Efficacious teachers, on the other hand, are more likely to explain bad events as:

Temporary ("This happened today"),

Specific ("Six students acted out") and

External in terms of cause ("When she understood my directions incorrectly") but

Internal in terms of ability to effect change ("If I had modeled the instructions I think she would have understood them.")

Less efficacious teachers may allow biases to enter their interpretations, while more efficacious teachers, who possess a positive self-image, are more likely to "own" or hold themselves responsible for the outcomes of teaching—whether high or low achievement.

Applying: The Projective Phase

At this stage, the teacher constructs new knowledge through analysis and applies that knowledge to future instructional situations or content. Experience can bring change, but experience alone is not enough. Experience is actually constructed: compared, differentiated, categorized, and labeled. This allows the teacher to recognize and interpret classroom events, departures from routines, and novel occurrences. Thus, the teacher can predict the consequences of possible alternatives and activities. Without this conceptual system, the teacher's perception of the classroom remains chaotic.

Autonomous teachers consciously reflect upon, conceptualize, and apply understandings from one classroom experience to the next. As a result of this analysis and reflection, they synthesize new knowledge about teaching and learning. As experiences with teaching and learning accumulate, concepts are derived and constructed. As a result, teachers become more routinized, particularized, and refined. They are capable of predicting consequences of their decisions and are therefore more experimental and risk-taking. They expand their repertoire of techniques and strategies to be used in different situations with varying content and unique groups of students.

Richard Shavelson[24] states:

> Any teaching act is the result of a decision, whether conscious or unconscious, that the teacher makes after the complex cognitive processing of available information. This reasoning leads us to the hypothesis that *the basic teaching skill is decision making.*

Many but not all of the cognitive or intellectual processes involved in the four components of the instructional act have been examined. Teaching is cognitively complex. Even the myriad decisions reported here are driven by even more deeply embedded conscious or subconscious beliefs, styles, metaphors, perceptions, and habits. In this chapter we have attempted to 1) refocus the definition of teaching away from an archaic, behavioristic model to a more modern and viable cognitive model and 2) thereby direct the focus of the coach away from only the overt behaviors of teaching to concentrate more on those invisible, inner thought processes of teaching. All the behaviors we see in the classroom are artifacts of these internal mental process.

If teachers do not possess these mental capacities, no amount of experience alone will create them. It is through mediated processing and reflecting upon experience that these capacities will be developed.[25] As coaches, therefore, we are interested in operating on the inner thought processes. Teachers possess wide and expanding bodies of information and skills and they make decisions about when to use what from the extensive range of their repertoire. Cognitive coaches assist teachers in becoming more conscious, efficacious, precise, flexible, informed, and skillful decision makers. Together, teachers and coaches create greater student learning.

Summary

In this chapter we report major findings influencing the work of the cognitive coach:
  • human behavior is based on simple maps of reality,

- talking aloud about one's maps energizes teachers and contributes to refinements in mental maps—and consequently behaviors, and
- certain invisible skills of cognition and perception drive teaching performance.

We have elaborated our beliefs that the craft of teaching is a cognitive process by presenting the research on teacher cognition. These cognitive processes were presented in four clusters of thought: Planning—the pre-active stage; Teaching—the inter-active stage; Analyzing and Evaluating—the reflective stage; and Applying—the projective stage.

It is based on this conception of teaching, that a model of coaching, presented in Chapter 2, directly parallels and is intended to enhance teacher's growth toward even more thoughtful teaching. The ultimate purpose, however, is not only to enhance teaching but to cause the teacher to grow toward higher states of holonomy, and to support the development of school cultures that value and are skilled in the dual goals of autonomy and interdependence necessary for Renaissance Schools. Thus the coach continually focuses on these longer-range goals in the use of cognitive coaching skills.

In addition to those trust-building skills described in Chapter 2, the additional linguistic skills presented in Chapter 3 included questioning with the intention of engaging and producing complex cognition, employing positive presuppositions, and probing for greater clarity and precision of language and thought.

Endnotes

1. Clark, C. and Peterson, P. "Teachers' Thought Processes," in Wittrock, M.C. (Ed.) *Handbook of Research on Teaching*, 3rd ed. New York, NY: MacMillan Publishing Co., 1986, pp. 255–296.

2. Jackson, P.W. *Life in Classrooms*. New York, NY: Holt, Rinehart, and Winston, 1968, p. 10.

    Coladarci, A.P. "The Teacher as Hypothesis Maker." *California Journal of Instructional Improvement* (March 1959): Vol. 2, pp. 3–6.

3. Dahllof, U. and Lundgren, U.P. "Macro- and Micro-Approaches Combined for Curriculum Process Analysis: A Swedish Educational Field Project." University of Goteborg, Institute of Education, 1970.

4. Clark, C. and Peterson, P. "Teachers' Thought Processes," in Wittrock, M.C. (Ed.) *Handbook of Research on Teaching*, 3rd ed. New York, NY: MacMillan Publishing Co., 1986, pp. 255–296.

5. Clark, C. and Peterson, P. "Teachers' Thought Processes" in Wittrock, M.C. (Ed.) *Handbook of Research on Teaching*, 3rd ed. New York, NY: MacMillan Publishing Co., 1986, pp. 255–296.

6. Costa, A. *Developing Minds: A Resource Book for Teaching Thinking*. Alexandria, VA: Association for Supervision and Curriculum Development, 1991.

7. Smith, E.R. and Tyler, R.W. *Appraising and Recording Student Progress*. New York, NY: Harper and Row, 1945.

   Costa, A. "Towards a Model of Human Intellectual Functioning," in Costa, A. (Ed.) *Developing Minds: A Resource Book for Teaching Thinking*. Alexandria, VA: Association for Supervision and Curriculum Development, 1991.

8. Wolfe, P. "Facilitator's Manual: Instructional Decisions for Long-Term Learning," ASCD Videotape Series, Alexandria, Va.: Association for Supervision and Curriculum Development, 1987.

9. Shavelson, R. "Teacher Decision Making." *The Psychology of Teaching Methods: 1976 Yearbook of the National Society for the Study of Education, Part I*. Chicago, IL: University of Chicago Press, 1976.

10. Zahorick, J. "Teachers' Planning Models." *Educational Leadership* (1975): Vol. 33, pp. 134–139.

11. Shavelson, R. "Teacher Sensitivity to the Reliability of Information in Making Pedagogical Decisions." *American Educational Research Journal* (Spring 1977): Vol. 14, pp. 144–151.

    Borko, H., Cone, R., Russo, D., and Shavelson, R. "Teachers' Decision Making," in Peterson, D. and Walberg, H. (Ed.) *Research on Teaching*. Berkeley, CA: McCutchan Publishers, 1979.

12. Taylor, P. *How Teachers Plan Their Courses*. Slough, Berkshire, England: National Foundation for Educational Research, 1970.

13. Miller, G.A. "The Magical Number Seven, Plus or Minus Two: Some Limits on Our Capacity for Processing Information." *Psychological Review* (March 1963): Vol. 2, pp. 81–97.

14. Ulich, E. "Some Experiments of the Function of Mental Training in the Acquisition of Motor Skills." *Ergonomics* (1967): Vol. 10, pp. 411–419.

15. Jansson, L. "Mental Training: Thinking Rehearsal and Its Use" in Maxwell, W. (Ed.) *Thinking: The Expanding Frontier.* Philadelphia, PA: The Franklin Institute, 1983.

16. Jansson, L. "Mental Training: Thinking Rehearsal and Its Use" in Maxwell, W. (Ed.) *Thinking: The Expanding Frontier.* Philadelphia, PA: The Franklin Institute, 1983.

17. Clark C. and Yinger, R. "Teachers' Thinking." *Research on Thinking.* Berkeley, CA: McCutchan Publishers, 1979.

18. Clark, C. and Peterson, P. "Teachers' Thought Processes," in Wittrock, M.C. (Ed.) *Handbook of Research on Teaching,* 3rd ed. New York, NY: MacMillan Publishing Co., 1986, pp. 255–296.

19. Harvey, O.J. "System Structure, Flexibility, and Creativity" in *Experience, Structure, and Adaptability.* New York: Springer Publishing Co., 1966, pp. 39–65.

20. Yinger, R.J. "A Study of Teacher Planning: Description and Theory Development Using Ethnographic and Information Processing Methods," unpublished doctoral dissertation, East Lansing, MI: Michigan State University, 1977.

21. Clark, C. and Peterson, P. "Teachers' Thought Processes" in Wittrock, M.C. (Ed.) *Handbook of Research on Teaching,* 3rd ed. New York, NY: MacMillan Publishing Co., 1986, pp. 255–296.

22. Perkins, D. *Smart Schools.* New York, NY: The Free Press, 1992.

23. Seligman, M. *Learned Optimism.* New York, NY: Alfred A. Knopf, Inc., 1990.

24. Hartoonian, B. and Yarger, G. "Teachers' Conceptions of Their Own Success," Washington, D.C.: ERIC Clearinghouse on Teacher Education, No. S017372, February 1981.

25. Shavelson, R. "Teachers' Decision Making." *The Psychology of Teaching Methods: 1976 Yearbook of the National Society for the Study of Education, Part I.* Chicago, IL: University of Chicago Press, 1976.

26. Feuerstein, R. and Feuerstein, S. "Mediated Learning Experience: A Theoretical Review," in Feuerstein, R., Kelin, P. and Tannenbaum, A. (Eds.) *Mediated Learning Experience (MLE) Theoretical, Psychosocial and Learning Implications.* London, England: Freund Publishing House, 1991.

Sidebar Endnote

1. McNeill, B. "Beyond Sports: Imaging in Daily Life: An Interview with Marilyn King," *Noetic Sciences Collection: 1980–1990, Ten Years of Consciousness Research,* Sausalito, CA: Institute of Noetic Science, 1991, p. 33.

1. Seligman, M. *Learned Optimism.* New York, NY: Alfred A. Knopf Inc., 1990.

6

Coaching Tools for Cognition

Thinking is an engagement of the mind that changes the mind.

Martin Heidegger

If teachers do not possess the mental capacities described in Chapter 5, no amount of experience alone will create it. It is through mediated processing and reflecting upon experience that these capacities will be developed.[1] The act of coaching engages, causes awareness of, develops, labels, and enhances these intellectual functions. For this reason, we sometimes refer to our model as "Brain Compatible Coaching." Let's look at the coach's role during each part of the process.

Planning Conference

The coach keeps in mind the types of invisible, intellectual processes that teachers perform during planning, and he purposely engages and mediates them. Thus, the Planning Conference is not merely about the forthcoming lesson but about the cognitive functions and processes of lesson planning.

We have discovered that what teachers pay attention to in planning is a matter of mental habit. Because the coach's questions focus their attention on learner objectives and ways of evaluating them, teachers begin to automate this way of thinking. The coach repeatedly asks: "What are your objectives and how will you know that you've achieved them?" Teachers gradually and spontaneously ask themselves these questions for all their planning, not just when they are being coached (see Figure 6-1).

Coaches mediate by having the teacher:

- Clarify lesson goals and objectives

- Determine evidence of student achievement

- Describe the lesson's relationship to the actual and/or hypothetical curriculum

- Anticipate teaching strategies and decisions

- Anticipate any concerns

- Identify the coach's data-gathering focus and procedures

Figure 6-1
An Extended Map of a Planning Conference

This kind of coaching leads teachers to be more flexible in their instruction. Although they have specific objectives, they also know they're looking for a variety of student behaviors, not just one event. Teachers know they can discuss with their coach why they deviated from their original plan. In a trusting, nonjudgmental relationship, teachers are free to take risks, use their intuition, be creative, and be vulnerable. Teachers come to realize that there is no such thing as a mistake; each lesson is an experience to be learned from.

Observation

Though the Observation is important, the coach's greatest help is offered to teachers in the Planning and Reflecting Conferences. In the Planning Conference, the coach asks a series of mediational questions to engage the teacher's metacognition during the teaching phase. For example:

- What are your plans for dealing with Jane's constant interruptions?

- What actions by the students will indicate to you that they're on task?
- How will you know when it's time to move from one stage of the lesson to another?

In the Reflecting Conference, the coach will return to these same types of questions to guide the teacher to recall his thinking during the lesson.

Reflecting Conference

Again, the coach's goal is to engage the teacher's analytic abilities. The coach invites the teacher to compare the actual and desired lesson. Is there a match or a mismatch? The coach might ask:

- What is it that you saw students doing to indicate to you that the lesson was successful?
- What is it that you did to cause the lesson to go as it did?
- What was it about the teaching strategy that produced the outcomes?

The coach also wants the teacher to apply experience to new situations:

- Based on your analysis, what next steps will you take?
- If you were to re-teach this lesson, how would you do it differently?
- What does this tell you about lesson planning?
- What does this tell you about your students?

Reflecting: Coaches mediate by having the teacher:

- Summarize their impressions and assessments of the lesson.
- Recall data supporting those impressions and assessments.
- Compare planned with performed teaching decisions, and student learning.
- Infer relationships between student achievement and teacher decisions/behavior.

Applying: Coaches mediate by having the teacher:

- Synthesize new learnings and prescribe applications.
- Reflect on the coaching process; recommend refinements.

Figure 6-2
Basic Reflecting Conference Map

The Language of Coaching

It becomes readily apparent that an important set of mediational skills are the coach's language tools. In Chapter 2 we explored the verbal foundational skills of coaching and in Chapter 3 the verbal and non-verbal behaviors for trust. Chapter 4 illuminated the need for flexibility in coaching. In Chapter 7 we will explore the coach's language tools that support teachers' to growth toward higher states of mind.

In addition to the nonjudgmental response behaviors of silence, paraphrasing, empathizing, clarifying, and providing data,[2] which were introduced in Chapter 3, cognitive coaches engage the intellectual functions of the four stages of instructional thought outlined in Chapter 5. The verbal skills of questioning, intonation, positive presuppositions, probing and clarifying, and providing data will be elaborated with their impact on cognition.

Questioning Skills

When an audience of teachers was asked, "How many of you teach at the elementary level? Where are our junior high teachers? Who teaches at the high school?" members of each group raised their hands even though they were not told to do so. When asked why they did that they responded, "Because you asked a question."

One of the great miracles of being human is the ability to decode language cues, and we pick up many of them in questions. Every time a coach poses a question, she is trying to cause analysis, application of learnings, and projections to the future. It's vital, then, that her questions take into account the subtle messages conveyed by intonation, sentence structure, and presuppositions.

Intonation

We interpret much of language simply from intonation. For example, a different word is italicized in each sentence below to indicate spoken emphasis on that word. As the intonation changes, what meaning or concept does your brain form?

I didn't steal that coat! (Not me!)

I *didn't* steal that coat! (What's going on here? How can

you suspect me?)

I didn't *steal* that coat! (I'm not a thief—I just borrowed it!)

I didn't steal *that* coat! (Ha ha—I took that other one!)

Our intonation greatly affects the mind of the person we're addressing. The skillful coach purposefully monitors—and uses—intonation as a language skill.

Sentence Structure

Embedded in our questions lie certain cues that signal various mental performances. If you're asked, "Who wrote *Leaves of Grass?*" you might answer, "Walt Whitman." The structure of that question signaled you to provide that answer because of the words "who" and the use of the past-tense verb "wrote."

When your brain hears "who, what, when, or where" and a past-tense verb, it knows that it should draw forth information from memory, to recall. For example:

Q. Who was the first man to set foot on the moon?

A. Neil Armstrong.

During coaching, a recall question might sound like: "What did you observe your students doing when you asked that question?"

We tap into higher levels of thought by posing questions with different structures. For example, you'll get a comparison type of answer if you ask, "What similarities do you see between Neil Armstrong's voyage to the moon and Christopher Columbus's voyage to the New World?" You're asking the person to draw forth and build upon previous knowledge, looking for similarities. As a coach, you might ask: "How did your students' reaction during the lesson compare with what you had planned?"

By posing the question using still a different structure, you get another level of thinking: "How do you think education would be affected if education received the same budget as that allocated for space exploration?" Now the brain is creating a new reality and judging how workable the ideas are. "Would/if" kinds of questions cause the brain to create, dream, visualize, evaluate, speculate, and imagine. Those two little words carry great power: They cause the brain to think hypothetically, to change circumstances, and to predict alternative outcomes. A coach can tap into this power by asking questions such as: "If you were to use these types of questions in a math lesson, what effects would they have on students' thinking?"

Note also that our answers to the various questions changed. The first kind of question prompts one- or two-word replies. Our answers became longer with the comparison. Finally, we had to answer in complete thoughts and whole sentences to envision new circumstances and outcomes. A distinct correlation exists between the structure of questions and the kinds of answers produced (see the sidebar "Question Syntax"). (Questioning strategies are further elaborated in the Appendix.)

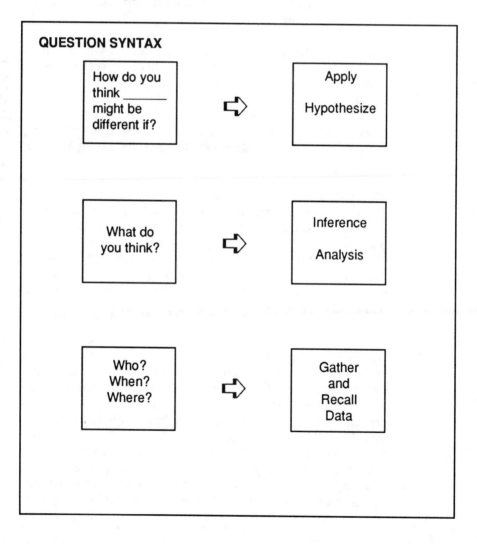

QUESTION SYNTAX

How do you think _____ might be different if?	⇨	Apply Hypothesize
What do you think?	⇨	Inference Analysis
Who? When? Where?	⇨	Gather and Recall Data

Presuppositions

Why did the audience of teachers raise their hands when asked their grade-level instead of standing up or calling out, "I am!"? They presupposed in that situation that they should provide an answer by raising their hands.

Questions can easily carry messages hidden below the surface meanings of the words used. Since limiting presuppositions have the potential to detract from and reduce teachers' resourcefulness, skillful coaches discipline themselves to avoid them. For example, "How would the results have been different if you had only listened?" implies that the results weren't good, the teacher didn't listen, she missed something, and she ought to feel a little guilty or ashamed. The question, "Doesn't it seem my objective is more practical?" contains the presupposition that something is wrong with the teacher's objective. If you simply ask, "Do you have an objective?" the presupposition is that there may not be one and a professional would certainly have objectives.

A question like "Why did you do that?" often creates a defensive reaction because it asks for a justification of behavior rather than an inquiry into the decision-making process. It is possible to ask "why" questions in other ways. For example, "What was your thinking that led up to that act? What were you considering at that time that led you to choose that particular piece?"

Empowering presuppositions extend and build trust with the teacher:

• What goals and outcomes do you have for your lesson? (The plural of goals and outcomes suggest that there will be more than one.)

• How will you know when you're successful? (This presupposes that the teacher will be successful, that she will hold the criteria for success in her mind, that she will read cues during the lesson by which to self-evaluate, and that she will find data to support her analysis.)

• As you consider alternatives, what seems most promising? (This implies that more than one alternative exists and that the teacher is considering and evaluating them.)

• What personal learnings or insights might you carry forward to future lessons? (This open-ended question can be very powerful because it gives the teacher an opportunity to reflect on his experiences and select what's most important to him.)

Probing and Clarifying

Our brain and central nervous system filters an enormous amount of sensory input. A million bits of information per minute come pouring into our brain—and we certainly can't attend to it all. Instead we:

- generalize, fitting information into already stored patterns and categories;
- delete, or literally stop data from coming in (for example, seeing bugs and dirt on a windshield, but looking through it to focus on the road and other cars);
- distort, shaping information to fit our preconceived structures and beliefs, similar to the man who thought he was a corpse. After six months, his psychiatrist asked him if corpses could bleed. The patient said, "Of course not," and the doctor pricked his finger and squeezed out some blood. The patient stared at it and exclaimed, "What do you know? Corpses do bleed!"

Knowing that our brains easily filter and distort information, it's important to understand some of the cognitive reasons why probing and clarifying is important. The skillful coach looks for the following:

Vague nouns or pronouns. When the teacher talks about "the textbooks," she has deleted information about which textbooks she's referring to. The coach can ask, "Which textbooks specifically?" Clarifying vague nouns and pronouns supplies missing data and provides more precise information. When the teacher says, "The girls in the class," the coach can get a better understanding by asking, "Which girls?"

Vague action words. These refer to unspecified verbs such as *think* and *understand* and also signal deleted information. When the coach hears, "I want students to understand," he can ask, "Understand what?" to clarify the content. "Which students?" will clarify the audience. "What will you see them doing if they are understanding?" tells the coach exactly what behaviors the teacher is looking for.

Comparisons. Distortions or generalities will sometimes be masked by comparisons. Often the teacher will not elaborate to whom or to what she is comparing students. For example, if the teacher says, "The class is much brighter," the coach can probe, "Brighter than what?" Or if the teacher says, "Franklin's getting along much better," the coach can ask, "Better than what?"

Rule words. Phrases like "I can't, we shouldn't, it happens all the time, nobody does that" should alert the coach that the teacher is limiting his thinking and possibly working with distorted perceptions. Skillful coaches challenge this mindset. When a teacher says, "I can't," the coach can respond, "What's stopping you?" When the teacher says, "We shouldn't," one response is, "What would happen if we did? Who made up that rule?"

Universal judgments. Phrases like "everybody, all the time, nobody, never, and always" also limit thinking. Those kinds of statements can be challenged with intonation. If the teacher says, "Nobody around here does that," the coach may simply respond, "Nobody?" Most people will recognize that they have overgeneralized. Or the coach can ask for an exception: "Nobody around here does that? Can you think of someone who does?" This too leads the teacher to see she has overgeneralized. If the relationship permits it, the coach can use a gentle exaggeration: "Nobody ever does that? Never in the history of this school has anyone done that?"

Providing Data

Inexperienced coaches, being quite proud of their data-gathering abilities, may tell the teacher so much information about the lesson that it just isn't possible for them to process it. Because of this, we'd like to offer some tips on data reporting.

Skillful coaches invite the teacher's recollection of data from the lesson rather than the coach providing it. This is done for at least two reasons:

 • Once you have the teacher's report, you know what is appropriate for you to give to the teacher to fill in the blanks, and

 • The teacher's ability to observe and remember what occurred in a lesson is a fundamental and essential cognitive skill necessary for self-reflection and self-coaching. Coaches are mindful that the purpose of coaching is not only to enhance the lesson but also the engagement and development of the habits and skills of self-coaching.

A trust-enhancing side-by-side seating arrangement works well for sharing data. In this way the teacher can look on the coach's notes directly and they can cooperatively review and assess what is there. Teachers appreciate being handed the observation notes before the post-conference is completed. This is symbolically important because it signals another distinction between coaching and evaluation and it leaves the teacher with a written reference she can pursue at her leisure. Occasionally it is appropriate to leave notes with the teacher prior to the reflective conference. This would be particularly helpful when the coach has gathered complex data such as student patterns of information. That allows the teacher to study the data prior to the reflective conference.

Sometimes coaches may decide *not* to discuss some of the data that they have gathered even though it has been requested in the pre-conference. This may occur when important but tangential problems or concerns are intro-duced by the teacher in the post-conference dialogue. When coaches remember that *the purpose of the post-conference is not to cover the post-conference map but to extend teacher thinking,* they are freed from mechanical adherence to that map. Having met their thinking objective, coaches may decide that it is not the best use of time to extend the conference to explore data that they have collected. The teacher could still review the data in the form of the coach's observation notes.

Beginning coaches often ask, "What if I see the teacher doing something wrong or that could have been done better?" Because the post-conference structure is one of objectively analyzing data and engaging the teacher in cause-effect thinking, teacher "errors" or uncorrected student behaviors will always be easily and nonjudgmentally addressed in the Reflecting Conference. Consider this dialogue in which students did *not* achieve the teacher's intended outcome:

> **Coach:** *How'd they do?*
> **Teacher:** *Miserably. Only half the class understood it.*
> **Coach:** *What do you suppose caused that?*
> **Teacher:** *Well, you saw the side talking going on. I couldn't get them to be quiet.*

Coach: *What do you think contributed to the side talk?*

The teacher is aware that students didn't achieve the learning objective, knows that student talking was the cause, and is now being invited by the coach to enter a problem-solving discussion which will lead to self-prescription for corrective action.

But what if the teacher *doesn't* know the students didn't reach the objective, nor why they did not?

> **Coach:** *How'd it go?*
> **Teacher:** *Great. They really loved it.*
> **Coach:** *So you're feeling good about their response. What are you recalling that indicates their enjoyment?*
> **Teacher:** *Well, they were all talking a lot.*
> **Coach:** *So you noticed a lot of engagement. How'd they do at mastering the concept?*
> **Teacher:** *Well, I'm not so sure.*
> **Coach:** *Would you like to see my data?*
> **Teacher:** *Sure.*
> **Coach:** *(Shows the teacher the coach's observation notes.) Notice that this half of the class responded correctly, this half had other answers. What do you make of that?*

What follows is an example of a Planning and Reflecting conference coded to explain the various language skills used and interactions illustrated. We hope coaches will use both sources of information as guidance and background knowledge in their actual interactions with teachers.

The Planning Conference

TEACHER'S COMMENTS	COACH'S COMMENTS	LINGUISTIC SKILLS EMPLOYED	ADDITIONAL COMMENTS
Hi, Javier, thanks for agreeing to come into my class today. I appreciate the time you're giving to me.	I'm looking forward to it. Tell me, Trish, what's your lesson going to be about?	The coach begins with an open-ended question to evoke the teacher's intentions.	The teacher has invited the coach in to observe—a strong indicator of a high level of trust.
Well, Javier, today I'm going to try a concept attainment lesson. I hadn't tried one before I attended the workshop that the District Thinking Skills Committee presented and I thought it would be great fun. I've tried it once with this class but they didn't respond too well and I think I need some help.	So, you're experimenting with some new techniques. Tell me what you hope to accomplish	Labels the teacher's behaviors then probes for specific outcomes	Another indicator of trust. The teacher is risking a new lesson format with the coach.
Well, I want the kids to verbalize their metacognition—to verbalize their thinking. We've never really done that before, and I don't know if they will be able to talk about their thinking.	So you're interested in having them talk about what's going on inside their head when they are thinking?	Paraphrasing	Matches verbal modality in language
Exactly. But I don't know if they can do that at this age.	What would you hear students saying if they were able to verbalize the inner thought processes?	Probing for specific student behaviors	

TEACHER'S COMMENTS	COACH'S COMMENTS	LINGUISTIC SKILLS EMPLOYED	ADDITIONAL COMMENTS
Well, if they reported that they were "observing" or "hypothesizing" or "changing their mind with more information"— something like that.	So, you're going to be listening for students describing what they're doing cognitively; you're listening for their use of cognitive terminology.	Paraphrasing	
Exactly!	What will you do to make that happen?	Questions to elicit intended teacher behaviors	
Well, I'll ask them to talk about what they are doing inside their head—their confusions, their strategies, their reasoning.	In other words, you'll invite them to talk out loud about their thought processes.	Paraphrasing	
Yes.	And you have a concern that they will not be able to do that?	Empathizes with the teacher's concern	
Yes. It's a new way of thinking for them—and for me. I've not asked them before; or if I have asked them to share their planning or their strategies, they just say, "I don't know, I just did it."	So tell me about your plan; how do you intend to structure your lesson?	The coach questions to elicit the teacher's strategies.	

TEACHER'S COMMENTS	COACH'S COMMENTS	LINGUISTIC SKILLS EMPLOYED	ADDITIONAL COMMENTS
Well, I'll start by reviewing our past concept attainment lesson. I'll tell them we're going to add to it. I'll explain the word, "metacognition" (they love those big words at this age). And I'll model it for them and ask them to explain to me what they are thinking as they are solving a sample problem I'll give them. Next I'll introduce another concept attainment lesson I've planned. I'll remind them of the rules about the two columns—the examples and non-examples— and how they must not give the concept but rather they must give another example as a test. I'm going to stop along the way and ask them to share their thinking and to describe why they are keeping or changing their hypotheses.	At what point in the lesson will you be interested in listening for their metacognition?	Probes for specific time	
After I have presented them with the two columns of the "examples" and "not examples" I hope to intrigue and make them curious and have to gather data more to support their conclusions.	What would you like me to do while I'm in your classroom?	Questions to establish the role of the coach.	

TEACHER'S COMMENTS	COACH'S COMMENTS	LINGUISTIC SKILLS EMPLOYED	ADDITIONAL COMMENTS
I want you to listen to the students and collect evidence of their metacognitive vocabulary—are they expressing what they're thinking using cognitive terminology.	So you want me to observe them. How should I collect the data in a way that would be most useful to you?	Paraphrases then probes for specific format of data collection	
I'll give you a seating chart and I'd like you to record all the cognitive words you hear each student expressing.	OK. By each student's name on the seating chart, I'll record the cognitive terminology that student uses. Is there anything else?	Paraphrases the role of the coach	
Yes. I'd also like to have you record my use of cognitive terminology—I want to know if I am modeling in my own language and labeling their cognitive language.	How should I do that?	Clarifies the task of the coach	
Well, I'd like you to record my use of thinking terms when I am modeling at the beginning; then during the discussion, do I label their cognitive processes; for example, if a kid says, "well, before I thought . . . . but now I'm thinking . . . ." I'd say, "OK, you've changed your mind with the addition of more information."	OK. I think I know what to do. I'm looking forward to this.	Shares personal information	

The Reflecting Conference

TEACHER'S COMMENTS	COACH'S COMMENTS	LINGUISTIC SKILLS EMPLOYED	ADDITIONAL COMMENTS
	Well, Trish, how do you think the lesson went?	Asks an open-ended question	Such an open-ended question allows the teacher to take the lead in interpreting the lesson from any approach the teacher wishes.
Well, I think it went pretty well, actually; I was impressed by how well these students could explain and describe their thought processes.			
	What did you hear that makes you think they succeeded?	Probes for recall of specific student behaviors to support interpretation	
I heard a lot of students saying things like "theory," "I'm changing my mind," "attribute"—words like that.			
	Would you be interested in seeing which students used which words?	Invites the teacher to consider the data that was requested	Does not dump the data; rather, the coach asks permission to share it if the teacher so desires.
Yes, I would.			

TEACHER'S COMMENTS	COACH'S COMMENTS	LINGUISTIC SKILLS EMPLOYED	ADDITIONAL COMMENTS
	You asked me to keep a seating chart and to record which students used which words. Here's what I recorded.	Provides data that was collected	Hands the record of observations to the teacher
Hmm. I didn't realize so many students used so many thinking words. Especially Ahmad and Shelley. And here, Alicia, too.			The teacher observes and analyzes the recorded data for herself.
	So, you are finding that many of the students did respond and did use thinking vocabulary. What did you do to make that happen?	Paraphrases the teacher's interpretations. Poses a question intended to have the teacher state a causal relationship between the teacher's behavior and the student's performance	Such a question stimulates growth toward even greater efficacy and an internal locus of control.
Well, I did try to model it, and, uh, I guess in this lesson I stated it as a goal at the beginning; I told students that that's what I wanted them to do. Then when I modeled it, I think they caught on— it freed them up to talk about what they were thinking because I modeled what I was thinking.			
	Why do you think that's so?	Questions to cause the teacher to infer a relationship	

TEACHER'S COMMENTS	COACH'S COMMENTS	LINGUISTIC SKILLS EMPLOYED	ADDITIONAL COMMENTS
Well, I guess making your objectives explicit and modeling the desired behaviors encourages them to do it themselves.			The teacher infers a relationship for herself.
	You were also interested in your own use of cognitive terminology and whether you labeled students' thinking. How do feel you did?	Recalls the teacher's concern about her own behavior from the pre-conference.	Does not yet volunteer the data; rather, invites the teacher to share her own recollections
Well, as a result of talking with you in the pre-conference, I found I was more aware of my own labeling; I was more alert to the students' cognitive performances and could identify which behaviors the students were using while I was teaching.			The teacher talks about her own metacognition and thinks about her own thinking.
	As you reflect back on the lesson, what were some examples of your labeling of students' thought processes.	Positive presupposition: (You are reflecting), and questions to cause the teacher to provide data.	
Well, one time was when Elena said, "I think the concept is 'animals with wings,'" and I said, "So you have a theory. How could you test it?" Then she said something like, "I could test it by adding another winged animal to the examples list, and if it stays there, then I will think my idea is a good one."			

TEACHER'S COMMENTS	COACH'S COMMENTS	LINGUISTIC SKILLS EMPLOYED	ADDITIONAL COMMENTS
	Would you like to know how many times you labeled students' thinking?	Offers the data to the teacher.	
Yes, I would			
	I counted eleven times that you labeled a student's thought processes.	Provides the data.	
Hmm. Maybe as students hear those words repeated and attach the names to their behaviors, they get used to hearing them and start using them.			The teacher forms her own inference about the effects of their behavior on the student's performance.
	As you envision the next step for these students in learning about thinking, what do you have planned?	Questions to cause application and prediction towards the future.	Uses positive presuppositions of envisioning and planning
Well, I've been thinking that it's not enough to just use the terminology. I want them also to bridge or apply these thinking processes to other situations in life.			
	So, you want them to use these words elsewhere?	Probes for clarity of purpose	
No, not just the words. I want them to talk about when they would use the processes of theorizing, experimenting, changing their mind with additional data. That's the real purpose for these types of thinking skills lessons.			The teacher corrects the coach's misinterpretation.

TEACHER'S COMMENTS	COACH'S COMMENTS	LINGUISTIC SKILLS EMPLOYED	ADDITIONAL COMMENTS
	As you are planning those lessons, I'd be interested in having you share your thoughts about how you'll do that. Tell me, Trish, as you reflect on our coaching today, what did this process do for you?	Invites the teacher to evaluate usefulness of the coaching process.	
It really helped. Our pre-conference made me more aware of the behaviors I wanted from the students; I also found that when I made them clear to you, I also made them clear to me. You know, we've done this coaching four times now, and I'm beginning to see that when I think through the lesson objectives as I plan the lesson, the clearer I become about what I'm trying to accomplish, the greater the likelihood that I'll accomplish it.			
	So becoming precise in your planning is helpful to you.	Paraphrases the teacher's conclusion	
Yes, in some ways I need you more to think through the plan with me, then I can analyze whether I've achieved my purposes for myself.			
	Thank you, Trish, I'd like to think through that lesson with you.		

Summary

Teachers have numerous tools of instruction in their class-rooms: computers, chalkboards, overhead projectors, maps, textbooks, etc. Likewise, coaches employ tools which are intended to enhance trust, contribute to learning, and build toward the holonomous and simultaneous states of autonomy and interdependence. These are the language tools of coaching. The types of language skills described in this chapter are not meant to be mastered in the few pages allotted here. Experimentation, practice, feedback and observation of results will obviously take time. You are invited to become conscious of, experiment with, practice, and discuss the effects of the use of these language tools.

These language tools are not restricted to classrooms or coaching. They are the basis of sound communication in problem solving, caring and understanding in many life settings—between parents and children, spouses, parents and teachers, administrators and teachers, school board members, etc. They are the basics of communication in the Renaissance classroom, school, and community.

Additional language tools will be presented in the next chapter as we discuss Five States of Mind toward which human beings aspire and the linguistic tools which effective coaches employ to produce such growth.

Endnotes

1. Feuerstein, R. and Feuerstein, S. "Mediated Learning Experience: A Theoretical Review," in Feuerstein, R., Kelin, P. and Tannenbaum, A. (Eds.) *Mediated Learning Experience (MLE) Theoretical, Psychosocial and Learning Implications*. London, England: Freund Publishing House, 1991.

2. Costa, A. *The Enabling Behaviors*. Granite Bay, CA: Search Models Unlimited, 1989.

7

Achieving Holonomy

The term holonomy comes from the Greek: *holos* meaning "whole" and *on* meaning "part." Autonomous also comes from the Greek: *auto* meaning "self" and *nemein* meaning "to hold sway." Both words are important to coaches, because the third goal of cognitive coaching is the development of autonomous individuals who exercise membership in holonomous systems.

Autonomous individuals set personal goals and are self-directing, self-monitoring, and self-modifying. Because they are constantly experimenting and experiencing, they fail frequently, but they fail forward, learning from the situation. But autonomous persons are not isolated or mechanical in their work; rather, they also participate significantly in their organization. They operate in the best interests of the whole while simultaneously attending to their own goals and needs. In other words they are at once independent and interdependent—they are holonomous.

Holonomous persons are, as are all autonomous organisms, self-referencing, drawing on their own unique systems, strengths, and origins to grow. Remarkably, in humans, this growth includes the capacity to transcend their own original patterns. But the growth always emanates from within, as a tree does from a seed. We define the sources of holonomy in terms of five states of mind: efficacy, flexibility, craftsmanship, consciousness, and interdependence.

I don't divide the world into the weak and the strong, or the successes and the failures, those who make it or those who don't. I divide the world into learners and nonlearners.
Carole Hyatt and Linda Gottlieb[1]

In her doctoral studies at Seton Hall University, Dr. Rosemarie Liebmann interviewed, both personally and by questionnaire, directors of Human Resource Development from twenty of the prime corporations deemed to be learning organizations as recommended by Dr. Peter Senge. She asked them to review descriptions of and to prioritize each of the five states of mind as valued attributes of both managerial and manual employees. Her findings were that all the attributes were deemed highly desirable for both managerial and manual employees. Consciousness was cited as most valuable. Interdependence, flexibility, efficacy, and precision followed in that order. Furthermore, these human resource developers were striving to create organizations in which these attributes were modeled, valued, and taught. While each agreed that their company had not yet succeeded entirely, they felt strongly that schools need to prepare young people to possess these five states of mind as necessary prerequisites not only for corporate productivity but also for employee satisfaction.

Liebmann's findings support the value of these five states of mind not only as attributes of vital, effective, growing members of learning organizations; they also support the value of including these states of mind in decisions school leaders make regarding curriculum, instruction, assessment, and educational reform.

States of Mind

The five states of mind are the catalysts, the energy sources fueling holonomous behaviors. For an individual, they represent the continuing tensions and resources for acting holonomously. For an organization, they form an invisible energy field, in which all parties are affected as surely as a strong magnetic field affects a compass. Taken together, they are a force directing one toward increasingly authentic, congruent, ethical behavior, the touchstones of integrity. They are the tools of disciplined choice making and the primary vehicles in the lifelong journey toward integration.

The five states of mind serve also as diagnostic tools, constructs through which we can assess the cognitive development of other individuals and groups and plan

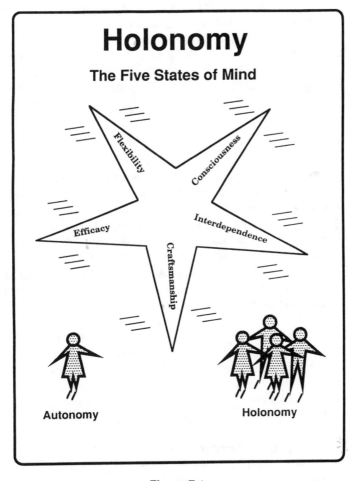

Figure 7-1
Holonomy: The Five States of Mind

interventions. But assisting others toward refinement and expression starts first with the self, your own states of mind. From there, it emanates to others, to the system in which you are a part, and even to students.

Three attributes characterize states of mind.
- They are **transitory**. They come and go. A person's state of mind varies depending on a variety of factors including familiarity, experience, knowledge, fatigue, emotion, etc.
- They are **transforming**. Dramatic increases in performance accompany heightened states of mind. Just as your current state of confidence will affect your in-the-moment competence, the states of mind access the personal resources required for peak performance. To be powerful, in other words, first think efficaciously.
- They are **transformable**, either by one's self or by another person. A colleague can cheer you up or encourage you, changing in that moment your state of mind and your capacity. Similarly, your own conscious awareness of your states of mind allows you to choose, and to change them.

Coach as Mediator of the States of Mind

A mediator is one who diagnoses and envisions desired states for others; constructs and uses clear and precise language in the facilitation of other's cognitive development; devises an overall strategy through which individuals will move themselves toward desired states; maintains faith in the potential for continued movement toward more holonomous states of mind and behavior; and possesses a belief in his or her own capacity to serve as an empowering catalyst of other's growth.

Coaches employ certain linguistic tools to enhance growth in the five states of mind. They also structure the environment to enhance growth. For example, a principal in California, Dave Schumaker, uses part of each faculty meeting for journal writing. In other settings, peer coaching and other forms of interaction are provided.

 The critical distinction between a mediator and a "fixer" is that the coach provides these experiences not to "teach behaviors" but to move that person to higher states of holonomy. Furthermore, the mediating coach will often collect evidence to indicate that person's growth. For example, Michael McCarthy, a middle school principal in Maine, compares teachers' annual goal statements in his search for developmental growth in teachers' states of mind.

Efficacy

Efficacious people believe their efforts make a difference. They do not think that things just happen to them due to chance or luck. When a situation needs a resolution, they take an active, responsive posture rather than a passive, blaming one. They are optimistic, self-actualizing, and self-modifying. Theorists have identified at least two important characteristics of efficacy: an individual's belief that she can successfully execute the behavior required to influence outcomes and a secure belief in one's own coping abilities.

Efficacy may be the most catalytic of the five states of mind because a person's sense of efficacy is a determining factor in the resolution of complex problems. If a teacher feels little efficacy, then despair, hopelessness, blame, withdrawal, and rigidity are likely to follow. But research indicates that teachers with robust efficacy are likely to expend more energy in their work, persevere longer, set more challenging goals, and continue in the face of barriers or failure.

Charles Garfield[2] in his ongoing study of peak performers has found that the primary locus of control for peak performers is not external, but internal. One element that stands out clearly among peak performers is their virtually unassailable belief in the likelihood of their own success, and their track records reinforce their beliefs.

Efficacy is important for a variety of reasons. School effectiveness research designates efficacy as one of five school conditions related to improved student learning. One study looking at the relationship between efficacy and curriculum implementation showed that teachers' efficacy and interdependence significantly predicted the implementation of the new curriculum guides.[3] Neither efficacy nor teacher interactions alone produced a significant difference in use of the curriculum, but together they brought about change. Fullan[4] regards teacher efficacy as a vital factor for successful implementation of change. Rosenholtz[5] also found that teachers' efficacy influenced students' basic skills and mastery. The more certain teachers feel about their technical knowledge, the greater students' progress in reading. The more uncertainty suffered by teachers, the less students learn.

In the Rand Corporation's seminal research on school effectiveness, Berman and McLaughlin[6] found that teacher efficacy was the single most consistent variable related to school success. The efficacy identified by the Rand Corporation study is what Fuller, Wood, Rapoport, and Dornbusch[7] label "organizational efficacy," or the link between what a person sees as valued goals and their expectation that those goals can be achieved by participating in the organization.

Research on efficacy has been pursued under several names: self-efficacy, personal efficacy, teacher certainty, peak performance, optimism, internal locus of control, and organization efficacy. What can the coach learn from this body of work?

Laborde and Saunders[8] report that people governed by an internal locus of control show initiative in controlling their environment. They control their own impulsivity, gather information, are cognitively active, eagerly learn information that will increase their probability of success, and show signs of humor. When compared with individuals who have an external locus of control, they are less anxious, less hostile, less angry, more trustful, less suspicious of others, less prone to suicide, less depressed, and less prone to psychosis.

Additionally, efficacious people are resourceful. They engage in cause-effect thinking, spend energy on tasks, set challenging goals, persevere in the face of barriers and occasional failure, accurately forecast future performances, are optimistic, are confident, have sound self-knowledge, feel good about themselves, control performance anxiety, implement curriculum in collegial environments, and translate concepts into action.

These descriptors provide a vision of the desired state toward which coaches can facilitate growth. One value of efficacy and the resulting self-confidence is that it frees the teacher to be more flexible. This is critically important for any creative work in which one wants to see the big-picture patterns as well as details.

Flexibility

We discussed flexibility in coaching in Chapter 4. Here we explore its source—the state of mind of flexibility. Flexibility involves the ability to step beyond yourself and look at a situation from a different perspective. This is what Piaget called the overcoming of egocentrism. Many psychologists believe that this is the highest state of intelligent behavior. As we shall see later, it is also a prerequisite state of the mind if one is to function interdependently.

Flexible people are empathic. They listen with their ears, eyes, heart, and mind. They hear beyond words and see beyond actions to the probable positive intentions beyond behaviors. They are cognitively empathic with their students, which enables them to predict misunderstandings, and they see through a variety of perspectives. The peak performers Garfield[9] studied had this quality of flexible attention, which he called *micro/macro attention*. Micro thinking involves logical, analytical computation and seeing cause and effect in methodical steps. It is important in the task analysis portion of planning a lesson or curriculum. It encompasses attention to detail, precision, and orderly progressions.

The *macro* mode is particularly useful for discerning themes and patterns from assortments of information. It is intuitive, holistic, and conceptual. Macro thinking is good for bridging gaps and enables us to perceive a pattern even when some of the pieces are missing. It is useful in searching for patterns in a lesson, or a week of lessons.

Peak performers have the flexibility required to trust their intuition. They tolerate confusion and ambiguity up to a point, and are willing to let go of a problem, trusting that their creative unconscious will work productively.

Flexibility is also strongly related to creative problem solving. When NASA was developing the Apollo and Mercury space capsules, they needed to deal with the tremendous heat of re-entry. A capsule literally glows cherry red as it encounters friction within the earth's atmosphere, and the scientists needed to develop a material that would withstand the heat. Finally, one scientist observed, "You know, we're doing it all wrong. Rather than trying to develop a material that would withstand the heat, we need to conduct the heat away from the space capsule." And to this day, ships like the space shuttle are lined with tiles that burn up on re-entry, conducting heat away from the spacecraft's surface.

That's an example of reconceptualizing a problem, and it's the kind of thinking that flexible people are able to do. In a classroom, the flexible teacher can deal with a variety of learning styles. She can handle visual, kinesthetic, and auditory learning. She can coordinate a variety of activities going on simultaneously and is as attuned to the Vietnamese as to the Spanish-speaking student.

The flexible teacher is a hypothesis maker who looks upon each experience as a learning opportunity. Flexible people can live with doubt because they have great capacity to look upon life as a series of problems to be solved. They enjoy the problem solving because it's a challenge.

Flexibility, just like efficacy, is related to risk-taking. David Perkins[10] describes creative people as living on the edge. They are not satisfied with living in the middle; they are always pushing the frontier. They generate new knowledge, experiment with new ways, and constantly stretch to grow into new abilities. The high jumper Richard Fosbury is a good example. Before Fosbury, high jumpers crossed the bar with a forward leap. But spectators at the 1968 Olympics in Mexico City saw a far different technique. Fosbury, in mid-air, turned his back to the bar. And cleared it. The stunned crowd broke into screams. Fosbury set an Olympic record with a leap of 7 feet, 4-1/4 inches, and his "Fosbury Flop" became the new standard. Because of Fosbury's novel approach, experimentation and mental flexibility, this unorthodox manner of getting over the high jump changed the world of high jumping forever. Since 1972, 13 of 15 men's Olympic medalists have used the Fosbury Flop.

Craftsmanship

(We regret the gender bias in this title. We searched for months for another word that would capture so precisely the attributes of this state of mind but could locate no better alternative. Because "craftspersonship" seemed artificial and awkward to us, we resigned ourselves to "craftsmanship." We hope readers will understand the dilemma produced by the current limitations of the English language.)

To appreciate this state of mind, think of the mindset of expert performers: musicians, artists, teachers, craftspersons, and athletes. They take pride in their work, and consistently strive to improve their current performance. Studies from the League of Professional Schools found that in schools where teachers are the most successful, they have the highest dissatisfaction with the results of their work.[11] The drive for elaboration, clarity, refinement, precision—craftsmanship—is the energy source from which persons ceaselessly learn and deepen their knowledge and skills.

Holonomous people strive for precision. They seek perfection and elegance, refinement and specificity. They generate and hold clear visions and goals. They monitor progress toward those goals. Perfection in performance is the soul of craftsmanship, and these teachers strive for exactness of critical thought processes and precise language for describing their work.

The holonomous person who is both flexible and craftsmanlike may attend to the big picture—or to detail. In one setting they may be excruciatingly detailed; in another, artfully vague.

Language plays a critical role in enhancing a person's cognitive maps and its impact on an individual's ability to think critically, have a knowledge base for action, and feel efficacious. The skillful coach, recognizing that language and thinking are closely entwined, consistently strives to enhance the clarity and specificity of teacher thought and language.

The craftsmanlike teacher is also precise in managing temporal dimensions. He or she orchestrates across six time dimensions: sequence (in what order), duration (for how long), rhythm (at what tempos, patterns, and speed), simultaneity (along with what else), synchronization (with whom and what), and finally across short and long time perspectives. (See the Appendix for greater detail on temporal dimensions.)

Consciousness

> *The function of consciousness is to represent information about what is happening outside and inside the organism in such a way that it can be evaluated and acted upon by the body.*
>
> M. Csikszentmihali[12]

Consciousness is prerequisite to self-control and self-direction. Webster defines consciousness as the knowledge of what is happening around oneself and the totality of one's thoughts, feelings, and impressions. To be conscious is to be aware of events both external and internal to oneself.

People who enjoy a state of consciousness metacogitate. They monitor their own values, thoughts, behaviors, and progress toward their own goals. They can articulate well-defined value systems, and they generate and apply internal criteria for decisions they make. They practice mental rehearsal and edit mental pictures as they seek to improve strategies.

Consciousness, like every other dimension of human behavior, is the result of biological processes. It exists only because of the incredibly complex architecture of our nervous system, which in turn is built up according to instructions contained in the protein molecules of our chromosomes. However, consciousness is not entirely controlled by biological programming; in many important respects it is self-directed. Nor is consciousness only a function of the neocortex. Intuition or kinesthetic awarenesses such as "gut feelings" are messages available to the attention of the conscious mind.

> The White people think the whole body is controlled by the brain. We have a word, umbelini (the whole intestines): that is what controls the body. My umbelini tells me what is going to happen: have you never experienced it?
>
> *Mongezi Tiso, Xhosa tribesman, South Africa*[13]

Conscious means that we are aware that certain events are occurring, and we are able to direct their course. While everything we feel, smell, hear, or remember is potentially a candidate for entering consciousness, the nervous system has definite limits on how much information it can process at any given time and the experiences that actually do become a part of it are much fewer than those left out.

"with-it-ness"

Teachers' ability to monitor and adjust in the classroom is based on their conscious capacities to read classroom cues and their own intentions and repertoire of strategies. Consciousness is the state of mind that explains what the research on teacher behaviors called "with-it-ness"—a teacher's ability to be aware of and respond to a variety of cues happening in the classroom while keeping students and themselves on task. (See sidebar on consciousness.)

Consciousness
A teacher in a third-period junior high English class notes a pattern beginning with two boys who speak to each other and others in the room without being called on during class discussion. She consciously makes note of this behavior, assesses the degree and nature of participation of other students in the room, makes a judgment about the appropriateness of their behavior related to criteria that she holds in general and criteria that she maintains for this specific lesson, reviews what has worked and not worked in the past with these two boys in redirecting their behavior, makes note of her own language and behaviors to check to see if she is in any way encouraging these behaviors, reviews strategies that she has access to, selects one, takes action, monitors the results, and is prepared with a follow-up intervention if her initial one does not produce the results that she wants.

Consciousness can also be the monitoring mechanism for each of the other states of mind. Should you become conscious that your personal efficacy is low at the moment, that you are rigidly seeing from only your own perspective, or that you are reacting impulsively, without thought, at that moment, the choice is yours to modify your state of mind, and your effectiveness.

Interdependence

Holonomous people have a sense of interdependence. They are altruistic, they seek collegiality, and they give themselves to group goals and needs. Just as they contribute to a common good, they also draw on the resources of others. They value consensus and are able to hold their own values and actions in abeyance in order to lend their energies to the achievement of group goals.

Interdependence is an essential state of mind for effective schools. For example, Rosenholtz,[14] in her study of elementary schools in Tennessee, found that the single most important characteristic of successful schools was goal consensus. Jon Saphier, of Research for Better Teaching, reports that the issue of good schools is so simple, that it's embarrassing. It is that people have common goals and people work together toward those goals.

Interdependence modifies working relationships. Saranson finds that "recognizing and trying to change power relationships, especially in complicated traditional institutions is among the most complex tasks human beings can undertake."[15] The school improvement agenda of the 1990s is moving all educators into more interactive and professional roles. So from both the perspective of what's good for schools and the perspective of what's good for individuals within the schools, we find that the fifth state of mind, interdependence, is a rich and essential resource.

The human organism grows in reciprocity with others. Lev Vygotsky, the Russian psycholinguist, reports, "Every function in cultural development appears twice. First, in the social level and later on the individual level. First, between people and then inside . . . . All the higher functions originate as actual relations between individuals."[16]

We have two forms of intelligence. One is the intelligence that we have in our own heads, our own experience. But the way that intelligence gets shaped is through reciprocity with others. Being a devil's advocate, having to justify, having to resolve differences, having to listen to another person's point of view, achieving consensus, receiving feedback actually increases our own intelligence. The individual and the organization continue to grow intellectually in reciprocity with others.

The principles of holonomy dictate that each autonomous unit in a system is not only influenced by the system, but influences the system. The latter is confirmed by Eleanor Roosevelt's potent statement that it only takes a small number of people to change the world. That's the way it has always been. Within the state of mind of interdependence, a two-way street exists; one gives help, receives help, one influences and is influenced.

Of course the goals of an idealized state of holonomy are never fully achieved. There is no such thing as perfect attainment of the states of efficacy, flexibility, consciousness, craftsmanship, and interdependence. These are utopian energies toward which we constantly aspire.

Mediating the Five States of Mind

In most cases, simply acting like a good friend will help others as they plan, solve problems, and learn from experience. However, there are also times when more complex strategies are necessary. A skillful coach, equipped with these strategies, can mediate in any—or all—of the five states of mind. The language of empowerment is one powerful form of mediation that draws upon three major communication maps useful to the coach mediating holonomy: Focus on the Desired State, Nine Principles of Intervention, and Pacing and Leading.

Focus on the Desired State

We have found that the broadest and most consistently useful intervention is focusing on the desired state. For example, Rob, a 4th grade teacher in his second year of teaching, is despondent, overburdened, and self-critical of his behaviors in the classroom. He confides in his coach that he is losing his temper when certain students use profanity.

The coach envisions short-range and long-range outcomes for Rob. Instead of being despondent, overburdened, and self-critical, the coach envisions a desired state. She would like to see Rob optimistic and feeling competent and confident. Rob would benefit from controlling his impulsivity instead of losing his temper, and he would gain by setting and applying classroom standards calmly and consistently instead of excessively reprimanding students.

In the long-term, the coach would like to help Rob develop efficacy instead of powerlessness and consciousness instead of lost access to larger goals and outcomes. He would benefit from developing flexibility in place of his egocentric views and his inability to envision alternatives.

 Having envisioned possible desired states for Rob, the coach now asks what internal resources Rob needs to move from the existing condition to the desired state—and what interventions might be employed to support Rob's growth.

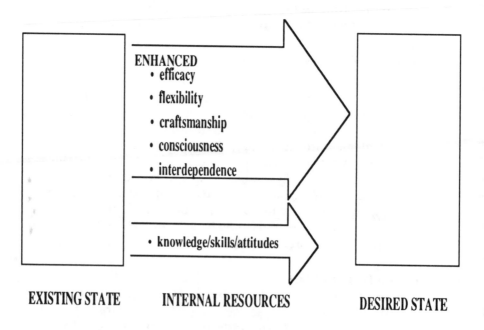

ENHANCED
- efficacy
- flexibility
- craftsmanship
- consciousness
- interdependence

- knowledge/skills/attitudes

EXISTING STATE   INTERNAL RESOURCES   DESIRED STATE

Figure 7-2
Desired State Map

Nine Principles of Intervention

Cognitive coaching is effective with a broad array of individuals who constitute a range of age, style, personal history, and current circumstance. The effective cognitive coach holds no uniform theory of why people behave as they do. Instead, they use nine principles of intervention, which taken together constitute a theory of intervention. Theories of personality or human behavior are useful, but they have shortcomings because resolutions are sought within the frame offered by the theoretical model. Since all models illuminate only selected views of human behaviors and place others in shadow, interventions based on theories of personality will always be doomed to partial success. In contrast, coaches working with the principles of intervention listed below will find themselves limited only by their own flexibility. The following are adapted from the work of Lankton and Lankton.[17]

1. People act on their internal map of reality and not on sensory experience. Each person perceives the world from his own unique vantage point, seeing it through frames of personal history, belief systems, representational systems, and cognitive styles. This principle reminds the coach to learn how the world appears to the other person and to sensitively gather data to understand the other person's maps and how they are constructed.

2. People make the best choice for themselves at any given moment. This principle does not suggest that people make the best choice possible, only the best choice available to themselves at the moment. High emotionality will limit choices as will strongly held positions or points of view.

3. Respect all messages from the other person. Empathy and respect are critical resources the coach brings to the coaching relationship. Skilled coaches attend to and respect both verbal and nonverbal messages. This requires being attuned to the more subtle elements of communication—voice tone, gestures, facial expressions, eye shifts, and speech metaphors.

4. Provide choice; never take choice away. In several cases, Erickson worked with suicidal persons. His approach was in effect, "Yes, that's one choice. What are others?"

When we attempt to limit a person's choice, they are often drawn even more stubbornly to the choice we've removed. Effective coaches exercise options.

5.   The resource each person needs lies within his or her own personal history. Erickson would frequently tell students or clients that their "unconscious contains a vast storehouse of learning, memories, and resources." Coaches need to be mindful that they are there to facilitate the teacher's access to these inner resources—not to offer a solution.

6.   Meet the other person in their own model of the world. The skills of rapport are especially helpful in connecting with another person psychologically. However, this does not imply the coach must stay in the other person's model.

7.   The person with the most flexibility or choices will be the controlling element in the system. The more repertoire teachers have, the greater flexibility and choice they have in terms of instructional strategies and classroom management. The same is true for the coach or any person in a helping relationship. When interventions fail, it is frequently due to the coach's inability to exercise the needed flexibility.

8.   A person cannot *not* communicate. Even if a person is not communicating verbally, he is still sending nonverbal messages. Some behaviors are very subtle, such as breathing shifts or a slight nod of the head. These behaviors are very important for the coach to attend to when using the language of empowerment.

9.   Outcomes are achieved at the psychological level. This principle is based on the reality that several levels of communication operate simultaneously. One of these is the social level message, which is usually reflected in the voice tone, gesture, or emphasis. When these two levels of communication are incongruent, the psychological message will determine the outcome of communication.[18] This principle reminds coaches to be conscious of and clearly intentional about their own levels of communication.

Pacing and Leading

Pacing and Leading is a strategic communication approach that incorporates many of the nine intervention principles. To pace means to meet the other person in their model of the world. Coaches pace when they communicate though their word choices and body language that they understand the other person's intention, point of view, or "reality." Leading relies on a variety of language tools to expand the teacher's model of the world and evoke the internal resources necessary to achieve the desired state.

The information on rapport becomes highly applicable now, as coaches pace by borrowing a gesture, matching posture, incorporating similar tones of voice, putting emphasis on the same words, and communicating to the other person through these and other out-of-awareness areas their empathy and understanding of the other person's reality. However, to meet the other person at their model of the world is not to live there with them. In the lead portion of pace and lead, the coach leads by using the linguistic tools of the *language of empowerment* to expand the teacher's model of the world, evoke the internal resources necessary to achieve the desired state, and expand choices available to the person.

 An effective pace includes four steps: expressing empathy, reflecting content, stating a goal, and presupposing a search for a pathway. The first two of these steps are embodied in any well-formed paraphrase. The fourth element marks the beginning of a statement that can lead the teacher to a new mental state. For example:

1. Express **empathy** by matching intonation and accurately describing the person's feeling: "*You're frustrated. . . . .*"
2. Accurately **reflect** the speaker's content: "You're frustrated *because they aren't really trying.. . . .*"
3. Infer the **goal** the speaker is trying to achieve: "You're frustrated because they aren't really trying *and you'd like them to give their absolute best. . . .*"
4. **Presuppose** a **search** for a **pathway** the person might take to attain the goal: "You're frustrated because they aren't really trying and you'd like them to give their absolute best *so you're searching for a way to cause them to apply themselves.*"

After pacing, a well-formed lead moves the conversation toward the natural desired state of the other person. A coach can listen for the desired states that the teacher communicates. Or sometimes the coach may infer from the teacher's communication a desired state, and articulate for the teacher a desired state he hasn't mentioned. If the lead doesn't stimulate movement toward the desired state the coach can pace again to be sure she is accurately communicating her understanding of the teacher's feelings and situation. A second strategy would raise the goal portion of the conversation to a higher logical level or an irrefutable goal. For example, a teacher says, "These kids are so messy. You should see their desks. At the end of the day my room is a disaster area." The coach paraphrases and then says, "You're interested in students learning neatness and valuing a healthy environment." The coach is not offering a solution or opinion but using a specific paraphrasing technique to help clarify the teacher's thinking.

These four elements of the pace are illustrated in the following conversation between two teachers. One teacher has asked another teacher to coach him in thinking through a problem.

> **Teacher:** *You know I've had it with my fourth period students. They come to class completely unprepared and then there goes my lesson plan, there goes my timing because I come expecting them to be ready to review their homework and they didn't do it.*
> **Coach:** *You are really frustrated.* **(empathy)** *You're frustrated because you plan carefully for this group, and repeatedly they come to the class unprepared, which throws your lesson plan out the window.* **(content)**
> **Teacher:** *It's really upsetting to me.*
> **Coach:** *What you want is that they will follow directions and get their homework done* **(goal)** *so that class time can be productive.*
> **Teacher:** *When they're given an assignment, I want them to care enough to do it.*
> **Coach:** *So, you want them to take an interest in their assignments and complete them. You're searching for a way that you can get them to come to class prepared.* **(pathway)**

In the example above, the second teacher (coach), having met her colleague at his model of the world (frustration, inefficaciousness, some implied blame of students, an intention for productive class sessions based in part on students' homework), is now ready to mediate her friend toward more efficacious thought and choices in resolving the problem. To do this she uses verbal strategies to "lead" toward greater personal resourcefulness.

Coaches develop language leads for each of the states of mind. Following are examples of leads in which the coach is mediating toward greater flexibility.

A continuum for flexibility might look like this:

Rigidity ——————————————— **Flexibility**
(I'm limited)   (I have unlimited choices)

Listed below are some verbal strategies when we choose to move ourselves or others from existing rigid states to more flexible states of mind. A flexible state of mind enables us to see things from varied perspectives and select behaviors appropriate to the occasion.

When stuck and feeling rigid:
    Try Entering Other Perspectives A verbal strategy that "leads" us to view a student or situation through the eyes of another person. Through this strategy we *set aside our own views to seek understanding of others'.*

Indicators of an inflexible state:	**A response to lead one toward greater flexibility:**
	Pace, then lead:
"That kid is a monster. He's absolutely impossible."	"What could he possibly be feeling when he behaves like that?"

When stuck and feeling rigid:
    Try Enlarging Frames of Reference A verbal strategy that leads us to refocus and *develop larger perspectives.*

Examples

Indicators of an inflexible state:	An example of response to move one toward greater flexibility:
"If I find 10 punctuation errors in a composition worth 10 points, the kid earns zero points, an F."	*Pace, then lead:* "What do you want kids to learn about writing and about putting forth effort? What messages about these learning goals might they possibly get from your grading policies?"

When stuck and feeling rigid:

Try Predicting Consequences: A strategy that "leads" (causes) one to think through probable consequences of his/her decisions. This strategy *allows one to consider data from multiple perspectives and generate more.*

Examples

Indicators of an inflexible state:	A response to lead one toward greater flexibility:
"I'm going to keep him in from recess until he completes his math."	*Pace, then lead:* "What long-range effect might that have on his feelings about math?"

In the Appendix, we offer a variety of verbal strategies for leading teachers in the five states of mind. Choice making, correcting fate control, enlarging frames of reference, predicting consequences, and mental rehearsal are just a few of the techniques discussed. Coaches will want to dedicate special time to that section to become familiar with the variety of tools available to the coach. Missing on those pages are the shifts in posture, eye movements, and breathing changes that are so important in understanding and mediating these kinds of interactions. Skillful coaches recognize that this information is only the basis for building a coaching repertoire.

Skillful coaches also recognize that these language skills are not mechanistic. A coach will not become skilled in the language of empowerment simply by reading these explanations and examples. Skill comes through the coach's own experience, practice, and self-referencing.

Beyond Technique

In this description of the language of empowerment's set of intervention strategies, the interventions are designed to elicit the internal resources that an individual (or group) needs to solve their own problems and direct their own growth. They are interventions that help a colleague get unstuck in the moment in ways that capacitate him or her for future self "unstucking." Self coaching is thus the ultimate goal of these interventions.

The danger in writing about this is that the examples can too easily be seen as mechanical formulae for given problems and desired states of mind. Nothing could be further from the truth. On these pages, we have displayed only what Lankton and Lankton[19] call the social message, carried in words. Missing on these pages are the postural shifts, inflections, breathing changes, and all the many ideomotor responses that send the psychological message—the message most important in contributing to achieving desired states. The skillful coach attends to these, again, not mechanically, observing and interpreting nonverbal signals, but caringly, intuitively, with his or her entire presence, being committed interdependently, one human being to another, to entering the other's model of the world, accessing resources and surfacing choice. The skillful coach does this not by formulae but with an ever-expanding repertoire, testing and devising new and more efficient ways to be catalytic in a colleague's growth.

As coaches become increasingly skillful in working with the language of empowerment, there is a reciprocal effect on themselves. In recognizing states of holonomy in others, the coach recognizes states of efficacy, consciousness, flexibility, craftsmanship, and interdependence in himself or herself. The *external* language of empowerment with others becomes *internal* in the coach, thus mediating himself or herself to higher states of holonomy. The model of cognitive coaching, then, becomes self-mediating, self-transforming, and self-modifying for coaches themselves. As Erich Fromm wrote:

In thus giving of his life, the mentor enriches the other person; he enhances the other's sense of aliveness. He does not give in order to receive; giving is in itself exquisite joy. But in giving he cannot help bringing something to life in the other person, and this which is brought to life reflects back to him; in truly giving, he cannot help receiving that which is given back to him.[20]

Summary

"Autonomous interdependence" may sound like an oxymoron. The transcendence of these two seemingly contradictory terms is in the concept of Holonomy—to be simultaneously an individual unit and at the same time a participant in a larger community. In this chapter we have elaborated the four states of mind of the autonomous individual: consciousness, flexibility, efficacy, and craftsmanship. The fifth state of mind, interdependence, transcends the sense of humans as isolated individuals and links them as recipients of and contributors to the larger organization of which they are a part.

Coaches strive to develop in themselves and others the skillful expression of holonomy—assisting others to grow not only as individuals but also as participants in a larger community. In this chapter we have described an additional set of linguistic tools which coaches employ to produce growth toward those five desired States of Mind.

To assess progress toward these States of Mind, a renaissance in assessment will be needed. In the next chapter, strategies will be explored for assessing the effects of Cognitive Coaching on coaches themselves, on others with whom they work, on classroom interactions, on the school, and on the community.

Endnotes

1. Hyatt C. and Gottlieb, L. *When Smart People Fail.* New York, NY: Simon and Schuster, 1988.

2. Garfield, C. *Peak Performers: The New Heroes of American Business.* New York, NY: William Morrow and Company, Inc., 1986.

3. Poole, M.G. and Okeafor, K.R. "The Effects of Teacher Efficacy and Interactions Among Educators on Curriculum Implementation." *Journal of Curriculum and Supervision* (Winter 1989), pp. 146–161.

4. Fullan, M. *The Meaning of Educational Change*. New York, NY: Teachers College Press, 1982.

5. Rosenholtz, S. *Teachers' Workplace: The Social Organization of Schools*. New York, NY: Longman, Inc., 1989.

6. Berman, P. and McLaughlin, M.W. *Federal Program Supporting Educational Change: Factors Affecting Implementation and Continuation*. Santa Monica, CA: Rand Corporation, 1977.

7. Fuller, B., Wood, K., Rapoport, T. and Dornbusch, S. "The Organizational Context of Individual Efficacy." *Review of Educational Press* (Spring 1982): 52, pp. 7–30.

8. Laborde G. and Saunders, C. *Communication Trainings: Are They Cost Effective?* Mountain View, CA: International Dialogue Education Associates, 1986.

9. Garfield, C. *Peak Performers: The New Heroes of American Business*. New York, NY: William Morrow and Company, Inc., 1986.

10. Perkins, D. *The Mind's Best Work: A New Psychology of Creative Thinking*. Cambridge, MA: Harvard University Press, 1983.

11. Garfield, C. *Peak Performers: The New Heroes of American Business*. New York, NY: William Morrow and Company, Inc., 1986.

12. Csikszentmihali, M. *Flow: The Psychology of Optimal Experience*. New York, NY: Harper and Row Publisher, 1990, p. 20.

13. Buhrmann, D. *Living in Two Worlds: Communication Between a White Healer and Her Black Counterparts*. Cape Town: Human & Rousseau, 1984.

14. Rosenholtz, S. *Teachers' Workplace: The Social Organization of Schools*. New York, NY: Longman, Inc., 1989.

15. Sarason, S. *The Predictable Failure of Educational Reform*. San Francisco, CA: Jossey-Bass, 1991.

16. Vygotsky, L. *Society of Mind*. Cambridge, MA: Harvard University Press, 1978.

17. Lankton, S. and Lankton, C. *The Answer Within: A Clinical Framework for Ericksonian Hypnotherapy*. New York, NY:

Brunner/Mazel Publishers, 1983, p. 17.

18. Garfield, C. *Peak Performers: The New Heroes of American Business*. New York, NY: William Morrow and Company, Inc., 1986.

19. Lankton, S. and Lankton, C. *The Answer Within: A Clinical Framework for Ericksonian Hypnotherapy*. New York, NY: Brunner/Mazel Publishers, 1983, p. 17.

20. Fromm, E. *The Art of Loving*. New York, NY: Harper & Row, 1956.

8

Assessing the Effects of Cognitive Coaching

The creative possibilities for the ideas and principles presented in this book depend on the coach's willingness to engage, inquire, experiment, and observe results. We cannot predict where this will lead, nor can we guarantee specific outcomes. Educational reform, indeed no systemic change, works that way. It is often our incapacity to tolerate ambiguity in the face of enormously complex problems that leads us to an almost automatic acceptance of anything that offers quick relief. Educational leaders must be extraordinarily patient with the process of change, rejecting simplistic solutions to complex problems.

We have only just begun the process of developing and inventing Renaissance forms of schools, instruction, coaching, curriculum, and organizations that will inhabit the twenty-first century. Educators may wonder if cognitive coaching would make a difference if it were adopted and implemented. Would teachers grow? Would the community change and students prosper? Would the coaches improve?

To answer those questions, effective coaches equip themselves and others with numerous strategies for collecting evidence that the vision is gradually being realized; that the principles and assumptions underlying Cognitive Coaching are becoming manifest throughout the community; that our ultimate charge of enhancing student learning is being achieved and that the Renaissance has begun.

We shall begin by sharing a growing research base for Cognitive Coaching. The presentation of this research is *not* intended to be conclusive or even persuasive. It is only suggestive of what to anticipate and it offers some models of how coaches might collect evidence of growth toward greater holonomy. We will offer a variety of alternative and authentic ways to assess self, teachers, the organization, and students as they progress toward increasingly higher degrees of holonomy.

These alternative forms of assessment can also serve as powerful environmental signals to staff, community, and students about what is valued. Renaissance leaders align assessment processes with program philosophy and goals. If we wish to truly change the way teachers teach and the way students learn, we must have a Renaissance in assessment practices as well.

Research on Cognitive Coaching

Several studies have demonstrated the obvious: the more engagement in coaching, the higher the benefits to the teacher. Findings suggest that these benefits may peak when the frequency of coaching reaches six or seven times a year. After that, we speculate that if the frequency of coaching were to decrease there would be no loss to teacher cognition as the process would be internalized. (A bibliography of research studies and literature on cognitive coaching is included at the end of this chapter.)

These research studies are classified into three categories: classroom instruction, teacher cognition, and relationships within the organization. Following is a brief summary of the research.

Classroom Instruction[1]

Study	Subjects	Results
Garmston, Hyerle (1988)	Eight university professors of mathematics, geology, communications studies, school administration, counseling and theater arts in a peer coaching, cognitive coaching project	• maximally effective at producing increased confidence about and enthusiasm for teaching • substantial improvements in expanding teaching repertoire • moderate improvements in producing greater student learning
Garmston, Linder, Whitaker (1993)	Two 7th and 8th grade English teachers being cognitively coached	• changes in teaching styles • expansion of teaching repertoire • more powerful lesson planning • greater student accountability
Sommers (1991)	Twelve high school teachers being cognitively coached	• teachers believed they improved in their ability to instruct students in higher order thinking skills
Flores (1991)	Case study of high school teacher having difficulties	• self-confidence improved, classroom management skills increased, behavioral referrals decreased and student-teacher relationships improved

Teachers' Cognitive Development[2]

Study	Subjects	Results
Foster (1989)	K-12 teachers being cognitively coached	• teachers report internalization of self-coaching questions after 6 or 7 cycles
Garmston, Hyerle (1988)	Eight university professors of mathematics, geology, communications studies, school administration, counseling and theater arts in a cognitive coaching, peer coaching project	• maximally effective in producing critical self-reflection • maximally effective in producing self-analysis and evaluation • maximally effective at attaining autonomous performance of 7 instructionally related cognitive skills • substantial improvements in language precision
Garmston, Linder, Whitaker (1993)	Two 7th and 8th grade English teachers being cognitively coached	• greater consciousness of own behaviors and options during teaching • teachers become more bi-cognitive, attending to relationship *and* task; student centered *and* teacher centered
Edwards (1992)	Sixteen 1st year teachers being cognitively coached	• a high correlation between the satisfaction with coaching and conceptual growth • a higher number of coaching contacts correlated with growth in reflectivity • a less direct style such as that used by cognitive coaching in their informal interactions with first-year teachers can influence growth in reflection • older teachers, those who had previous careers, and those with a higher number of semester hours beyond the B.S. degree tended to show more conceptual growth

Study	Subjects	Results
Lipton (1993)	Seventeen educators being trained in the cognitive coaching leadership model	• cognitive coaching model increased repertoire of choices and informed their actions • suspended egocentricity in viewing problems • decreased impulsivity at crucial decision points • enhanced ability to generate alternative approach to problem solving • metacognitive awareness of use of cognitive coaching model in internal dialogue

Relationships with Others in the School[3]

Study	Subject	Results
Garmston, Hyerle (1988)	Eight university professors of mathematics, geology, communications studies, school administration, counseling and theater arts in a cognitive coaching, peer coaching project	• moderate improvements in increased instructional dialogue with faculty not involved in the cognitive coaching project
Garmston, Linder, Whitaker (1993)	Two 7th and 8th grade English teachers being cognitively coached	• participants contributed professionally by writing articles for professional journals, presenting at state-wide conferences and initiating influence with district decision makers to provide cognitive coaching for other teachers

Study	Subject	Results
Sommers (1991)	Twelve high school teachers being cognitively coached	• teachers reported talking to their colleagues more about teaching
Midlock (1991)	High school teachers in a cognitive coaching, peer coaching project	• teachers participating in cognitive coaching reported more positive perceptions about collegiality, staff development, and the climate of the work site than colleagues who were not involved in coaching
Lipton (1993)	Seventeen educators being trained in the cognitive leadership model	• cognitive coaching model increased repertoire of choices and informed their actions
Naylor (1991)	75 teachers from three high schools engaged in cognitive coaching as an alternative to teacher evaluation	• administrators, particularly department chairpersons, had a more collegial relationship with their staffs • teachers improved collegial relationships within and across departments • teachers and department chairs were more likely to try something new as a result of peer coaching

Toward Renaissance Assessment

"When you cannot measure it, when you cannot express it in numbers, your knowledge is of a very meager and unsatisfactory kind." Until recently, this archaic, technological, and reductionist theorem by Lord Kelvin, the 19th-century British scientist who devised a scale for measuring temperature, influenced our efforts to translate educational goals into observable, measurable outcomes.

As schools move toward becoming communities for developing the five states of mind, they are also reorienting their thinking about outcomes, curriculum, policies, practices, organization of time, and assessment of progress. They set aside some of their outmoded, 19th-century procedures to make room for Renaissance practices.

> *When you can measure it, when you can express it in numbers, your knowledge is STILL of a meager and unsatisfactory kind!*
>
> Jacob Viner

The assessment process will be relevant to all individuals and units in a holonomous community because it will be used as elements in feedback loops which guide and inform reflective practice about progress toward the five states of mind.

Four Principles of Renaissance Assessment

As a new conception of assessment is envisioned, the following principles may serve as guidelines.

1. **Every unit within the holonomous system is a participant in assessment.** These include the individual, the school, the classroom, the district, and the community. Students, teachers, community members, administrators, support staff, parents, school board members are in a constant state of self-assessing, self-learning, and self-modifying.

2. **Interactive Assessment of Holonomous Units.** Because the concept of holonomy is interactive, no assessment of any one unit is complete without assessing the qualities of the other surrounding units. To assess student progress, the quality of classroom conditions must be monitored as well. To assess teacher performance, the quality of school workplace conditions must be examined; and to assess the quality of the school district, the community support and commitment must also be assessed. Thus, a well-conceived assessment design includes a search for consistency and integrity of surrounding conditions which directly influence each one of the units in a holonomous organization.

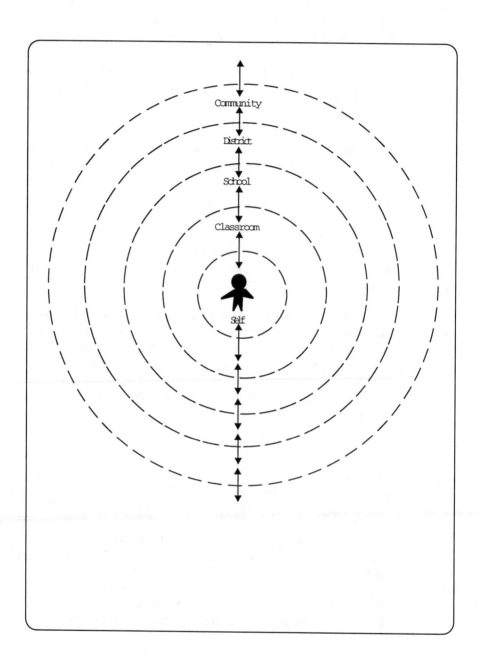

Figure 8-1
Autonomous Units Interacting in a Holonomous System

3. Feedback Loops are components of continued learning. Learning requires continual feedback. Being able to clarify and construct internal meaning implies deriving information from an external world. Renaissance organizations act and gather evidence by scanning their environment for clues about the results of their actions.

Feedback loops are cyclical strategies for gaining information about the effects of actions so that those actions may be modified to better meet desired outcomes. (See sidebar on feedback loops for more details.)

Feedback Loops

Some feedback loops are *internal:* The artist mixes colors on a palate. When the color is still not to her liking, she tells herself, I'll mix a little more blue.

Some are *external:* The artist displays her works and then interviews patrons about their reactions.

Feedback loops can be intricately *entwined:* A teacher poses a higher-level question and then searches his students' verbal and nonverbal responses for evidence of mental engagement. In response, a student gives an answer and searches her teacher's face, verbal response, and body language for clues which may signal acknowledgment.

Feedback loops can be *complex, systematic, and long-range* in design: A school system implements a whole language program and designs a system for gathering evidence of its impact and achievements.

Feedback loops are not intended to define the "bottom line" summative, terminal conditions or behaviors. Rather they are used as guides to continued progress toward desired goals. The components of a feedback loop may include at least the following steps or decisions in a cyclical pathway:
- clarifying goals and purposes
- designing action/experimentation
- selecting data for assessment
- studying, reflecting, and deriving meaning
- modifying actions, and
- revisiting and redefining goals

Participants in learning organizations who are in a constant state of improvement, design feedback loops by which to gather data through

---

conscious observation of their own feelings, attitudes and skills; through observation and interviews with others; and by collecting evidence of the effects of their efforts on the environment. These data are analyzed, interpreted, internalized. Based on this analysis, actions are modified in order to more closely achieve the goals. Thus, individuals and organizations are in a constant state of self-learning, self-renewal, and self-modification.

Organizations and individuals who think and act in terms of feedback loops remain alert to the data coming to them. They are sensitive to feedback, consider and reflect on incoming data, and are open to self-modification. Individuals and organizations who lack these characteristics would stagnate because they have no feedback loops to guide self-improvement. Some organizations no longer exist because they were insensitive to feedback from their customers; they failed to keep abreast of market trends, or to keep a close and running inventory of their merchandise.

4. Systematizing Assessment Procedures. Alert teachers can readily describe their intuitive feelings of students' progress: The lights that go on in students' eyes, the exuberant voice inflections of students when they've "got it," the "ah-ha" of discovery. What is needed is a systematic way of collecting and reporting such evidence. Leaders help staff members refine their skills of consistent, meaningful, and sustained observation. Teachers, parents, administrators, and students will all need clear understanding of the school's objectives and purposes, and all will become more involved in systematically collecting and interpreting data, revising perceptions, and realigning practices.

Four Cornerstones of Renaissance Assessment

With the new goals and procedures of the Renaissance school and community in mind, Cognitive Coaches are challenged with the assessment of growth toward the five states of mind in four arenas: in coaches themselves, in others who are coached, in the organization, and—since our ultimate goal is student learning—in students as well.

How Coaches Assess Their Own Growth

Carl Rogers expressed the view that "The degree to which I create relationships which facilitate the growth of others as separate persons is a measure of the growth I have achieved in myself."

Because of the transformational nature of cognitive coaching, coaches themselves will experience change in their own holonomy. They should acquire feelings of greater efficacy, enhanced flexibility, heightened consciousness, more elegant precision, and an increased sense of community.

Holonomous people gather data through conscious observation of their own feelings, attitudes, and skills; through observation and interviewing others; and through collecting evidence of the effects of their efforts on the environment. These data are analyzed, interpreted, internalized. Thus, the coach is in a constant state of self-learning, self-renewal, and self-modification.

Coaches Interview Colleagues for Self-Evaluation

At the close of every coaching session, the coach invites the teacher to provide feedback about the coaching process and about the coach's skills. The coach asks, "What can I do to make our time together more productive?" "What can I do to assist you in your continuing work toward your full potential?" "What might I improve to be of greater assistance to you?" "What is your understanding of the purposes and expectations of this coaching process?" These questions not only build trust, they are also requests for information and feedback to help the coach evaluate growth in his own coaching skills.

Coaches Keep Journals

Writing is a powerful form of learning for adults as well as for students because it is a way of sharing their craft knowledge. It promotes reflection, clarification, and discussion. Coaches keep journals, and they encourage others to keep journals as well. Journal writing richly serves the principles and purposes of cognitive coaching because it engages such intellectual skills as fluency of thought, precision of language, formulation of theories, sequencing of tasks, analysis of concepts, synthesis of skills, inducing from experiences, deducing from generalizations, and creating metaphorical and personal analogies.

A journal can be a powerful means for producing intellectual growth when it is used in at least three ways: for sharing selected entries with trusted colleagues, making journal entries and reflecting on them, and comparing personal journal entries over time. Returning to entries made in the past, reflecting on thoughts over time, and examining where coaches are today invites self-evaluation. During such reflection, coaches may ask themselves: How have my thoughts matured? How have my questions become more focused and complex? How many of my initial questions have I answered? What new questions am I posing? What patterns and connections do I perceive? What ideas have I tried and what have I learned from that trial?

Coaches Personally Reflect

Coaches inquire about their own growth in the states of mind:

Efficacy. What evidence do I perceive that I am increasing in my own ability to produce results, to think and act with greater effectiveness, confidence, and optimism? What have I done that indicates I am continuing to learn how to learn? What new challenges am I posing for myself? What is next for me?

Flexibility. What are evidences of my greater creativity? Which are indicators that I am increasingly able to achieve shifts in perspectives and points of view? What am I noticing about my communications with those of different beliefs, styles, modality strengths, intelligences? In what areas of flexibility might I next improve?

Consciousness. What am I noticing about my self-monitoring practices? To what degree am I aware of and directing my thoughts, emotions, behaviors, and strategies? What new knowledge about myself and my relationship to others am I producing? What am I aware of in my own growth in problem solving, decision making, questioning strategies, and metacognitive abilities? What am I noticing about my ability to be conscious of nonverbal cues, social dynamics, and the intentions of others? What consciousness-building tasks might I assign myself?

Craftsmanship. How am I developing in my ability to clearly express my values, personal goals, goals for others, and for my school? As I reflect upon my language, am I expressing ideas and feelings with appropriate precision, clarity, meaning, thoughtfulness, and elegance? What am I noticing about my drive for mastery, improvement, refinement? How can I further enhance my sense of precision and craftsmanship?

Interdependence. What am I realizing about myself as a listener, communicator, and trust builder? In what ways am I expanding my resource base with other educators, parents, community agencies? What indicates a greater sense of community in my organization? In what ways am I linking with—giving and receiving help from others? Which skills of group interaction might I develop and refine?

Assessing Teachers' Growth

If you believe that teaching is an intellectual process of decision making, and the work of teaching is the application of cognitive processes, then the evaluation of teaching should be evaluation of decision making. The teacher evaluation process in the Renaissance school will become aligned with this modern concept of both the science and artistry of instruction. This view, along with the other changes, may constitute yet another paradigm shift in personnel policies and procedures.

In the Renaissance school, teachers are knowledgeable, skilled, collaborative, professional decision makers. Teaching teams assume responsibility for knowledge management, selection of content, creation of instructional strategies, design of research and assessment techniques, and all the curriculum decisions that orchestrate the complex implementation of effective learning. Teachers take responsibility for what is increasingly regarded as teachers' professional work: learning, teaming, coaching and teaching colleagues; educating and networking with the school community, and making contributions of professional knowledge to the larger professional community. A Renaissance assessment system would focus on the degree to which teachers are competent at professional problem finding and solving.

Beginning teachers do not assume their first teaching assignments as autonomous professionals. And even some

veteran teachers experience situations in which their resourcefulness is at a low ebb. Teacher development in a
Renaissance school occurs developmentally and individually over time. Growth is supported through mediated
experiences by skilled leaders in workshops, course work,
reading, study, and collaboration and modeling in the
school environment.

One Washington State school district has developed a scale
to assess beginning teachers' cognitive development toward
autonomy. At the California State Department of Education,
a beginning teacher assessment scale is being used to help
mentors work with new teachers.

If the goals of cognitive coaching are to support teachers in
becoming more efficacious, flexible, precise, conscious and
interdependent, then the assessment of teacher growth will
focus on the degree to which teachers develop the capacity
to analyze, evaluate, and self-prescribe their own growth
toward these ends, and to modify their own behavior accordingly. Ultimately, teachers will assume responsibility for
evaluating themselves. The role of the coach becomes one
who facilitates teachers' capacities to evaluate themselves.
(For an elaboration of this form of assessment, see A. Costa,
R. Garmston, and L. Lambert, "Evaluation of Teaching: The
Cognitive Development View," in S. Stanley and W.J. Popham,
Teacher Evaluation: Six Prescriptions for Success, Alexandria, VA.: The Association for Supervision and Curriculum
Development, 1988.)

Taxonomies to Assess Growth in Reflectivity

Taxonomies for assessing teachers' growth toward more
reflectivity may be useful to Cognitive Coaches. Taxonomies
are theoretical constructs arranged in a hierarchical fashion
to analyze incremental stages of growth toward higher, more
complex levels.   Such developmental stages can be arranged sequentially into identifiable phases through which
people grow. While there may be great variation in the speed
through which people progress through these stages, the
sequence with which they grow is probably constant.

Coaches may collect evidence of stage growth by listening to
teachers' comments during the Planning and Reflecting
Conferences, by observing their comments in group meet-

ings and problem-solving sessions, by reading their journal entries, and by analyzing collections of teaching artifacts such as lesson plans, teacher-made tests, and homework assignments. The coach may gather such evidence in the concerns teachers raise, the rationales they give in defense of their opinions, and the reasons they express for structuring and selecting the lessons they create.

Two taxonomies that coaches might find useful in analyzing teachers' growth toward greater reflectivity are:
- Van Mannen's Levels of Reflectivity,[4]
- The Pedagogical Language Acquisition and Conceptual Development Taxonomy of Teacher Reflective Thought (RPT) developed by Sparks-Langer, Simmons, Pasch, Colton, and Starko.[5]

Our purpose is not to advocate these taxonomies. Instead, we invite coaches to become knowledgeable about such taxonomies as possible diagnostic aids regarding teachers' developmental movement toward higher levels of holonomy. We also encourage coaches to flexibly draw from a repertoire of strategies pacing each teacher's level of concern while they provide developmentally appropriate assistance. Some of these are elaborated in the appendix.

Recording Critical Incidents

Critical incidents are serendipitous, spontaneous events that happen in the day-to-day life of the classroom, school, and community. Cognitive coaches watch for and record small pieces of verbal and nonverbal evidence to serve as indicators of individual and group growth toward higher states of holonomy.

Following are some examples of critical incidents shared by Diane Zimmerman, Principal of the West Davis Intermediate School in Davis, California and Bill Sommers, Vice-Principal of Wayzata High School, Wayzata, Minnesota. (Teacher's names have been changed.) These incidents serve as indicators of shifting values, thinking, or collaboration of staff members toward one or more of the five holonomous states of mind.

- While walking though my building one evening, long after the staff and students had left, I found the primary teachers discussing some problem. Being surprised to find them, I said, "I didn't call a grade level meeting." "Oh, no," they replied. "We decided to get together ourselves to plan and talk. We set our own time and meeting agenda."

• Tom, a foreign language teacher, initiated a discussion about his instruction. He asked for at least an hour of my time. We spent three! He was using story and metaphor, and his students were doing better than ever. He shared his approach with other teachers and now they have begun to team and share these instructional strategies. Tom, usually a loner, tells me when he wants more time to discuss instructional approaches and problems. While some staff members thought he was difficult to get along with, he has started coming to our monthly group meetings and contributes ideas. He has found new enthusiasm in students' writings, in having them make societal connections, and observing students become thinkers, not parrots. Coaching Tom and listening to his ideas has given him a connection to the educational system that did not previously exist.

• Barb is a teacher who voluntarily organizes, hosts, and encourages 10 to 15 other teachers, secretaries, and administrators to meet once a month to share new readings, books, stories, and to share strategies related to improved learning and instruction.

• Mario, a math teacher, is writing his doctoral dissertation on student achievement using cognitive coaching as a direct teaching method. His research design is to have the students observe the coaching session at the front of the room. Mario's hypothesis is that having students "listen in" while the teacher describes the lesson's framework will increase their achievement.

• Alicia, a biology teacher, and Roger, an English teacher, were among the first teachers I coached. During a reflective conference with Roger, after a cooperative learning lesson, I asked if he had been in the science department where the biology and chemistry teachers were also using cooperative learning. After Roger observed in Alicia's class, they became very excited about working together and decided to team teach their English and biology classes. The two classes meet together twice a week. They are using the novel, Jurassic Park. Alicia is having the students keep journals in biology. One standing journal question is: What connections are you making to every day life?

Paragraph Completion

Some coaches assess teachers' increased reflectivity on the Hunt Paragraph Completion Method,[6] which is designed to test conceptual growth. Participants read a sentence stem and write at least three sentences on each topic. They may spend three minutes on each stem, which gives sufficient time to quickly write the required number of sentences but does not permit them to create an elaborately rationalized account.

The sentence stems are:
1. What I think about rules . . .
2. When I am criticized . . .
3. When someone does not agree with me . . .
4. When I am not sure . . .
5. When I am told what to do . . .

To score Hunt's Paragraph Completion Test, a numerical value from zero to three is assigned to each response. The three highest scores are then averaged to determine an overall score. Scores of 0 indicate individuals who tend to be impulsive and concerned about themselves. Scores of 1 indicate individuals who are concerned about behaving in socially accepted ways, evaluate situations in simple, concrete terms, and are sensitive to figures of authority.

People who receive scores of 2 tend to be open to the ideas of others and to evaluate alternatives. They have an increased tolerance for uncertainty, and need independence.

A score of 3 suggests that the individual weighs alternatives before deciding on the best solutions to problems, shows concern for the consequences of decisions, and is securely independent.

Portfolios

Art's son-in-law is an architect. When he has applied for various jobs he has taken with him his portfolio, a collection of artifacts which display his standards of excellence: craftsmanship, creativity, precision, innovation, repertoire, artistry, versatility, and his rich background of knowledge and experience.

Portfolios can be powerful tools to assess growth toward the five states of mind. Coaches may invite teachers to keep portfolios of their finest work: yearly goal statements, lesson plans, worksheets, homework assignments, tests, communications to parents, writing samples.

Coaches may invite teachers to meet periodically to share their portfolios. The essence of keeping a portfolio is to generate numerous artifacts and then to select out of them those which demonstrate their core values. In such meetings, teachers are invited to share these examples and describe why they selected these particular exemplary artifacts.

Dialogues and Interviews

In Planning and Reflecting conferences, in problem-solving discussions and in informal dialogues, teachers' statements, goals and concerns may indicate a movement toward higher levels of autonomy. Since more complex, abstract, and empathic teachers produce students who think at higher levels, coaches will be alert to indications that teachers are moving toward 1) valuing process goals of thinking, creativity, and collaboration; 2) valuing conceptual development more than content coverage, 3) becoming more empathic toward students, and 4) striving for more lofty and global societal goals. Following are some examples of teacher statements which might indicate their progress along these continuums.

From Content goals . . .

"I want them to understand economic concepts to help them be successful in this economy. They need to understand how these public laws affect them. Because some of the gifted students are at a higher level, I expect them to pick up more content and relate it to the principles of economics we are discussing."

To Process goals

"I want them to use their analytic skills to think through a problem for themselves. It really bugs me when students don't think for themselves. To survive effectively in our society, we need people who can think, who can become somewhat skeptical, who will take risks and who will question the political and advertising messages coming at them. The human mind is a terrible thing to waste."

From Content coverage . . .   **To Conceptual depth**

"I'm interested in exposing kids to a wide variety of ideas. I try to squeeze as much information as possible into my course. If they know a little vocabulary and have a grasp of the field, they can go farther as they get older. While I can't cover it all, I can, at least, expose them to the major ideas."

"I don't try to teach all the chapters in the book. Instead, I teach whatever I teach well and carefully. It's ridiculous to try to cover all the scientific content in one year. I focus on concepts. I figure that if I can turn kids on to science, they can pursue other ideas later. Actually, it doesn't matter where in science you start since all the sciences are interrelated anyway."

From Indifference toward students . . .   **To Empathic attitide toward students**

"Students aren't interested in learning. They just want to fool around. They don't put much effort into their studies and their attention span is minimal. Some of the more gifted kids are just as apathetic as the slow ones."

"A lot of kids have gotten the message over the years that they can't—that they have limitations. I believe that all kids can become better thinkers—we all can. I believe my job is to get inside that mind and turn it on. It requires a lot of effort, but they're worth it."

From Immediate issues . . .	**To Larger, more global societal issues**
"In my class, kids know they can't just speak out. They have to take turns. It's so difficult for them to listen to me and to each other. I've tried rewards, taking away privileges and positive reinforcement. Nothing seems to work. They're just going to have to learn to straighten out."	"It's so interesting how different kids are in my classroom. It's a real melting pot of cultures, languages, races and backgrounds. They are having a rich experience in getting accustomed to dealing with diversity — like it really is in our society. I try to help them take responsibility for themselves and others. Sometimes kids come to school and they really don't know how to act in a classroom like mine. But I encourage them to help each other learn the ropes. Its amazing how kids can teach each other ideas more efficiently than I can sometimes."

Through coaching, arranging group interaction, and providing an organizational climate conducive to teacher growth, coaches use opportunities for dialogue to observe growth of teachers toward higher states of mind.

Assessing the Holonomous Learning Community

As community members become more informed and involved, leaders can observe them employing more systemic thinking. They may inquire about how the effects of one change in the system will influence another part of the system. Their suggestions will increasingly be of long duration—three to five years rather than quick fixes. Communities become willing to provide resources to support change over time. They will seek information as to the causes of problems, study alternative solutions, employ clear values as ways of prioritizing. They will design feedback loops to monitor progress and remain informed about indicators of change. They will investigate how other districts and communities have handled similar problems; they will attend forums and organizational meetings to learn how they can assist in the change process.

Assessing Organizational Growth

The following figures provide one means of collecting evidence about the evolutionary development of the organization. They provide snapshots of some desirable attributes of each of the units of the Renaissance community—Self, Classroom, School, District, and Community—in relation to the five holonomous states of mind.

We offer such an assessment schema, *not* for adoption but as an example of a criteria matrix that a staff might develop and adopt based on their collective vision of a Renaissance School. Communities could develop indicators, collect, interpret, and own the data from such a matrix. An holonomous faculty could develop improvement strategies and commit to move each level of the organization to even higher states of holonomy. Such matrices could also be used like an environmental impact study—to anticipate what influences proposed programs or practices might have on the states of mind.

ORGANIZATIONAL CLARITY AND CRAFTSMANSHIP

	As decisions are made, how are the five states of mind kept in the forefront, applied, and evaluated?	In what ways are members employing strategies to monitor and assess their progress toward the five states of mind?	What are indicators that progress is being made toward the commitment to achieving the vision of a Renaissance school?
Self			
Classroom			
School			
District			
Community			

ORGANIZATIONAL EFFICACY

	What are indicators that leadership skills are being learned, practiced and applied?	What evidence exists that members shape the goals and allocation of human, financial, and material resources of their unit in the organization?	What evidence exists that members of the Renaissance unit are becoming more persevering, productive, and confident?
Self			
Classroom			
School			
District			
Community			

ORGANIZATIONAL CONSCIOUSNESS

	What degrees of alignment exist between policies, practices, and the five states of mind?	How are the five states of mind becoming more visible in communications, environmental symbols, artifacts, and celebrations?	How are the five states of mind being used as criteria for decisions about curriculum, instruction, and assessment?
Self			
Classroom			
School			
District			
Community			

ORGANIZATIONAL FLEXIBILITY

	What are indicators that a spirit of inquiry, curiosity, risk - taking and experimentation exists?	What are indicators that an increasingly diverse range of viewpoints are being sought and valued?	What evidence suggests that people are increasing their adaptability to change?
Self			
Classroom			
School			
District			
Community			

ORGANIZATIONAL INTERDEPENDENCE

	What are indicators of improvements in such interpersonal and group skills as communication, problem solving, conflict resolution, and decision making?	What are examples of how personnel are contributing to and relying on one another while solving problems?	By what indicators are members better understanding the holonomic nature of the total organization and their connectedness to it?
Self			
Classroom			
School			
District			
Community			

Evaluating Student Growth Toward Greater Holonomy

In his book, *Schools of Thought*, Rex Brown[7] argues that the most active, thoughtful learning, involving the most energized students happens in schools that use no standardized tests. He asks: "Do we want thoughtfulness in schools? Do we want learning that means something? Do we want learning that can be taken into the world?"

You may take the examination alone, with another person, or with as many other people as you would like. I frown on cheating. In fact, I go blind with rage if I catch anyone cheating. I define cheating as the failure to assist others on the examination if they request it. . . . You may refer to notes and reference materials during the exam. You may bring friends, relatives or associates to help you. You may also bring equipment, such as typewriters, computers, musical instruments, sewing machines, cookstoves, cameras or any other contrivance which will provide assistance to your work. You may not cheat. If possible, have fun. If not, be competently miserable.

Jerry Harvey. "Class Syllabus: Individual and Group Dynamics"
George Washington University, 1983.
Washington, D.C.

Growth toward the five states of mind as desired goals of the Renaissance curriculum requires new, more authentic and appropriate forms of assessment for students. One of the main reasons why coaches encourage and employ the various and alternative developmental forms of assessment described above is because they are environmental signals to employ more authentic alternative, developmentally appropriate, individualized assessments of students.[8]

In the same manner that coaches, teachers, and the environment are assessed using such diverse strategies as portfolios, journals, critical incidents, inventories, direct observations, or interviews, so, too, will teaching teams employ such diverse assessments of students. In the same manner that coaches help teachers self-evaluate and self-modify, so, too, will teachers coach students toward greater self-evaluation and self-modification.

Summary

This chapter invites the reader to consider ways of collecting evidence regarding the benefits of cognitive coaching and the contribution of cognitive coaching practices toward the development of Renaissance Schools. The chapter begins with a summary of the beginning research base on cognitive coaching to serve as springboards for educators who wish to construct ways of assessing growth toward greater holonomy. Four Principles of Renaissance assessment are offered, followed by suggestions and examples for how coaches might assess their own growth, assess teacher growth, assess the development of holonomy in the community and the educational organization, and, finally, how coaches might broaden the range of assessment strategies for student growth toward greater holonomy.

Chapter 9 will extend the principles, values and visions of cognitive coaching into images of what might be—Renaissance Schools operating as holonomous organizations in an increasingly dynamic and interrelated universe.

Cognitive Coaching Research Studies and Literature

Albert, S. (1991). "Developing Beginning Teacher Autonomy: Gender Differences on Observer Ratings of Cognitive Coaching Elements." Professional Paper. Federal Way School District, Federal Way, WA.

Costa, A. (1991). Supervision for Intelligent Teaching. Search Models Unlimited, Sacramento, CA, 40–50.

Costa, A. & Garmston, R. (1985, February). Supervision for Intelligent Teaching. Educational Leadership, 42 (5), 70–80.

Costa, A. & Garmston, R. (1986, December). Cognitive Coaching Supervision for Intelligent Teaching. Pedamorphosis, Inc., P.O. Box 271669, Tampa, FL. Wingspan, 3 (1), 38–42.

Costa, A. & Garmston, R. (1986, March). Reviewing the Difference Between Supervision and Evaluation. Better Teaching Through Instructional Supervision: Policy and Practice. Compiled by Tye, K. & Costa, A. California School Boards Association, Sacramento, 9–12.

Costa, A. & Garmston, R. (1987, Fall). Student Teaching: Developing Images of a Profession. Action in Teacher Education. University of Houston, Texas, 9 (3).

Costa, A. & Garmston, R. (1993). The Art of Cognitive Coaching: Supervision for Intelligent Teaching. Training Syllabus, Institute for Intelligent Behavior, 720 Grizzly Peak Blvd., Berkeley, CA 94708.

Costa, A. & Garmston, R. (1992, Spring). Cognitive Coaching: A

Strategy for Reflective Teaching. *Journal for Supervision and Curriculum Improvement.* California ASCD.

Costa, A. & Garmston, R. (1991, Fall). Cognitive Coaching: Developing the Individual and the School. *Leadership.* Council of Supervisors & Administrators of The City of New York, 72–77.

Costa, A., Garmston, R., & Lambert, L. (1988). Evaluation of Teaching: A Cognitive Development View. In Popham, W.J. & Stanley, S.J. (Eds.), *Teacher Evaluation: Six Prescriptions for Success.* Association for Supervision and Curriculum Development, Alexandria, VA, 145–172.

Costa, A., Garmston, R., & Zimmerman, D. (1988). *Helping Teachers Coach Themselves.* Videotape Script, Association for Supervision and Curriculum Development, Alexandria, VA.

Donnelly, L. (1988, Spring). *The Cognitive Coaching Model of Supervision, A Study of Its Implementation,* Masters Thesis, California State University, Sacramento, CA.

Edwards, J. (1992). "The Effects of Cognitive Coaching on the Conceptual Development and Reflective Thinking of First Year Teachers." Unpublished Doctoral Dissertation, Fielding Institute, Santa Barbara, CA.

Flores, J. (1991, Spring). *Cognitive Coaching: Does it Help?,* Master's Thesis, Educational Administration, California State University, Sacramento, CA.

Foster, N. (1989). *The Impact of Cognitive Coaching on Teacher's Thought Processes As Perceived by Cognitively Coached Teachers in the Plymouth-Canton Community School District.* Doctoral Dissertation, Michigan State University, Detroit, Michigan.

Garmston, R. & Garmston, S. (1992, Summer). Supporting New Teachers. *KASCD Record.* Kansas Association for Supervision and Curriculum Development, *10* (1), 9–16.

Garmston, R. & Hyerle, D. (1988, August). *Professor's Peer Coaching Program: Report on a 1987–88 Pilot Project to Develop and Test a Staff Development Model for Improving Instruction at California State University,* Sacramento, CA.

Garmston, R., Linder, C. & Whitaker J. (1993, October). Reflections on Cognitive Coaching. *Educational Leadership,* Association For Supervision and Curriculum Development, Alexandria, VA. Vol. 51, No. 2, p. 57–61.

Garmston, R., Linder, C. & Whitaker J. (1993, In press). Learning How to Coach. *Journal of Staff Development,* National Staff Development Council, Oxford, OH.

Garmston, R. & Prieskorn, J. (1990, May/June). Leadership for Intelligent Teaching: Superintendents' Responses to Cognitive Coaching. *Thrust for Educational Leadership,* Association of California School Administrators, *19* (7), 36–38.

Garmston, R. (1986, November). How Do Teachers Coach? *SERNews,* The Special Education Resource Network. California State Department of Education, Sacramento, CA, 3, 4.

Garmston, R. (1986, November/December). Improve Conference Results . . . . Not Performance. *Thrust for Educational Leadership,* Association of California School Administrators, *16,* (3), 34.

Garmston, R. (1987, December). Support Peer Coaching. *School*

Administrator. American Association of School Administrators, *11* (44), 36–37.

Garmston, R. (1987, February). How Administrators Can Support Teachers Who Coach. *SERNews,* The Special Education Resource Network. California State Department of Education, Sacramento, CA, 4, 12.

Garmston, R. (1987, February). How Administrators Support Peer Coaching. *Educational Leadership,* 44 (5), 18–28.

Garmston, R. (1987, March). Teachers as Coaches: Training for Peer Coaching Success. *SERNews,* The Special Education Resource Network. California State Department of Education, Sacramento, CA, 5, 13.

Garmston, R. (1988, August). A Call for Collegial Coaching. *The Developer,* National Council of Staff Development, 1, 4–6.

Garmston, R. (1989, July). Peer Coaching and Professors' Instructional Thought. Pedamorphosis, Inc., P.O. Box 271669, Tampa, FL. *Wingspan, 5,* (1), 14–16.

Garmston, R. (1990, Spring). Is Peer Coaching Changing Supervisory Relationships?: Some Reflections. *California Journal of Curriculum and Supervision.* California ASCD, *3,* (2), 21–27.

Garmston, R. (1991, February). Cognitive Coaching: Leadership Beyond Appraisal. *Instructional Leader.* Texas Elementary Principals and Supervisors Association, Austin, TX, IV, (1), 1-3,9.

Garmston, R. (1991, April). The Cognitive Coaching Postconference. *Instructional Leader.* Texas Elementary Principals and Supervisors Association, Austin, TX, IV (2), 10–11.

Garmston, R. (1992). "Cognitive Coaching: A Significant Catalyst," in *If Minds Matter: A Foreword to the Future,* Skylight Publishing, Palatine, IL, Vol. I, 173–186.

Liebmann, R. (1993). "Perceptions of Human Resource Developers as to the Initial and Desired States of Holonomy of Managerial and Manual Employees." Unpublished Doctoral Dissertation. Seton Hall University, South Orange, NJ.

Lipton, L. (1993). "Transforming Information into Knowledge: Structured Reflection in Administrative Practice." Paper Presented at American Educational Research Association National Conference, Atlanta, GA.

Martinez, Rick. (May 10, 1991). Professors Offered Assistance Through Peer Coaching Program. *The Hornet,* California State University, Sacramento, CA, 9.

McDonough, S. (1991, Spring). *The Supervision of Principals: A Comparison of Existing and Desired Supervisory Practices as Perceived by Principals Trained in Cognitive Coaching and Those Without Cognitive Coaching Training.* Master's Thesis, Educational Administration, California State University, Sacramento, CA.

McDonough, S. (1992, Spring). How Principals Want To Be Supervised. *Visions.* Washington State Staff Development Council, Seattle, WA, *9* (3), 4–5,7.

Midlock, S. (1990). *Peer Coaching of High School Teachers.* Doctoral Dissertation, Leadership and Educational Policy Studies, Northern Illinois University.

Naylor, J. (1991). *The Role and Function of Department Chairper-*

sons in the Collegial Peer Coaching Environment. Doctoral Dissertation, University of Illinois at Urbana/Champaign.

Pajak, E. (1993). *Approaches to Clinical Supervision: Alternatives for Improving Instruction.* Christopher-Gordon Publishers Inc., Norwood, MA.

Prieskorn, J. (1990, Winter). Cognitive Coaching Raises Teachers' Self-Esteem. *Self-Esteem Today.* National Council for Self-Esteem, Sacramento, CA, *3* (3), 2.

Sommers, William. (1991, January). "Cognitive Coaching Sustains Teaching Strategies." *Minnesota Association of Secondary School Principals Newsletter,* 7.

Sparks, D. (1990, Spring). Cognitive Coaching: An Interview With Robert Garmston. *National Staff Development Council Journal,* 11 (2), 12–15.

Weatherford, D. & Weatherford, N. (1990). *Professional Growth Through Peer Coaching: A Handbook for Implementation.* Master's Thesis. California State University, Sacramento, CA.

Wood, Stillman W. (1991, March/April). Cognitive Coaching: Leadership Style for 21st Century. *THE PRINCIPAL NEWS,* The Association of Washington School Principals, Olympia, Washington, 19, (4), 12.

Endnotes

1. Garmston, R. and Hyerle, D. "Professor's Peer Coaching Program: Report on a 1987–88 Pilot Project to Develop and Test a Staff Development Model for Improving Instruction at California State University." Sacramento, CA, 1988.

    Garmston, R., Linder, C. and Whitaker, J. "Reflections on Cognitive Coaching." *Educational Leadership* (1993 October) . Alexandria, VA: Association for Supervision and Curriculum Development.

    Sommers, W. "Cognitive Coaching Sustains Teaching Strategies." *Minnesota Association of Secondary School Principals Newsletter* (1991): 7.

    Flores, B. "Cognitive Coaching: Does it Help?" Unpublished Master's Thesis, California State University, Sacramento, CA, 1991.

2. Foster, N. "The Impact of Cognitive Coaching on Teachers' Thought Processes as Perceived by Cognitively Coached Teachers in the Plymouth-Canton Community School District." Doctoral Dissertation, Michigan State University, Detroit, MI, Dissertation Abstracts International, 1989, 27, 54381.

    Garmston, R. and Hyerle, D. "Professor's Peer Coaching Program: Report on a 1987–88 Pilot Project to Develop and Test a Staff Development Model for Improving Instruction at California State University." Sacramento, CA, 1988.

Garmston, R., Linder, C. and Whitaker, J. "Cognitive Coaching: Two Teacher's Perspectives." *Educational Leadership* (1993 October, in press). Alexandria, VA: Association for Supervision and Curriculum Development.

Edwards, J. "The Effects of Cognitive Coaching on the Conceptual Development and Reflective Thinking of First Year Teachers." Unpublished Doctoral Dissertation, Santa Barbara, CA: Fielding Institute, 1992.

Lipton, L. "Transforming Information into Knowledge: Structured Reflection in Administrative Practice." Paper presented at American Educational Research Association National Conference, Atlanta, GA, 1993.

3. Garmston, R. and Hyerle, D. "Professor's Peer Coaching Program: Report on a 1987–88 Pilot Project to Develop and Test a Staff Development Model for Improving Instruction at California State University." Sacramento, CA, 1988.

Garmston, R., Linder, C. and Whitaker, J. "Reflections on Cognitive Coaching." *Educational Leadership* (1993 October) . Alexandria, VA: Association for Supervision and Curriculum Development.

Sommers, W. "Cognitive Coaching Sustains Teaching Strategies." *Minnesota Association of Secondary School Principals Newsletter.* 1991, 7.

Midlock, S. "Peer Coaching of High School Teachers." Doctoral Dissertation, Leadership and Educational Policy Studies, Northern Illinois University, 1990.

Lipton, L. "Transforming Information into Knowledge: Structured Reflection in Administrative Practice." Paper presented at American Educational Research Association National Conference, Atlanta, GA, 1993.

Naylor, J. "The Role and Function of Department Chairpersons in the Collegial Peer Coaching Environment." Doctoral Dissertation. University of Illinois at Urbana/Champaign, 1991.

4. Van Mannen, M. "Linking Ways of Knowing With Ways of Being Practical." *Curriculum Inquiry* (1977): 6, pp. 205–228.

5. Sparks-Langer, G.M., Simmons, J., Pasch, M. , Colton, A. and Starko, A. "Reflective Pedagogical Thinking: How Can We Promote It and Measure It? *Journal of Teacher Education* (1990): 41 (4), 23–32.

6. Hunt, D. E., Greenwood, J., Noy, J. and Watson, N. *Assessment of Conceptual Level: Paragraph Completion Method.* Toronto,

Canada: Ontario Institute for Studies in Education, 1973.

7. Brown, R. *Schools of Thought.* San Francisco, CA: Jossey-Bass, 1991.

8. While alternative forms of assessment are not elaborated here, further sources of information include:

    Burke, K. *Authentic Assessment: A Collection of Articles.* Pallatine, IL. Skylights Pubs, 1992.

    Herman, J.L., Ashbacher, P.R. and Winters, L. *A Practical Guide to Authentic Assessment.* Alexandria, VA. Association for Supervision and Curriculum Development, 1992.

    Perrone, V. (Ed.) *Expanding Student Assessment.* 1991 Yearbook of the Association for Supervision and Curriculum Development. Alexandria, VA.

    Tierney, R., Carter, M. and Desai, L. *Portfolio Assessment in the Reading–Writing Classroom.* Norwood, MA. Christopher-Gordon Publishers, 1991.

9

Renaissance Schools As Holonomous Organizations

No problem can be solved from the same consciousness that created it. We must learn to see the world anew.
                                              Albert Einstein

We came to call our new vision of schools the Renaissance School because we were inspired by the emotional power of the word. Renaissance represents rebirth and reawakening, a reenergizing of values, a reconnecting with natural forces found in the universe, a recognition of the innate capacities for human development, both individually and in groups. The Renaissance School is at once a celebration of the limitless potential and creativity of the human spirit and a means of continuous movement toward ideals.

Two core values form the centerpiece of this organization. First, that each person is on an unending journey toward authenticity, integration, wholeness, self-expression, and morally sound contributions to fellow human beings. Second, that each person has the capacity to influence the multiple systems of which they are part, and, therefore, can make the world a better place.

But how are cognitive coaching and Renaissance schools related? Findings in the new sciences—world views unlocked first by Einstein and later by the formation of quantum theory—have moved us beyond a linear view of the universe to new, more complex and integrated explanations of how things work.

Through such fresh lenses as quantum physics, complexity theory, chaos theory, the study of fractals and so forth, scientists are examining anew the natural order of the universe and, consequently, management theorists are reexamining human social order. Several conclusions, conjectures, and possibilities for human organization are emerging.[1]

1. Tiny initial inputs into a system can produce far-reaching and unpredictable results. Human organizations, like natural systems, are composed of so many interacting elements that they are tremendously sensitive to even the tiniest factor. Briggs[2] says about this phenomena that everything influences everything else because everything is interacting with everything else. Cognitive coaching, along with other well-focused practices in staff development, curriculum development, organizational decision making, and so on, can, as we have repeatedly seen, produce tremendous changes throughout the entire system. These changes are rarely predictable in a linear fashion.

2. Many natural systems have a fractal quality; that is, they share similar details on many different scales and levels. Consider the endless duplication of the patterns of a cauliflower, or the repetitions in the shape of a fern. Focusing on any part of the system reveals a reproduction of the system itself.

We contend that Cognitive Coaching is just such a potent force—through mediation, facilitation, nonjudgmentalism—for the empowerment of individuals capable of independence and harmonious, skillful living with others. Cognitive coaching produces a fractal quality reproducing these values and attributes throughout the entire organization: self, classroom, school, district, and eventually the community.

3. Subatomic elements spontaneously change in relationship to each other. This *is* a world of relationships, not of things. Wheatley[3] reports that her diagnosis of the health of

organizations increasingly focuses on the quality of relationships between individuals and not on material resources, organization charts, or leadership theories. Furthermore, at the subatomic level, matter changes simply by its relationship to other matter. Light waves are simultaneously waves *and* particles and can change back and forth to either form.

So we see a natural extension of Cognitive Coaching as being a prime (not the only, but a significant) catalyst to the development of Renaissance schools.

The Renaissance School, influenced at its very core by Cognitive Coaching and the new scientific concept of the "chaos of nature,"[4] is a holonomous enterprise. It operates autonomously with site-based goal setting, resource allocation, curriculum development, assessment procedures, staff development, shared leadership—and at the same time interdependently as part of the entire educational system influencing and being influenced by the district and the community. The school values inclusion, democratic principles, diversity of style, personal history, capacities, interests, and—within certain moral boundaries—opinions. The function of leadership is to capacitate others. The function of teaching is to activate in students' minds and souls the indefatigable butterfly wings of the five states of mind. The function of learning is to become all that you can be.

The Renaissance School governs itself by using guidelines of a learning community:
- Exists equally for its members and its clients.
- Questions itself about its purpose and its process.
- Takes joy in the success of its members.
- Demonstrates care for its members.
- Shares a common set of norms, values, and goals.
- Has a process for mediating its values to new members.
- Enables freedom of expression.
- Displays a spirit of inquiry.
- Values challenges to the group.
- Uses resources in alignment with its values.
- Has a core learning content.
- Views itself flexibly through many lenses.
- Provides a forum for thinking.
- Has a common foundation of experience and knowledge that keeps on developing.

- Values conflicts as developmental opportunities.
- Fights openly, passionately, and gracefully.
- A learning community has taboos and makes these taboos conscious.

It is not acceptable, for example, to dictate how others should think; it is not acceptable to engage in activities that weaken the five states of mind; it is not okay to chastise, demean, or limit the growth of anyone It is unacceptable to vegetate and not be a continual learner.

Visions of the Renaissance School

Writings by Senge, Block, Toffler, Pascarella, Covey, Demming, Wheatley, Bracy, and numerous others indicate that there is need for a greater caring for the personal growth of each individual, a desire to enhance individual creativity, to stimulate collaborative efforts, and to continue learning how to learn. Wheatley[5] reports that "as we let go of the machine models of work, we begin to step back and see ourselves in new ways, to appreciate our wholeness, and to design organizations that honor and make use of the totality of who we are." The Renaissance School is such an organization.

Up to the present time, most organizations have been constructed on notions derived from 17th-century Newtonian physics, on cherished assumptions that this is a world of things, of mechanics, of leverage, of hierarchies and rigid organizations. Through the new sciences, however, within the fresh discoveries and hypotheses in biology, chemistry, and quantum physics, we are being challenged to reshape our fundamental world views. We are discovering that this is not a world of things; it is a world of relationships.

> To live in a quantum world, to weave here and there with ease and grace, we will need to change what we do. We will need to stop describing tasks and instead facilitate *process*. We will need to become savvy about how to build relationships.[6]

Five States of Mind Pervade The Renaissance School

Recent efforts to bring a more thoughtful and collaborative focus to our schools most likely will prove futile unless school environments signal the staff, students, and commu-

nity that the development of holonomy is of prime importance as the community's goal. While tremendous energy
may be invested in efforts to enhance the staff's instructional competencies, develop curriculum, and revise instructional materials and testing procedures, it is crucial
that the school climate in which educators make decisions
also be aligned with the Renaissance goals. Thus, teachers
will more likely teach toward student holonomy if teachers
are in environments which stimulate growth toward teacher
holonomy.

Coaches have not only the responsibility for developing the
fullest capacities of each player, they also have the responsibility for weaving those individual talents into synergistic
holonomous teams. The educational leader is not only one
who works with other school personnel in face-to-face
interactions but who also mediates the larger school and
community environment. In this role the leader is mindful
of the broader, longer-term goal: To develop and enhance
the fullest potentials and interrelationships of all the inhabitants of the school community. This includes teachers,
administrators, support staff, students, parents, community members, non-certificated personnel, and para-pro-
fessionals. To accomplish this, the Renaissance leader constantly mediates school culture[7] by employing group processes, arranging environmental conditions, and embracing
problems, challenges, and crises as learning opportunities.

As the mediator of the intellectual ecology, the school leader
maintains faith in the potential of group interaction as a
means for all team players to continue growing toward
desired states. She is clear that under the right group
conditions, adults can continue to develop cognitively toward the five states of mind. The coach has a repertoire of
strategies to produce organizational growth toward the five
states, and has faith in her own skills and competencies in
assisting that growth.

Following are glimpses of classrooms, views of schools, and
visions of communities in which the five states of mind are
valued. We offer them as visions of what might be. Indeed
each of these views are images that do exist now, in various
settings. Some readers will recognize portions of what they
already have and visions of what they might aspire to.

Windows of Efficacy

Efficacious organizations are self-renewing and have an internal locus of control. The locus of decision making is within the organization rather than mandated from "above." Communities of classrooms, schools, districts, and parents are involved in decision making; problem solving; assessing; and reporting progress, envisioning outcomes, and determining curriculum. In Renaissance Schools, efficacious persons experiment with new ideas in ongoing quests for improvement. They operationalize their findings into policies and practices. They produce and report new knowledge gained from their experimentation.

Leaders of Renaissance Schools invite teachers and community members to take membership in governance groups. They assist them in publishing articles and research findings in local newspapers, state journals, and professional publications. Parents, support staff, and community members are invited to make presentations at meetings of professional organizations. The school initiates assistance networks for members of the community by bringing together community resources and agencies with parents and students who are in need of counseling, legal assistance, welfare, parenting skills, medical and psychological help, and child-care.

Traditionally, leadership skills have been the province of a few people "at the top of the hierarchy." In the Renaissance School, however, efficacious leadership is shared by all. Everyone, at one time or another, in various situations, is called upon to teach, to lead, to coach, to present, to consult, to conduct action research, and to network. Therefore, leaders provide opportunities for all members of the learning organization to learn, practice, employ, and receive feedback about these leadership skills.

Knowing that the school's mission is to develop efficacy in all members of the organization, leaders strive to invest thoughtful learning, reflection, and metacognition not only into the classroom but also in the district office, the board room, and in the larger learning community as well. All stakeholders continue to expand their skills of reasoning, creating, and cooperating. Teachers, administrators, support staff, and parents are encouraged to continue learning throughout their lifetimes and to strive to improve their own cognition, parenting skills, leadership skills, communication abilities, and instructional strategies.

In the classroom, students expand their range of efficacious behaviors by learning what to do when solutions to problems are *not* immediately known. They learn persistence, they learn how to learn, to reason, problem pose, and engage in creative decision making.[8] They learn more about their own cognitive styles, modality preferences, and intelligences and how to cooperate with others who have differing styles and intelligences. They learn how to cause their own "creative juices" to flow by brainstorming, inventing metaphors through Synectics,[9] and concept mapping.

Staff development purposes in the Renaissance School include a major investment of leadership skills for all personnel. Teachers, students, custodial staff, parents, bus drivers, secretaries—all the members of the school community—continually develop their skills of teaching, parenting, presenting, consulting, coaching, facilitating, networking, and researching. Numerous opportunities are provided for teaching team members to perform in a variety of roles: leader, consultant, researcher, coach, teacher, manager, and networker.

• Teachers in Hueneme High School in Oxnard, California, were dissatisfied with their class schedule and a disjointed, compartmentalized curriculum. They experimented with innovative ways of restructuring time. They divided the school year into trimesters, and classes met for three periods for one third of the semester. Teachers teamed and taught thematically. Evaluative comments from teachers and students demonstrated the merits of giving students time to complete labs in science; brainstorm, compose, revise, edit and deliver original compositions in English; and pursue to a satisfactory conclusion dialogues in social studies.

• In Worthington, Ohio, custodians are coached in making presentations to students about their responsibilities in caring for the school building. Students learn to facilitate school-community councils and advisory committee meetings.

Since the full community shares in the responsibility for student learning and school improvement, understanding feedback loops, data gathering, research design, and assessment techniques becomes the province of the total community.

• In Pinellas Park, Florida, for example, parents are invited to observe students at home and collect indicators of their child's growth in intelligent behaviors.[10]

• In Adrian, Michigan, a project entitled, *Communities for Developing Minds*,[11] bus drivers, custodians, secretaries, teachers, parents, and administrators are trained to facilitate meetings, to coach and to communicate not only with each other, but with students, at home, and with their staffs.

• In one California high school, students had been learning the strategies of Creative Problem Solving.[12] As a senior project, they interviewed employees of a local savings and loan association and discovered some problems. The students then met with the managers and applied some of their creative problem-solving strategies to assist the managers in solving the problems (an example of corporate world education cooperation in reverse!).

Windows of Flexibility

In Renaissance Schools teachers' strengths are used in many different ways. Most people have strengths in some areas, but they are not especially good in others. That's legitimate and human. Renaissance organizations learn to allow for that and even nurture it.

Renaissance School leaders help staff, students, and parents become aware of, value, and know how and when to draw upon and manage the multiplicity of their own and others' unique forms of intelligence. They illuminate a vision of an educational community where each member's range of multiple capacities would be maximally developed and utilized.

In a Renaissance School, the faculty provides assistance to teaching teams to work effectively with heterogeneously grouped students. Students of diverse cultural backgrounds, socioeconomic levels, learning abilities, developmental levels, and talents work and learn together. Teachers organize classrooms, plan instruction, and assess students' growth on a personalized basis providing each child developmental opportunities in the five states of mind.

In the Renaissance School, growth is found in "disequilibrium," not balance. Out of chaos, order is built, learning takes place, understandings are forged, and organizations function more consistently with their mission, vision, and goals.[13] In these schools codes of discipline, school rules, and policies are examined for their consistency with the goals of interdependence, self-evaluation, and self-modification. Kriegel and Patler's book, *If it Ain't Broke, Break It,*[14] bears the wonderful title that elegantly sums up what Renaissance school leaders do with crystallized, plateaued organizational thinking.[15]

Numerous strategies are employed to break mental models. Conditions exist in which people can take risks and experiment. Job assignments are rotated, tasks are assigned to stretch the imagination and cognition of staff members.

Teachers are researchers in Renaissance Schools. Alternate classroom and instructional strategies are tested. Experiments are conducted with various lesson designs, instructional sequences, and teaching materials.

The classroom climate, too, fosters risk-taking as students experiment with ideas, share their thinking strategies with each other, and venture forth with creative thoughts without fear of being judged. Value judgments and criticism are replaced with acceptance of, listening to, empathizing with, and clarifying each other's ideas. Students learn and use the Cognitive Coaching skills of interaction.

In the past, archaic compartmentalization of the disciplines kept school staffs separated. In the Renaissance School, development of the five states of mind is the capacitating core of the curriculum. Traditional content and subject matter boundaries become increasingly obscure and selectively abandoned. In their place, relevant, problem-centered, integrative themes are judiciously selected because of their contributions to the thinking, learning, and community-building processes.

Principals often feel bound by traditions, laws, policies,

rules, and regulations that tie them to past practices, obsolete policies, and archaic metaphors. We are often asked, "How can I use cognitive coaching when, by state law, I have to evaluate teachers twice a year?" "How can I go into teacher's classrooms when the teacher's association has negotiated only two classroom visits per year?" "How can I employ cognitive coaching when we have to award merit pay by observing a teacher with a checklist of sixty-five state-adopted competencies?" "I believe that cognitive coaching is the way to go; now how do I convince the district administration when they really want us to go in and "fix" or terminate inadequate teachers?"

Elegant cognitive coaches use creative insubordination: strategies that "stay within the law" but produce imaginative solutions to meeting the spirit, not the letter, of the law. Following are some examples:

• In some districts, it is written into policy that administrators must complete teacher evaluations by a certain date (April 15, for example). There is nothing to say, however, that evaluations could not be performed before that date. Flexible administrators conduct their mandated evaluations by October 1 for tenured teachers so that all classroom visitations thereafter are for coaching purposes.

• In several states (New York, Illinois, Texas, California), it is possible to request permission to waive the legal regulations for the purpose of experimentation, restructuring, or educational reform. Flexible cognitive coaches beat a path to the State Department of Education door with requests in hand.

Numerous school districts have encouraged flexible pathways to continued teacher learning. Osseo, Minnesota; Dawson Creek, British Columbia; Anchorage, Alaska; Carrollton-Farmers Branch, Texas, High School District 230, Illinois; Dauphin, Manitoba, Canada, and Teanac, New Jersey are examples. They allow teachers to choose each year how they wish to grow. Among the choices are in-house mini-sabbaticals, coaching and being coached, evaluation, staff development, or curriculum revision projects, to name a few options. The only option teachers cannot choose is to stagnate.

Windows of Craftsmanship

As schools work to reinvent themselves, they commit human resources to modify the systems in which people work.[16,17] Organizational change is as important as the development of the individual, perhaps more important because of the incredibly powerful mediating capacity of the environment. Certainly, the two interact with one another, and they mutually influence student learning. In the holonomous school community, twin goals must exist: development of the organization's capacities for growth *and* the development of individual's capacities for learning.[18]

Renaissance organizations devoted to craftsmanship continually clarify their mission: Why we exist and what business we are in; our culture/philosophy. What we believe, and therefore how we do things consistently with what we believe, or vision. What our organization will look like in the future, and how we work toward that vision, along with specific goals and outcomes: How will we operationalize and measure our effectiveness?

• All systems support the organization's direction. Personnel practices, for example, reflect the desire to infuse the five states of mind. Job specifications for hiring new personnel include skills in teaching processes of thinking and collaboration. Teachers are empowered to make decisions that affect their jobs. Staff development practices are directed toward enhancing the five states of mind and enhancing the perceptions and intellectual growth of all staff.[19]

• Selection criteria for texts, tests, instructional materials, and other media include their contribution to enhancing efficacy, flexibility, craftsmanship, consciousness, and interdependence. Counseling, discipline, library, and psychological services are constantly evaluated for their enhancement of and consistency with thoughtful practice.[20]

• In schools, cafeterias and classrooms, discipline practices appeal to students' thoughtful and empathic behavior. Students participate in generating rational and compassionate classroom and school rules and continually strive to monitor and evaluate their own holonomous behavior in relation to those criteria.[21]

In Hawaii, the State Department of Education developed The Hawaii Continuum for Teacher Development, based on the five holonomous states of mind. This model is used to guide their vision of the effective teacher for the 21st century, to focus their professional development support for beginning and experienced teachers, and as a classification for areas of teachers' self-analysis and self-improvement.

Colorado's Jefferson County School District has six explicit outcomes for students. They expect that as a result of the school's program each student will have the knowledge, skills, and attitudes to be:

1. **An effective communicator** who expresses ideas using a wide variety of methods, including written and spoken languages, math, and the arts.
2. **A complex thinker** who analyzes, evaluates, and synthesizes information and ideas from multiple resources to make responsible, informed decisions, and who applies flexible and creative ideas and approaches to identify and solve problems.
3. **A responsible citizen** who develops an awareness and an understanding of his or her own cultural and ethnic heritage, as well as that of others, and who promotes and supports attitudes, practices, and policies that enhance the quality of life in our multicultural, interdependent world.
4. **A self-directed learner** who takes responsibility for self-improvement and ongoing learning and who plans, evaluates, and adapts using the lessons of the past and forecasts of the future.
5. **An ethical person** who uses a strong sense of his or her own identity and personal values to make responsible decisions that balance self-interest with the interests of others and who displays qualities the community values, including caring and respect for others, honesty, integrity, loyalty, and fairness.
6. **A quality worker** who creates high-quality products, services, and performances through both independent actions and teamwork.

These six outcomes are the focus for lessons taught in that school district. If a lesson cannot be shown to support one or more of these outcomes, the lesson is discarded.

• At the school level, Dave Schumaker, principal of the New Brighton Middle School in Soquel, California, instituted a Philosophy Club. He shared articles of interest with his staff and invited them to meet on Friday after school for a professional discussion of the article. At first, few staff members attended. Then, gradually, more and more of his staff appeared, became engaged, and started to lead the discussions. Then teachers began finding articles and sharing them. Now there is a parents' philosophy club as well.

In the school dedicated to precision and craftsmanship, writing samples, materials manipulation, open-ended multiple answer questions, portfolios, interviews, performances, and exhibitions are more useful and "authentic" than traditional testing procedures. They mirror situations in which real problem-solving and creativity are demanded. They allow teachers to more accurately diagnose students' abilities. They take place *during* instruction rather than *after* instruction. They provide more immediate results that assist teaching teams in evaluating the effectiveness of their own curriculum decisions and instructional efforts. Of most importance, they provide "real-time" feedback to students themselves who are (or who must become) the ultimate evaluators of their own performance.

Windows of Consciousness

We are learning that power in organizations—power to get work done, to teach, to learn, to transform lives—is energy. Energy needs to flow through the entirety of organizations; it cannot be confined to positions, functions, levels, titles, or programs. As Wheatley reports,

> What gives power its charge, positive or negative, is the quality of relationships. Those who relate through coercion, or from a disregard for the other person, create negative energy. Those who are open to others and who see others in their fullness create positive energy.[22]

While a quiet revolution is taking place across America in corporate offices and industrial settings, there is a corresponding revolution in the sources of power in schools as well. It is a revolution of consciousness, relationships, and valuing of a revolution of the intellect, placing a premium on our greatest natural resource—our human minds in relationship with one another. Increasingly, those attributes of a climate conducive to intellectual growth and self-fulfillment are becoming universally recognized and accepted. The conditions that maximize creativity are being described, understood, and replicated in classrooms, schools, districts, and communities.[23] This consciousness permeates Renaissance Schools.

Compelling influences that act on teachers' thought are the norms, culture, and climate of the school setting. Hidden but powerful cues emanate from the school environment. They signal the institutional value system that governs the operation of the organization.[24] Similarly, classroom cues signal a hidden, implicit curriculum that influences student thinking as well.

Knowing that developing holonomy is the important goal, Renaissance leaders facilitate the consciousness of all inhabitants of the school regarding their right to think. Coaches keep this primary goal in focus as they make day-to-day decisions. Teachers' rights to be involved in the decisions affecting them are protected, as are the rights of those who choose not to be involved in decision making.

• In one district, leaders learned to recognize and respond to vague language and probed each other for specificity. The staff made an agreement that every time someone used the word "they," others would stop them to probe who "they" was.

Consciousness of a school's values are carried in an organization's traditions, celebrations, and humorous events. Staff members share humorous anecdotes, jokes, and stories about students who, as a result of instruction, display growth toward holonomous behaviors. ("I observed two sixth grade boys on the playground yesterday. I could tell a scuffle was about to break out. Before I got to them another boy intervened and I overheard him say, 'Hey, you guys, restrain your impulsivity.'")

Jon Saphir of the Research for Better Teaching in Carlisle, Massachusetts, tells of a school where each teacher is provided with a $100 account. The money cannot be spent; it can only be given away to another teacher who has in some way helped the teacher giving the money. Furthermore, it cannot be given away in private; it is only given away in public, at a faculty meeting.

As a school journeys toward a more conscious expression of the five states of mind, the vision increasingly pervades all of its communications. In Palmdale, California; Wayzata, Minnesota; Maple Valley, Washington; Pinellas Park, Florida; Novato, California; and Burlington, Wisconsin, report cards, parent conferences, and other progress reports include indicators of the growth of students' autonomous behavior: habits of mind, questioning, making connections, metacognition, flexibility of thinking, persistence, listening to others' points of view, and creativity.

The staff of the Bleyl Junior High School in Houston, Texas refer to themselves as "The United Mind Workers."

Student growth toward the five states is assessed and reported in numerous ways, including teacher-made tests, structured observations, and interviews. Students maintain journals to record and reflect on their own growth. They share, compare, and evaluate their indicators of growth toward the five states of mind over time. Parents, too, look for indicators that their children are transferring efficacy, craftsmanship, consciousness, flexibility, and interdependence from the classroom to family and home situations. In Westover Elementary School in Stamford, Connecticut, for example, portfolios of students' work show how their organizational abilities, conceptual development, and creativity are growing. Assessment data report such critical thinking skills as vocabulary growth, syllogistic thinking, reasoning by analogy, problem solving, and fluency.

Parents and community members in Sorento, Illinois, receive newspaper articles, calendars, and newsletters informing them of the school's intent and ways they can engage children's intellect.[25] "*The Rational Enquirer*" is the name given to the Auburn, Washington School District's Thinking Skills network newsletter. In Verona, Wisconsin, parents attend evening meetings to learn how to enhance their children's thoughtful capacities and behaviors.[26]

Cognitive coaches monitor the school's many forms of communications to search for ways the school's and the district's values can be made ever more conscious and clear to the staff, students, parents, and community.

Windows of Interdependence

> *"To be" is to be related.*
>
> *Krishnamurti*

The final holonomous state of mind is interdependence—a sense of community. Never in the history of the planet has there been a time of greater interdependence and a feeling of world community. In Europe, South America, Asia, North America, and the Pacific Rim, nations are struggling to form trading blocs and common markets. The United Nations takes unanimous actions against acts of terrorism and aggression. The World Health Organization provides forums in which developed and developing nations can proactively address health concerns. Countries are banding together to solve environmental problems as they realize the oceans into which toxic wastes are being dumped are not one country's resource but the world's resource; as they realize that the thin layer of oxygen we breath and which protects us from the sun's ultraviolet rays is being destroyed, and is a limited resource available to all of us. To solve these problems, nations must act in concert.

So, too, must educators work together. But time limitations, isolation, and minimal peer interaction in traditional school settings have prevented teachers of different departments, grade levels, and disciplines from meeting together. Renaissance School leaders realize that humans grow toward holonomy by resolving differences, achieving consensus, and stretching to accommodate dissonance. They realize there is a greater possibility for making connections, stimulating creativity, and growing the capacity for complex problem solving when such differences are bridged.

Educators are also prone to be conflict avoiders. If everything runs smoothly—in classrooms, schools, and communities—we think we're doing a great job. Many educators are valued because they "don't cause grief." They neither disrupt the equilibrium nor disturb the balance. Consequently, many great ideas failed to become operationalized because they were in conflict with existing practice.

Renaissance leaders boldly engage staff members in forging interdependence and a true community by addressing issues, conflicts, and challenges as they continually question traditional ways of working.

Being committed to enhancing interdependence and a sense of community, everyone in the school becomes more aware of and is willing to discuss strategies for improving the school climate, the quality of their interactions, and interpersonal relationships.[27] Students and school personnel practice, evaluate, and improve their listening skills of paraphrasing, empathizing, and clarifying and understanding.

At school board, administrative, and faculty meetings, decision-making processes are discussed, explained, and adopted. Process observers are invited to give feedback about the group's effectiveness and growth in decision-making, consensus-seeking, and communication skills.

In the community, teachers, administrators, parent, students, and support staff continue to discuss and refine their vision of the Renaissance School. Networks and coalitions study and debate community issues and problems. Support groups are formed to help others in need. Community agencies work together to develop the capacities of all members of the community.

In schools, teaching teams plan, prepare, and evaluate curriculum materials. Teachers visit each other's classrooms frequently to coach and give feedback about the relationship between their instructional decisions and student behaviors. Together they prepare, develop, remodel, and rehearse lessons. Definitions of, teaching toward, and assessment of students' and staff's growth toward their five states of mind are continually clarified.

Interdependence in the classroom is nurtured as students work together cooperatively with their "study-buddies," in learning groups, and in peer problem solving. In class meetings, student teams set goals, establish plans, and set priorities. They generate, hold, and apply criteria for assessing the growth of their autonomous behavior. They take risks, experiment with ideas, share thinking strategies, and venture forth with creative thoughts without fear of being judged.

Through dialogue, at all levels in the Renaissance organization, feelings of friendship and camaraderie replace defensiveness and division.

Towards a Larger Vision

> The most important thing we can do is to trust and love one another.
>
> George Land and Beth Jarman
> *Break-Point and Beyond. Mastering the Future Today.*

The theories, principles, and skills in this book have been aimed at stimulating, enhancing, and growing the states of mind and intellectual resources of teachers, students, and all who work with schools. Yet we have a still larger vision. It is a dream of world interdependence. In a holonomous universe, all things are connected. The butterfly wings of the five states of mind do influence the school community, but they reach far beyond that. In all of history, educational practices have reflected society, and vice versa. We would like to believe that cognitive coaches, and those they influence, would use the principles of cognitive coaching locally, but continue to think and act globally.

Over the past three decades numerous educational innovations have come and gone: the "back to basic movements," the educational reforms of the Sputnik era, the accountability movement, and the age of Aquarius. School improvement efforts have been initiated by federal grants, legislative mandates, and corporate philanthropy. Curriculum projects, staff development, and in-service training in myriad instructional strategies, have been part of the innovations and changes in education since the early 1960s. But in all the changes in education, few if any corporate or governmental dollars have supported a curriculum to help students understand the meaning of *love*. Few staff development programs are intended to develop the human capacity to produce a more loving relationship. No instructional strategies are unashamedly designed to teach people how to give and receive love.

Of course, when we say love, there is the possibility for misunderstanding. In some communities, if "Love" were included in a mission statement, some parents would be irate. If a national test were developed to assess love, the resulting debates would bury its implementation.

Unfortunately, our English language lacks the richness to communicate the meaning of love we wish to convey. Interestingly, in other cultures whenever there is an abundance of something, there are multiple labels for it. It is often said that Eskimos have numerous words for snow. Italians have unique labels for each type of pasta: spaghetti, vermicelli, fettucini, ziti, penne, fuscelli, macaroni, tortellini, to name a few. South Pacific islanders have many names for *coconut* and can discern their distinguishing characteristics. Americans have many types and names of firearms.

Philos, for the Greeks, connoted love: philosophy, the love of wisdom; philharmonic, the love of music; philology, the love of words. They use the word *storgy* to refer to love of animals. *Filias* is the familial love between siblings and parents. *Eros* is the physical love between man and woman. They also have the word *Agape*, which is the love of fellow human beings.

Love of humanity cannot be mandated, funded, or taught. It is experienced and lived. In many respects, the behaviors employed by cognitive coaches are the behaviors of Agape:

Accepting, non-judgmentally. A loving relationship is one where you know all about a person and love them just the same. It is a relationship of unconditional acceptance and empathy. It is a relationship in which energy is positively charged and changes both partners. It is a relationship in which, despite differences in approaches to problem solving, philosophies, or ways of processing information, we non-judgmentally accept each other. Power and growth are accomplished, and the relationship fosters and stimulates growth.

Clarifying and probing intensifies the relationship and communicates love. It means that you care, wish to understand, and value the other person. When you love someone, you want the bonds to grow deeper and stronger. A relationship that does not grow deeper grows shallower, dries up, and dies. When the coach probes and clarifies, in a very real way, his or her actions are an expression of *love*.

Open-ended questioning implies a loving relationship. It presupposes confidence that the other person has the resources for his/her own development. These questions are gifts in which the questioner sets aside his or her own agendas and solutions to help another person work from his or her own interests, mental maps, and resources. Inquiring together builds more information and a stronger bond over time.

Sharing information and providing data—being honest about yourself and your own emotions and feelings—reveals the vulnerability on which a loving relationship exists. Information is unique as a resource because of its capacity to generate itself. It is the inexhaustible cosmic energy of relationships and organizations as well.

We live in an age of miracles. We have fax machines in our cars, telephones in our briefcases, live viewing of world events. We have probed the ocean depths and the far reaches of space. With special photography, we can watch the brain process information. We have machines that can compute instantly what would take a hundred persons thousands of hours to compute. We have sent men and women soaring into orbit like demigods. And yet with all our achievements, our humanity, and our resources, starvation, despair, poverty, violence, pessimism, drugs, war, racism, bigotry, homelessness, and crime are still persistent companions to humankind. In this global village, in this holonomous universe, we can learn—in fact are learning—to help each other live together with the grace, beauty, potential, and agape accorded to human beings.

Margaret Wheatley[28] states that quantum physicists are discovering that the world is a world of relationships, a world of energy and information constantly interacting with and changing one another. She describes her understanding of her relationship to the world in these terms:

> A quantum universe is enacted only in an environment rich in relationships. Nothing happens in the quantum world without something encountering something else. Nothing is independent of the relationships that occur. I am constantly creating the world—evoking it, not discovering it—as I participate in all its many interactions. This is a world of process, not a world of things.

Educators, then, have a larger, more global agenda: to build the 21st Century as a quantum world—a learning community where all people are continually discovering ways to live together, trust each other, learn together, provide for each other, nurture this environment, and grow toward higher states of holonomy. The Association For Supervision and Curriculum Development, until very recently an American-based organization, exemplifies this commitment to world collaboration in its newly adopted mission statement and one of its six strategic goals for the years 1994–2001.

ASCD Mission

"A diverse, international community of educators, forging covenants in teaching and learning for the success of all learners."

An ASCD Goal

"By the year 2001, ASCD will work together with educators and educational organizations worldwide to promote quality education through structures that address both national and international issues."

We envision a world where the states of mind of efficacy, flexibility, craftsmanship, consciousness, and particularly interdependence are valued and supported. We see educators striving to become more holonomous themselves and teaching others to be more autonomous, self-assertive, and interdependent. We envision a world which is moving toward ever more holonomous individuals, communities, organizations, and nations, making more possible a caring, interdependent global community. We envision a critical mass of people moving toward:

WORLD EFFICACY—believing we can and generating increasingly more effective approaches to solving world problems using peaceful, cooperative solutions instead of power solutions.

WORLD FLEXIBILITY—transcending generations of ethnocentrism, to see truly and value the abundant diversity of other cultures, races, religions, language systems, time perspectives, political systems, and economic views to develop a more stable world community.

WORLD CONSCIOUSNESS—developing our collective capacity for conscious attention to the effects we have on each other and on the earth's finite resources in order to live more respectfully, graciously, and harmoniously in our delicate environment.

WORLD CRAFTSMANSHIP—striving for clarity and congruence between our democratic ideals and our decisions and actions, and striving for precision in our communication with others regardless of what language they speak.

WORLD INTERDEPENDENCE—by caring for, learning from, sharing with others, and helping one another manage ourselves and our earth's resources in ways that link all humans into a global community.

Alan Kay says, "The best way to predict the future is to invent it."[29] If we want a holonomous future that is much more thoughtful, vastly more cooperative, greatly more compassionate, and a lot more loving, then we have to invent it. The future is in our schools and classrooms today.

Endnotes

1. Wheatley, M. *Leadership and the New Science.* San Francisco, CA: Berrett-Koehler Publishers, 1992.

2. Briggs, J. *Fractals–The Patterns of Chaos.* New York, NY: A Touchstone Book, 1992.

3. Wheatley, M. Presentation to ASCD Executive Council, Washington, D.C., March 1993.

4. Briggs, J., proposes that the old scientific concept of the "balance of nature" is quietly being replaced by a new concept of the dynamic, creative, and marvelously diversified "chaos of nature."

5. Wheatley, M. *Leadership and the New Science.* San Francisco, CA: Berrett-Koehler Publishers, 1992.

6. Wheatley, M. *Leadership and the New Science.* San Francisco, CA: Berrett-Koehler Publishers, 1992.

7. While the term "culture" is often thought of in an anthropological or sociological sense, we like to think of culture using a biological metaphor. In biology, a culture is considered a *growth medium* which supplies the nutrients to produce maximum and rapid growth of the organisms which it hosts.

8. Costa, A. "The Search For Intelligent Life." *Developing Minds: A Resource Book For Teaching Thinking.* Alexandria, VA: Association for Supervision and Curriculum Development, 1991a.

9. Gordon, W.J. *Synectics: The Development of Creative Capacity.* New York, NY: Collier Books, 1961.

10. Palmer, C. "Twelve Ways Your Child/Student Shows Growth in Thinking Skills." *Developing Minds: A Resource Book For Teaching Thinking.* Alexandria, VA: Association For Supervision and Curriculum Development, 1991.

11. "Communities For Developing Minds" is the name given to the school improvement project of the Adrian, Michigan Public Schools and |I|D|E|A|—the Institute for the Development of Educational Activities of Dayton, OH.

12. Parnes, S. "Creative Problem Solving." *Developing Minds: Programs For Teaching Thinking.* Alexandria, VA: Association For Supervision and Curriculum Development, 1991.

13. Peters, T. *Thriving on Chaos: A Revolutionary Agenda For Today's Manager.* New York, NY: Alfred E. Knopf, 1987.

14. Kriegel, R.J. and Patler, L. *If It Ain't Broke, Break It!* New York, NY: Time/Warner Books, 1991.

15. Bardwick, J.M. *The Plateauing Trap.* New York, NY: Bantam Books, 1986.

16. Glickman, C. *Renewing America's Schools.* San Francisco, CA: Jossey-Bass Publishers, 1993.

17. Frymier, J. "Bureaucracy and the Neutering of Teachers," *Phi Delta Kappan* (1987): 69 (1), pp. 9–14.

18. Garmston, R. and Wellman, B. *How to Make Presentations That Teach and Transform.* Alexandria, VA: Association For Supervision and Curriculum Development, 1992.

19. Costa, A. *The School as a Home For The Mind.* Palatine, IL: Skylight Publishing, 1991.

20. Curwin, R. and Mendler, A. *Discipline With Dignity.* Alexandria, VA: Association for Supervision and Curriculum Development, 1989.

21. Saphier, J. and King, M. "Good Seeds Grow in Strong Cultures." *Educational Leadership* (1985): Vol. 42 (6), pp. 67–74.

22. Wheatley, M. *Leadership and the New Science.* San Francisco, CA: Berrett-Koehler Publishers, 1992, p. 39.

23. Perkins, D. *Smart Schools.* New York, NY: The Free Press, 1992.

Kohn, A. "Art for Art's Sake." *Psychology Today* (September 1987): Vol. 21, pp. 52–57.

Deal, T. Presentation made at the 1987 ASCD Annual Conference, New Orleans, LA, 1987.

Boyer, E. "On the High School Curriculum: A Conversation With Ernest Boyer." *Educational Leadership* (September 1988), Vol. 46, (1).

McClure, R. *Visions of School Renewal.* Washington, DC: National Education Association, 1988.

24. Frymier, J. "Bureaucracy and the Neutering of Teachers," *Phi Delta Kappan* (1987): 69 (1), pp. 9–14.

25. Diamandis, L. and Obermark, C. *Bright Ideas –A Newsletter for Parents: Critical Thinking Activities for Kindergarten Children.* Sorento, IL. 1987–1988.

26. Feldman, R.D. "25 Ways to Teach Your Child to Think." *Woman's Day* (November 11, 1986): pp. 60–68.

27. Garmston, R. "Is Peer Coaching Changing Supervisory Relationships?—Some Personal Impressions." *CASCD Journal* (Winter 1990): pp. 21–28.

28. Wheatley, M. *Leadership and the New Science.* San Francisco, CA: Berrett-Koehler Publishers, 1992.

29. Kay, A. "The Best Way to Predict the Future is to Invent It." Title of keynote presentation delivered at the Annual Conference of the Association for Supervision and Curriculum Development, San Francisco, CA, 1990.

Appendices

Appendix A
A Metacognitive Strategy for Setting Aside Bias in Cross-Cultural Communications

We have selected the following vignette from case studies regarding teaching diverse students collected by the Far West Laboratory for Educational Research. Space limits us to selecting but one example. The selection criteria we used was the teacher's rich metacognition that so amply illustrates the set-aside strategy we will present later.

In this case study, the teacher is a first-year returnee after 15 years of home making. The setting is in a ghetto high school and her third period students are primarily Afro-American. As you read, we invite you to appreciate that the unfolding drama could be involving any teacher, any grade level, any race, or any socio-economic setting. It is the differences between the perceptions and expectancies of the students and those of their teacher which creates extremely complex communication dynamics. It is to the teacher's handling of her own metacognition and resulting decision that we wish to call the reader's attention.

A first-year teacher writes about her first day of teaching in an inner city high school:

Nothing in the first three-week orientation I'd been through, or the first two classes of the day, seemed to prepare me for what I was about to meet third period. The students were much noisier coming in. When I launched into my idealistic speech about how they were the star players, the performers, and I was their coach, they laughed and someone called out, "Who's the quarterback? Where's the ball?" Whereas the first two classes had been quiet and attentive as I explained the special opportunities that lie ahead for qualified "minority" peoples in the decades to come (as American whites decrease in number while all minorities increase), this class seemed totally uninterested. The more I tried to explain the "new high school"—with genuine new expectations—the more restless they became. Someone mumbled that the old school was just fine.

Fifteen minutes into the hour, big trouble entered the room. Stout, black, stuffed into a flame-red dress, Veronica saun-

tered slowly, insolently past me and took a seat as con-
spicuously as possible. She grinned slyly and said in a
loud, husky tone, "What are you, some kind of fake white
preacher lady?" The class burst out laughing and three
large black boys suddenly jumped out of their seats and
began literally dancing around the room, spontaneously
rapping about the situation, clapping their hands, calling
out "Yea, Sister!" This was how I met Veronica, Travis, Lee,
and "Larry Luv." Before long I had named then "The Gang
of Four."[5]

This extremely difficult situation illustrates a common
problem; how to select a communications response most
appropriate to the persons and situation. This situation is
made more complex because of the mix of cultural differences in the situation—age, race, values, positional authority, and socioeconomic class.

Obviously, selecting an appropriate response in this situation is important for the welfare of the students and the
teacher. Yet even when conditions are less inflammatory,
selecting appropriate responses are important, because
inappropriate ones can result in anger, hurt, suspicion,
anxieties, fear, resignation, or a host of other feelings or
thoughts which interfere with achieving one's intentions.
The greater the differences between the coach and person
being coached in patterns of perceiving, processing and
communicating, and the more unconscious one's own patterns are, the greater the value of the metacognitive set-
aside strategy we shall describe here.

Figure A-1 displays several important dynamics present in
any cross-cultural communication. Each person engages in
dialogue from the perspectives of their own sense of identity.
Identity is constructed from both consciously and unconsciously held beliefs about goals, personal worth, identifica-
tion with a profession, gender, race, religion, theories of
learning, perceived status, interpretations of the motivations of others, etc. Consistent with this sense of personal
identity are the moment-to-moment intentions of what one
wants to communicate or "get from" a relationship. These
also live at unconscious and conscious levels, the unconscious intentions contributing to the metamessages (I am
capable, you are less so, therefore I will guide you to
solutions; or as the man, I'm expected to be helpful, therefore I'll offer a solution; I hear your discomfort, I want you to

know you're not alone, therefore I'll tell you about a similar experience I've had).

Frequently it is the metamessages that cause the most difficulties in communication. We believe that this is mainly so because of their unconscious nature, both for the sender and the receiver. The Anglo male holds the door open for a Hispanic woman. The intention of which he is conscious may be that he is being generous and that holding the door open for her is polite behavior. His unconscious intention may be to signal a difference in status through a metamessage of control: the woman gets to proceed not because it is her right but because the man has granted her permission, therefore she is being framed as a subordinate. If the woman's identity, which is comprised of the sum total of her conscious and unconscious beliefs, picks out the man's unconscious intention to respond to, she is likely to protest his polite gesture and he to be confused and angry about her response.

Finally, as shown in Figure A-1, all the filters of perception we have explored in Chapter 4—representational systems, cognitive styles and others—will form the lenses through which communications will be encoded and decoded. Readers will appreciate how richly complex these communications may become across multiple cultural differences, particularly when knowledge of other ways of processing and interpreting communications is absent. An Anglo coach, for example, may misinterpret an Asian colleague's quietness for nonassertiveness, not recognizing that perseverance may be valued more highly by this colleague than speaking out. Deborah Tannen, reports that "Americans in Greece often get the feeling that they are witnessing an argument when they are overhearing a friendly conversation that is more heated than such a conversation would be if Americans were having it."[6] As another example, linguist Deborah Schiffrin showed that in the conversations of working-class Eastern European Jewish speakers—both male and female—in Philadelphia, friendly argument was a means of being sociable. Persons outside this culture might well misinterpret these conversations.

This brings us to a consideration of the set-aside strategy presented in Figure A-2. To illustrate this, let us return to the inner city classroom example cited earlier. The teacher writes,

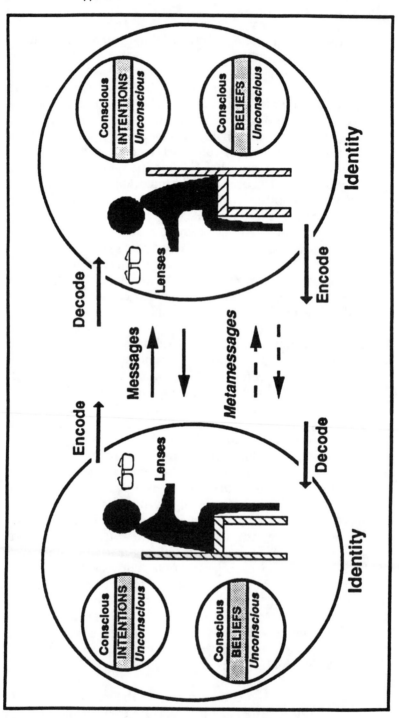

Figure A-1
Cross Cultural Communications

During those first nightmarish days, I felt I had run into the worst of everything I had heard about in the ghetto: crude, foul language, rudeness, low achievement, blatant sexuality, continual talk of violence, guns, drugs—the works. These students would have been a fearsome group in any color, but their blackness seemed at first to be a barrier. I was not sure what <u>really</u> to expect from them. Were they truly capable of decent behavior? Did they need some other kind of schooling?

What saved me from indicting <u>all</u> the black students was the obvious fact that in my first two classes I had wonderful students of all ethnic groups who defied these ghetto stereotypes, who were courteous, well-behaved and capable. Their skills in speech and writing would certainly enable them to compete successfully for placement in a job or college. I was delighted to know and work with them.

What I gradually realized was that the antics of 'The Gang' simply represented bad behavior—period. The cultural ways they expressed defiance of authority were only on the surface, where color is. Basically, success in school or anything else depends on certain attitudes that are universal. The high expectations the school held for its students were without regard to color. For the sake of The Gang, myself, and the rest of the class, I had to get control of the situation.[7]

In this setting, the teacher, over time, intuitively exercises a metacognitive, set-aside strategy. She does this by first **focusing her consciousness** on her own reactions—her anger, fear, judgment and prejudice. Then from a more detached, observer's position, she becomes aware of factors that are contributing to her prejudice and examines what data supports and does not support her feeling that "their blackness seemed at first to be a barrier."

Second, she **processes data** about her own internal state and the external stimuli, and decides that her intention is to find a solution:

One day as I looked into their faces, I saw that the misery I was feeling was mirrored in their eyes. The good students were powerless to do anything about all the trouble. And the Gang of Four seemed incapable of actually exerting positive leadership. I realized that I, myself, was the only person in that room who could solve the problem. <u>It was my responsibility!</u> Even though I hadn't deliberately started the

> *trouble, it was my role to find a solution. I needed to be not just a teacher, but a true leader in solving a group problem.*

She considers options and decides to reveal to the class how miserable she was feeling and engage them in a search for a solution.

Third, she **develops and tests** that plan, ultimately becoming successful.

Later, she comes to the conclusion that

> *It is poverty that is the real enemy. What I strive to do every day is to help students get over what I call the poverty mentality—the apathy, laziness, hopelessness that will surely doom them to perpetual poverty if they can't see beyond it. Do we truly feel that an individual, by his own efforts, can succeed? Most of my students do feel they can, and so do I.*

We have described the use of the set-aside strategy in a fairly complex situation, with events and communication happening between multiple persons and over time. Skilled coaches also use the set-aside strategy in one-on-one settings.

For example, Kimberly and Kevin are in the faculty room munching on Friday snacks. Kevin is telling about a discussion he had with four female colleagues. He had expressed to them his understanding of Joseph Campbell's premise that women do not need initiation rites into adulthood because natural physiological developments bring external manifestations of passage. He said to Kimberly, "I really got blasted when I said women don't need initiation rites, that it just happens for them." Kimberly became conscious of her own discomfort with Kevin's statement, and was able to activate a strategy to set aside her own bias in responding to Kevin.

As shown in Figure A-2, the three major phases of this strategy correspond to the input, processing, output stages in the model of human intellectual functioning described in Chapter 5. First, **focusing her consciousness** on her reactions to what has been said and moving away from an egocentric state, Kimberly carefully observes Kevin and speculates, with positive presuppositions, about his perspective in communicating what (and the way) he did. Second, she **processes data about the internal and external environment** by once again scanning Kevin's and her own nonverbals, she decides what her intention will be in responding to Kevin, inventories her communication repertoire to select a type of response appropriate in this setting and does a check for the safety of this response, should she actually use it. Third and finally, she **develops and tests a response** to Kevin by engaging in one of several powerful communication states (such as being curious or a detached observer, or communicator of love, or speaking to the presumed goodness within the other person, or borrowing a style of response modeled by another), she encodes her message into words and nonverbals, communicates her response, and then calibrates the effect it has on Kevin.

This faculty room conversation is a fairly simple transaction, uncomplicated by the use of different nonverbal codes such as culturally learned patterns of averting eyes or maintaining eye contact. Nor is it encumbered by culturally based value differences such as a Native American's valuing of patience as contrasted with a non-Native American's valuing of quick action. Neither is there a confusion about meaning of message type as in Greece, where people often show they care by telling people what to do, which to many Americans would be annoying and construed as presumptuous. Yet, the strategy we have been describing for setting aside bias in communication works as well in in-the-moment cross-cultural settings as it does in the earlier discussion example which took place over several days.

While the set-aside strategy we have described may seem cumbersome and complicated—and it is when reduced to a linear description on paper—in practice it is lightning quick and requires only one resource to successfully employ it. That resource is *consciousness*. We know to begin the strategy the moment we experience any discomfort in a cross-cultural, cross-gender discussion, or any other discussion for that matter. For example, when we feel a shift in our internal state, when we notice feeling threatened, or misunderstood, or angry, when we notice ourselves puzzled about what is going on, or fidgeting or hear changes in the patterns of our voice, we can use that information as a cue to focus our consciousness. This starts the process and with only one or two practices with the set-aside strategy, the rest becomes automatic.[8]

1. **FOCUS CONSCIOUSNESS**
   a) Kimberly notices her own discomfort. Kevin's statement does not match her own experience, so she regards it as a partial truth.
   b) She shifts to a dispassionate observer position. In this state she becomes aware of what part of Kevin's message initiated her discomfort (nonverbals or a certain part of his verbal message).
   c) She notices that she values the work of Joseph Campbell, the source of Kevin's information, and notices that she regards Kevin as sometimes having a lack of respect for women. She also notes that she believes Kevin to be a well-intentioned and thinking person, and that she feels safe in this dialogue because she has information about this topic and considers Kevin's motivations to be benign, and she believes his intentions are simply to impart information.

   All of this emotionally initiated cognitive activity has happened in less than a second or two. This incredibly rapid pace of processing will also be the case during phase two.

2. **GATHER DATA**
   The purpose of this phase is to make meaning of the situation and select a course of action.
   a) Kimberly tests the tentative conclusions she has drawn from her reflections so far by scanning again her external environment (Kevin's remembered and current nonverbals and verbals), her own feelings and explanatory self-talk, and she checks for congruence. Because her current data scan confirms her earlier conclusions she moves forward and . . . .
   b) Decides that her intention is to educate Kevin. She will tell him that in addition to the physiological manifestations of the girl-woman transformation, external social recognition is also important to get emotional validation. An unconscious intention on her part, she realizes later, is also to sound smart.
   c) Kimberly now inventories her conscious repertoire of response patterns appropriate to her intention and this situation. She selects one and . . . .
   d) Checks the safety of the response she has selected by predicting whether Kevin's reaction will be dangerous to her or not.

3. **TEST RESPONSE**
   The purpose of this phase is to communicate safely and satisfy her communication intentions.
   a) Kimberly enters a mental state of speaking to what she presumes to be Kevin's reasonable nature.

b) She encodes the message she has previously decided to send, and says, "I see your point," and then elaborates on the initiation into womanhood by giving an example of an initiation ritual she knows about which was carried out in an American desert. She concludes by saying that in every culture there is a biological passage, but in this and other cultures it is often shamed and hidden. While she is saying this she is carefully calibrating Kevin's verbal and nonverbal responses to determine whether she is safe in the communication and is meeting her intentions. Since some of her communication intentions are below her own level of consciousness (to sound smart), part of this calibration and resulting adjustments in the way she delivers her message are also unconscious. Because Kevin says, "Yeah, that's just what Campbell meant," she feels heard and validated, at both her conscious and unconscious levels of intention.

Figure A-2
A Meta-Cognitive Set-Aside Strategy

Appendix B
Teachers and Time

Six rather distinct temporal dimensions have been identified in teachers' thinking. Every instructional thought, event, occurrence, or situation can be defined in terms of sequence, simultaneity, synchronicity, duration, rhythm, and temporal logic. These six time dimensions interact constantly with our other thoughts and values and influence our daily decisions.

Sequence refers to the ordering of instructional events within a lesson. Most teachers tend to think sequentially about what they will do at the beginning of the lesson, what will happen after that, and, if the lesson is successful, how the lesson will end. Furthermore, teachers think of where this lesson fits into an overall sequence: What came before today's lesson and what will happen as a follow-up, whether that occurs tomorrow or next month or next year. Highly holonomous teachers plan sequences because they perceive how today's lesson fits into long-range goals. They can perceive relationships between the day-to-day student behaviors and their cumulative progress toward long-range educational outcomes and can prioritize goals and objectives so they know which student behaviors to reinforce and which to ignore.

Simultaneity refers to the capacity to operate under multiple classification systems at the same time. This means teachers can teach toward multiple objectives, coordinate numerous and varied classroom activities at the same time, plan a lesson incorporating several learning modalities, and think about multiple time frames. The research indicates that there are as many as six time dimensions that affect how teachers plan: weekly, daily, long-range, short-range, yearly, and long-term.

Synchronicity describes the ability to make all those multiple, various, and sequenced activities come together in time. For example, the teacher knows that the bell is going to ring in 15 minutes, but the remainder of the lesson as planned requires 20 minutes. What should be left out or sped up to make it all come out right? Can she carry some of the lesson over to tomorrow? Where is a good stopping point?

Duration refers to how long an activity will take. Within a given amount of time for a lesson, teachers must decide how to allocate that time to the various activities or phases of the lesson. New teachers are often inexperienced with these temporal dimensions of duration and synchronicity. They often plan for a 10-minute discussion that ends up consuming the entire class period. This tacit knowledge matures with experience.

Rhythm refers to the pacing, tempo, or speed at which the lesson is conducted. Teachers must constantly juggle decisions about what to include, what to leave out, and how much time is available. Teachers often feel the pressure of time in their teaching. One middle school history teacher once despaired, "I just don't know what I'm going to do! I'm only up to the Civil War and it's almost Easter. I don't think I'm going to make it to the present by the end of the school year!"

Temporal logic refers to our cultural perspective of time. Western culture is more "chrono-logic," being somewhat linear, immediate, sequential, and finite in our view of time. People of other cultures may be referred to as "poly-logic"; they live moment to moment. Their view of time is more emergent, flowing, transcendent, and infinite. While other cultures, such as Eastern, South Pacific, and Native American, value the meditative, reflective experience where time may have little meaning, our Western technological culture tends to value speed. We have timed tests and competitive races to see who can finish first and fastest. We complain when our trains and planes are late. We purchase labor-saving devices to allow us more time for other pleasures.

The Iroquois see themselves as servants of the past and stewards of the future. They ask, "How does the decision we make today conform to the teachings of our grandparents and to the yearnings of our grandchildren?" They consider, "Will this be to the benefit of the seventh generation?" By contrast, many other cultures tend to strive for immediate results and satisfaction. All of this, of course, transfers to school.

Appendix C
The Language of Coaching: Questioning

A direct correlation exists between the levels and syntactical structure of questions and the production of thought. Effective coaches deliberately use questions in ways that produce desired mental processes in the mind of the teacher.

Following are some examples of desired mental processes and the syntactical signals in a question that might produce them.

Planning Conference

If the desired thought process in the teacher is to:	Then the coach might ask: (the syntactical cues are in boldface)
(Describe) State the purpose of the lesson.	"**What** is your lesson going to be about today?"
(Translate) Translate the purposes of the lesson into descriptions of desirable and observable student behaviors.	"As you see the lesson unfolding, **what will** students be doing?"
(Predict) Envision teaching strategies and behaviors to facilitate student's performance of desired behaviors.	"As you envision this lesson, **what do you see** yourself doing to produce those student outcomes?"
(Sequence) Describe the sequence in which the lesson will occur.	"**What will** you be doing **first? Next? Last?** How will you close the lesson?"
(Estimate) Anticipate the duration of activities.	"As you envision the opening of the lesson, **how long** do you anticipate that will take?"

(Operationalize criteria)
Formulate procedures for
assessing outcomes
(envision, operationally
define, and set criteria).

"What will you see
students doing or hear
them saying **that will
indicate** to you that your
lesson is successful?"

(Metacogitate) Monitor
their own behavior during
the lesson.

"What will you look for
in students' reactions **to
know if** your directions
are understood?"

(Describe) Describe the
role of the observer.

"What will you want me
to look for and give you
feedback about while I
am in your classroom?"

Reflecting Conference

If the desired cognitive
process in the teacher is to:

Then the coach might
ask: (the syntactical cues
are in boldface)

(Assess) Express feelings
about the lesson.

"As you reflect back on
the lesson, **how do you
feel** it went?"

(Recall and Relate) Recall
student behaviors observed
during the lesson to
support those feelings.

"What did you see
students doing (or hear
them saying) **that made
you feel** that way?"

(Recall) Recall their own
behavior during the lesson.

"What do you recall
about your own behavior
during the lesson?"

(Compare) Compare
student behavior
performed with student
behavior desired.

"How did what you
observe **compare** with
what you planned?"

(Compare) Compare
teacher behavior performed
with teacher behavior
planned.

"How did what you
planned **compare** with
what you did?"

(Infer) Make inferences
about the achievement of
the purposes of the lesson.

"As you reflect on the
goals for this lesson,
what can you say about
your students'
achievement of them?"

(Metacogitate) Become aware and monitor one's own thinking during the lesson.

"What were you thinking when you decided to change the design of the lesson?"

OR

"What were you aware of that students were doing **that signaled you** to change the format of the lesson?"

(Analyze) Analyze why the student behaviors were or were not achieved.

"What hunches do you have to **explain why** some students performed as you had hoped while others did not?"

(Cause-effect) Draw causal relationships.

"What did you do (or didn't do) **to produce the results** you wanted?"

(Synthesize) Synthesize meaning from analysis of this lesson.

"As you reflect on this discussion, **what** big ideas or **insights are you discovering**?"

(Self-prescription) Prescribe alternative teaching strategies, behaviors or conditions.

"As you plan future lessons, **what ideas** have you developed that **might be carried forth** to the next lesson or other lessons?"

(Evaluate) Give feedback about the effects of this coaching session and the coach's conferencing skills.

"As you think back over our conversation, **what has this** coaching session **done for you?** What is it that I did (or didn't) do? What assisted you? **What could I do differently** in future coaching sessions?"

These questions are only examples and not meant to be prescriptive or complete. The purpose is to show how skilled coaches intentionally pose questions. Their intent is to engage, mediate, and thereby enhance the cognitive functions of teaching. The questions, therefore, are adroitly focused on, composed, and posed to deliberately engage the intellectual functions of teaching.

Appendix D
Some Verbal Strategies

Following are examples of language patterns that can lead teachers to states of efficacy, precision, consciousness, and interdependence.

Efficacy

When someone is stuck and feeling powerless, try *Self-prescribing*, a verbal strategy that shifts misplaced responsibility from others to self and pre-supposes that personal action produces outcomes. Through self-prescribing, a person works to intentionally influence the outcomes of a problematic situation.

For example, when a teacher says, "If the parents can't motivate them to learn, how do you expect me to teach them?" the coach can ask: "What might you do within your own classroom to motivate them?"

Another approach is *Choice Making*, a verbal strategy that initiates an invitation to brainstorm possible approaches for a problematic situation. This strategy acknowledges the state of not knowing alternatives and supports the person in generating alternatives from which he/she can make practical choices appropriate to the situation. Coaches use this lead only when a friend, colleague, or student has reached a dead end in his or her own thinking.

For example, someone says, "I have just run out of ideas! I can't seem to get students to come in, sit down, and get to work." The coach answers, "Would you like to hear about a few things that I have seen other teachers do? I saw one teacher write an exercise on the board at the beginning of the class. Another teacher immediately began class with a group response to three oral questions. Another teacher tells the assignment to kids when they are lined up outside the door before reentering the classrooms. Which one seems most appropriate to you?"

The coach can also use *Correcting Fate Control*, a strategy that attributes success to specific efforts rather than to fate or luck. This strategy elicits awareness of the personal resources that contributed to the teacher's success. If the teacher exclaims, "It was my lucky day," the coach can probe, "What did *you* do to cause the day to go so well?" Another technique is *Drawing from Past Experience*, which encourages the teacher to access and apply his or her resources from past settings to the current situation. "I want him out of here!" exclaims the teacher. "He constantly disrupts the class. He leaves without permission." The coach can answer, "Think back to a time when you were successful with him. What were you doing at that time that you can apply in this situation?"

Craftsmanship

When someone's comments seem vague, try *Communicating with Specificity*, a verbal strategy that invites a person to elaborate what he or she means. For example, a teacher might say, "Wow! We really had a great faculty meeting!" The coach can probe, "How, specifically, was it great?" or, "When you say great, what are you thinking about?"

Or if a teacher says, "I really want to learn the new stuff in education," the coach can probe, "When you say 'new stuff,' what do you have in mind?"

Eliciting Specific Criteria is a verbal strategy for judging events. A teacher may vaguely ask, "Just tell me if I'm doing a good job with restructuring my math program." The coach can probe, "What criteria would you use to determine that it was a good job?"

Or if the teacher says, "I care deeply that students learn," the coach can answer, "What would be some indicators that would verify that they are learning?"

Sometimes it's necessary to deal with temporal vagueness. Certain verbal strategies will assist with *Managing time*. If the teacher says, "This lesson will be a review," the coach can ask, "What events led up to the review? **(sequencing)** How long do you plan to spend on each of the major concepts? **(duration)** During the review, what will those students be doing who have already mastered the content? **(simultaneity)**"

Consciousness

Metacogitation leads people to consider the relation between internal values, goals, thoughts, and feelings and decisions about external events. In the Planning Conference, the coach might ask:

What will be your important decisions during this lesson?

You value debate. Why is this so important to you?

How will you know what types of responses to give?

What will you be monitoring in your questions?

In the Reflecting Conference, the coach might ask:

What led to your decision to modify your teaching plan?

What went on in your head when the students responded like that?

What was your intention when you said . . .?

Mental Rehearsal is a strategy that leads someone to envision and mentally enact a planned activity.

Coach: *How will you know the lesson is successful?*

Teacher: *By student responses.*

Coach: *What criteria will you use to determine a satisfactory student response?*

Coach: *What data can I gather for you?*

Teacher: *Collect examples of the questions I ask.*

Coach: *How will you know when to ask different types of questions?*

Flexibility

Considering Intention is a strategy that leads one to examine the positive intentions of someone else's behavior by considering data from other perspectives and generating new linkages. For example, a teacher might say, "This administration doesn't care what happens to students. All schools are forced to use the same math text." The coach answers: "What benefit do you think that has for students transferring from other district schools?"

Style Check is a strategy that leads to awareness of our own and others' styles, modalities, beliefs, values, and behaviors in the moment. Questions that promote this awareness include:

What learning styles are used most in your class?

How do you compare your own learning preferences with hers?

What philosophic position might cause Mrs. Sanchez to say that?

Interdependence

Values Search focuses on the potential value of different points of view and conflict. When a teacher says, "Their disagreements with this project are slowing us down," the coach can answer, "In the long run, if there were any value to getting these disagreements out now, what might that be?"

A *Talent Search* leads to envisioning potential capacities of the group and its members. When the teacher says, "This group seems unable to complete its tasks," the coach can answer, "What would you see or hear from them if they were completing them?" or "What skills are needed to complete the task?" or "What are the existing strengths within the group that could be built upon?"

Resource Banking moves people from positions of isolation to seeking and giving help. When someone admits, "I'm stuck," the coach can answer, "What help do you need? Who do you know here who has experience with that?" Or, "If this were Sally's problem, how might she approach it? What else might she do? Want to ask her?" Or "How could the group working together help resolve this?"

The strategy of *Group Support* raises a problem to a level of team awareness and solution. When a teacher says, "I teach the kids to think, they go to the next grade and there's no follow through," the coach can ask, "What would it take to build staff commitment to critical thinking? Would you raise this issue at our next department meeting?"

Appendix E
Taxonomies to Assess Growth in Reflectivity

A taxonomical approach to assessing teachers' growth toward more reflectivity may be useful to coaches as they search for the effects of their efforts to coach teachers and to enhance the environment. Taxonomies are theoretical constructs arranged in a hierarchical fashion, and they may prove useful in analyzing growth or in planning a sequence of a lesson or a change strategy.

Educators are probably most familiar with Bloom's taxonomy. Following are two other taxonomies that coaches might use to analyze teachers' growth toward greater reflectivity. They are Van Mannen's *Levels of Reflectivity,*[1] the *Pedagogical Language Acquisition and Conceptual Development Taxonomy of Teacher Reflective Thoughts (RPT)* developed by Sparks-Langer, Simmons, Pasch, Colton, and Starko,[2] We provide information about these taxonomies so coaches can draw from a wide repertoire of strategies to pace staff members' present levels of concern and to provide developmentally appropriate mediation that leads to further growth toward higher developmental levels.

Van Mannen's Levels of Reflectivity
Van Mannen[3] distinguishes between different forms of reflection, each embracing different criteria for selecting among alternative courses of action. The three levels are presented below with examples.

Level 1: The teacher examines techniques to reach given objectives. The teacher is concerned mainly with means rather than ends, issues of improving specific, externally defined technical skills. On this level, "practical" refers to the technical application of educational knowledge. *Reflections are on teaching objectives, strategies, lesson plans, classroom control, and student progress.* In short, reflection is limited to issues of improving specific, internally defined technical skills.

For example, the teacher might say, "I want the children to read critically—to clarify and critique the textual material. I want the children to begin to learn how to question as they read. In the lesson today we will read and critique two stories. I want them to read and talk about what they read, explaining and developing their own ideas. I want them to tell what questions they are asking about the story."

Level 2 demonstrates higher reflectivity. *The teacher establishes relationships between principles and practices.* He expresses a need to assess the educational, aesthetic, and psychological implications and consequences of his actions in a social context (for example, organization structure, established curriculum, work expectations, and belief systems). Knowledge is often presented as problematic rather than absolute. It is assumed that every educational choice is based on a value commitment to some interpretive framework by those involved in the curriculum practice. At this level, "practical" refers to the process of analyzing and clarifying individual and cultural experiences, meanings, perceptions, assumptions, prejudgments, and presuppositions in practical terms. Curriculum and teaching-learning are perceived as processes of establishing communication and common understandings. *At this level, the focus is on interpreting and understanding experience in terms of practical choices.*

For example, a teacher might say, "I believe the reason some students are not comprehending the math instructions is because I am presenting it too abstractly. I must find ways to introduce concepts concretely, and then move to more abstract presentations. I'm beginning to realize that teachers should see themselves as developing professionals. We must become lifelong students of our own teaching. During this lesson, I learned from my students just as they learned from me."

Level 3 is the point at which the teacher uses *deliberate rationality as the ideal to pursue worthwhile educational ends in self-determination, community, and on the basis of justice, equality, and freedom.* This third level of reflection incorporates both ethical and political concerns of social justice, equality, and emancipation. *Teachers may express the links between professional activity and social and political forces in society.*

For example, a teacher might say, "As I reflect on our conference, I'm realizing how much change has taken place in me. It's been a slow but steady change in and out of my classroom. After all these sessions I realize that some of the dimensions of critical thought have been awakened in me. Before, I never realized they were there, and I used them without thinking about it.

"Just this week at home I found myself having a discussion with my family about public justice. and why human needs are not taken care of in other parts of the world like Cuba and China. Human rights? How can we change them? What is right and wrong? As we continued to talk about it, we asked deeper questions and evaluated actions and policies in other countries. My children and husband became involved and I realized how they were probing deeply into the subject, looking for answers from other people and different sources.

"Lately I find myself using many critical thinking strategies with my own children, trying to develop some of the attitudes and values of critical thinkers in them. As a result, a few days ago after the visit of relatives, my family engaged in a discussion on the rights and justice of the people. My children asked many questions about how and why these things happen. We compared ourselves to other countries. We asked ourselves how we could develop and improve our system to obtain even greater social justice."[4]

The Taxonomy of Teacher Thought

Using the *Pedagogical Language Acquisition and Conceptual Development Taxonomy of Teacher Reflective Thought*, teachers are asked to describe an instructional incident, writing everything related to it that comes to mind. The description—which can be broad or narrow—is then scored at one of seven levels:

Descriptive Stage

Level 1—Teacher is unable to describe a recent example of teaching.

Level 2—Teacher is able to describe a recent example of teaching but without using pedagogical concepts. (For example, "I taught this lesson on bats, and the students really enjoyed it.")

Classification Stage

Level 3—Teacher describes a recent example of teaching using pedagogical concepts to label the events. (For example, "I taught this lesson on bats, and we brainstormed on the board all the things we know about them. It's a guided reading technique called KWL. The K stands for prior knowledge."

Level 4—Teacher describes a recent example of teaching using pedagogical concepts to label events. But when asked to explain why the lesson was successful or unsuccessful, he is unable to relate effects to an established, relevant pedagogical principle. (For example, "It works because all the students participate.")

Explanation Stage

Level 5—Teacher describes a recent example of teaching using pedagogical concepts to label the events. When asked to explain why the lesson was successful or unsuccessful, she is able to relate effects to one or more established relevant pedagogical principles. (For example, "The prior knowledge activity works because it gets everyone on a level field as far as background knowledge is concerned. It sets up a framework inside everyone's head that we can then use to understand the reading on bats.")

Conditional Stage

Level 6—Teacher describes a recent example of teaching using pedagogical concepts to label the events. When asked to explain why the lesson was successful or unsuccessful, he is able to relate effects to one or more established, relevant pedagogical principles. In addition, the teacher relates the lesson to the students, classroom, community, and/or larger society. (For example, "Kids in this community are at different levels of background. Some have very rich parents who take them to museums and zoos and travel with them. Other kids have very little exposure to the outside world. The guided reading activity gives everyone an opportunity to say something.")

Level 7—In addition to the previous levels, the teacher relates the lesson to universal moral/ethical/socio-political principles. (For example, "If urban education is going to be successful, it's crucial to encourage children to learn from each other. Competition between students who have all the advantages and students who lack these advantages will, predictably, be unfair. The guided reading activity is a great way to even things out a little as far as background knowledge is concerned. Everyone begins to read about bats with approximately the same level of prior knowledge.")

Endnotes

1. Van Mannen, M. "Linking Ways of Knowing With Ways of Being Practical." *Curriculum Inquiry* (1977): 6, pp. 205–228.

2. Sparks-Langer, G.M., Simmons, J., Pasch, M., Colton, A. and Starko, A. "Reflective Pedagogical Thinking: How Can We Promote It and Measure It?" *Journal of Teacher Education* (1990): 41 (4), pp. 23–32.

3. Van Mannen, M. "Linking Ways of Knowing With Ways of Being Practical." *Curriculum Inquiry* (1977): 6, pp. 205–228.

4. Appreciation is expressed to Alicia Moreyra who assisted with this description and used this taxonomy in her doctoral dissertation: *The Role of Thinking Frames in Developing Teacher's Critical Thinking Skills and Dispositions.* University of Miami, 1991.

5. Shulman, J.H., and Mesa-Baines, A. (1993). "Fighting for Life in Third Period," in *Diversity in the Classroom: A Casebook for Teachers and Teacher Educators,* Hillsdale, NJ: Lawrence Erlbaum Associates, pp. 45–54.

6. Tannen, D. *You Just Don't Understand: Women and Men in Conversation.* New York: Ballantine Books, 1990, p. 160.

7. Shulman, J.H., and Mesa-Baines, A. (1993). "Fighting for Life in Third Period," in *Diversity in the Classroom: A Casebook for Teachers and Teacher Educators,* Hillsdale, NJ: Lawrence Erlbaum Associates, pp. 45–54.

8. Garmston, R. Cross Cultural Communications. Unpublished manuscript. Facilitation Associates. 337 Guadaloupe Drive, El Dorado Hills, CA 95762. 1991.

Photo by Bruce M. Wellman, Science Resources, Lincoln, Mass.

Arthur L. Costa, Ed.D.

Arthur L. Costa is co-director with Dr. Bob Garmston of the Institute for Intelligent Behavior, and Professor Emeritus, School of Education, California State University, Sacramento.

He is the author of The School as a Home for the Mind (1991), published by Skylight, The Enabling Behaviors, and Teaching for Intelligent Behaviors, coauthor of Techniques for Teaching Thinking (1989), published by Critical Thinking Press & Software, and the editor of Developing Minds: A Resource Book for Teaching Thinking (1991), published by the Association for Supervision and Curriculum Development. He has also written numerous articles and publications on supervision, teaching strategies, thinking skills, and assessment.

Dr. Costa has made presentations and conducted workshops for educators throughout the United States, Canada, Mexico, Central America, Europe, Africa, the Middle East, Asia, Australia, and the South Pacific. He taught in the Bellflower School District, worked as a curriculum consultant in the Los Angeles County Superintendent of Schools Office, served as Director of Educational Programs for the National Aeronautics and Space Administration for the Western States, and was Assistant Superintendent of the Sacramento County Office of Education.

Active in many professional organizations, Dr. Costa served as president of the California Association for Supervision and Curriculum Development and as president of the national ASCD from 1988 to 1989.

Photo by Bruce M. Wellman, Science Resources, Lincoln, Mass.

Robert J. Garmston, Ed.D.

Robert J. Garmston, Emeritus Professor of Educational Administration at California State University, Sacramento, is executive
director at Facilitation Associates, an educational consulting firm
specializing in leadership, learning, personal and organizational
development. He is co-developer of Cognitive Coaching and co-
director with Dr. Art Costa of the Institute for Intelligent Behavior.
Dr. Garmston is author of numerous publications on leadership,
supervision and staff development. He conducts seminars throughout the United States and in Canada, Europe, Asia and the Middle
East.

Formerly a teacher and administrator in several school districts,
he is active in many professional organizations. He is past president of the California ASCD and currently a member of the
Executive Council for the Association for Supervision and Curriculum Development.

Dr. Garmston has served as consultant to over 200 schools and
educational agencies and such diverse groups as the Arabian
American Oil Company, the Danforth Foundation, American Soci-
ety for Training and Development, National Association for Court
Administration, the Department of Defense Schools, United States
Air Force, and the World Health Organization.

Although his work requires an extensive amount of traveling, he
still finds time to enjoy backpacking, hiking, and relaxing with his
wife, Sue, at their home near Sacramento, California and spending
time with his children; Kimberly, Judy, Kevin, Michael and Wendy.

Index